Lab Manual to Accompany Essentials of Health Information Management: Principles & Practices
Third Edition

Mary Jo Bowie, MS, BS, AAS, RHIA, RHIT
Consultant and Owner
Health Information Professional Services
Binghamton, New York
Associate Professor in Health Information Management
Program Director
Mount Wachusett Community College
Gardner, Massachusetts

Michelle A. Green, MPS, RHIA FAHIMA, CPC
SUNY Distinguished Teaching Professor
Department of Physical and Life Sciences
Alfred State College
Alfred, New York

CENGAGE
Learning·

Australia • Brazil • Mexico • Singapore • United Kingdom • United States

Lab Manual to Accompany Essentials of Health Information Management: Principles & Practice, Third Edition
Mary Jo Bowie, Michelle A. Green

SVP, GM Skills & Global Product Management: Dawn Gerrain

Product Manager: Jadin B. Kavanaugh

Senior Director, Development: Marah Bellegarde

Product Development Manager: Juliet Steiner

Senior Content Developer: Elisabeth F. Williams

Product Assistant: Mark Turner

Vice President, Marketing Services: Jennifer Ann Baker

Marketing Manager: Erica Glisson

Senior Production Director: Wendy Troeger

Production Director: Andrew Crouth

Senior Content Project Manager: Kara A. DiCaterino

Managing Art Director: Jack Pendleton

Cover image(s): © Sergey Nivens/Shutterstock.com

© 2016, 2011 Cengage Learning

WCN: 01-100-101

For product information and technology assistance, contact us at **Cengage Learning Customer & Sales Support, 1-800-354-9706**

For permission to use material from this text or product, submit all requests online at **www.cengage.com/permissions.**
Further permissions questions can be e-mailed to **permissionrequest@cengage.com**

ISBN: 978-1-285-17735-9

Cengage Learning
20 Channel Center Street
Boston, MA 02210
USA

Cengage Learning is a leading provider of customized learning solutions with employees residing in nearly 40 different countries and sales in more than 125 countries around the world. Find your local representative at **www.cengage.com.**

Cengage Learning products are represented in Canada by Nelson Education, Ltd.

To learn more about Cengage Learning, visit **www.cengage.com**

Purchase any of our products at your local college store or at our preferred online store **www.cengagebrain.com**

Printed in the United States of America
Print Number: 01   Print Year: 2015

Contents

Preface

Welcome to *Lab Manual to Accompany Essentials of Health Information Management*, third edition. This student lab manual contains application-based assignments organized according to textbook chapters. These assignments will reinforce learning and encourage skill building. The lab assignments allow students to apply concepts learned from reading and studying corresponding textbook chapters. Completing each assignment will prepare the student for related health information tasks assigned during professional practice experiences (internships). Because the lab assignments simulate on-the-job experiences in a health information department or physician's office, the student can also feel confident applying for the following entry-level positions:

- Abstractor
- Assembly clerk
- Analysis clerk
- File clerk
- Receptionist
- Release of information processing clerk

These positions allow students to earn income while attending school, and perhaps more important, when a technical position becomes available in the health information department or physician's office, the student (or graduate) is considered an internal candidate.

OBJECTIVES

The objectives of this lab manual are to allow students to:

1. Apply health information management concepts common to allied health professionals.
2. Visit a health care facility and interview a professional to explore career opportunities.
3. Analyze actual patient records for documentation deficiencies.
4. Sequence patient record numbers in straight numeric and terminal-digit order.
5. Redesign an outdated patient record form.
6. Calculate patient record storage based on case scenarios.
7. Abstract patient cases for health data collection.
8. Process requests for release of information.
9. Complete a hospital financial report using DRG base rates to calculate total reimbursement rates.
10. Update a clinic encounter form by verifying/editing codes.
11. Investigate the implementation of ICD-10-CM and ICD-10-PCS.

This lab manual is designed to be used by college and vocational school programs to train allied health professionals (e.g., cancer registrars, coders, health information administrators and technicians, medical assistants, medical office administrators, medical transcriptionists). It can also be used as an in-service training tool for new health care facility personnel and independent billing services, or individually by health information specialists.

FEATURES OF THE LAB MANUAL

- Introduction at the beginning of each chapter provides an overview of content.
- Lab assignments provide students with an opportunity to apply textbook chapter concepts.
- Objectives for each lab assignment clearly indicate purpose of application-based activity.
- Step-by-step instructions for each lab assignment communicate exactly how each is to be completed.
- The accompanying Student Companion website at www.CengageBrain.com includes practice records and more.

• Lab Assignments marked with this world wide web icon include a fillable form or other online activity.
- New! Appendix II includes additional lab activities using Neehr Perfect® VistA EHR software. A separate subscription is required. For more information on using Neehr Perfect® with the lab manual, please go to neehrperfect.com/Cengage.

SUPPLEMENTS

The following supplements accompany this lab manual.

INSTRUCTOR'S MANUAL

The instructor's manual consists of two parts, one for the text and one for the student lab manual. Lesson plans, answers to chapter exercises and reviews, chapter quizzes, and answers to student lab manual assignments are included.

STUDENT COMPANION WEBSITE

Additional resources can be found online at www.CengageBrain.com. Search by author name, ISBN, or title to locate the Student Companion website for *Essentials of Health Information Management*, third edition. Resources include downloadable files to support the student lab manual and textbook, product updates, related links, and more. The student resources include Adobe pdf files of assignments that can be completed as forms and sent as an e-mail attachment to instructors for evaluation. (Go to www.adobe.com to download the latest version of Adobe Reader to fill in forms.) Save completed forms as electronic files using the naming convention required by your instructor.

FOR CUSTOMER SERVICE:

For technical issues with accessing or using Neehr Perfect® (already using product):
Neehr Perfect® Help Desk (24/7):
support@neehrperfect.com
877-907-2186

For questions about an activity in the Lab Manual:
Contact your Cengage Learning sales representative

For general information about Neehr Perfect®:
Neehr Perfect® Sales and Customer Service (8am–5pm Central):
contact@neehrperfect.com
877-742-3926

Chapter 1

Health Care Delivery Systems

❦ INTRODUCTION

This chapter focuses on the historical development of medicine and health care delivery from prehistoric/ancient medicine to modern times, familiarizing the student with the Hippocratic Oath, seventeenth-, eighteenth-, and nineteenth-century medical discoveries, hospital ownership, organizational structure and accrediting organizations, and committee composition and minutes.

LAB ASSIGNMENT 1-1   Organizational Charts

OBJECTIVES

At the end of this assignment, the student should be able to:

- Prepare an organizational chart
- Interpret the organizational relationship among health care facility departments

Overview

An organizational chart (Figure 1-1) illustrates formal relationships among departments. It also depicts lines of authority within a department or between a department manager and facility administration. This assignment will familiarize the student with the creation of an organizational chart.

Instructions

1. Review the following case scenario, which depicts the organizational structure of a health information department.

   The health information manager is head of the department. An assistant manager reports directly to the health information manager. A coding supervisor and a document imaging supervisor report to the assistant manager. The department secretary reports directly to the health information manager. The following employees report to the coding supervisor: the inpatient coder, the outpatient coder, the ED coder, and the abstractor. Two document imaging clerks and an analysis clerk report to the document imaging supervisor.

2. Create an organizational chart that accurately illustrates the lines of authority depicted in the case scenario.

   NOTE: Organizational charts can be hand drawn by hand or with software such as OrgPlus (www.orgplus.com), an automated organizational chart creation program. The site contains an OrgPlus free trial.

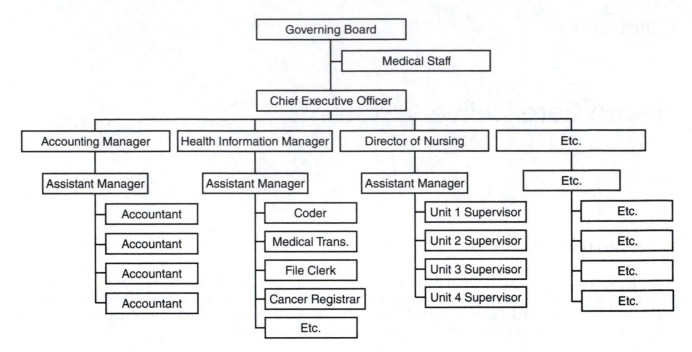

Figure 1-1   Portion of Facilitywide Organizational Chart

LAB ASSIGNMENT 1-2   Information Literacy

OBJECTIVES

At the end of this assignment, the student should be able to:

- Develop and increase information literacy skills
- Select, search, and evaluate information resources
- Prepare an annotated bibliography

Overview

Information literacy expands upon essential technical skills (knowing how to use computers and access information) to include critical thinking about the nature of information and its cultural, philosophical, and social context and impact. The purpose of this assignment is to assist you with developing and increasing your information literacy skills, which will, in turn, allow you to select, search, and evaluate information resources. You will prepare an annotated bibliography (Figure 1-2), which contains a brief description for each citation that summarizes the accuracy, quality, and relevance of the reference source, followed by the citation. (An annotation is *not* an abstract, which is a descriptive summary of a citation.) The annotated bibliography is descriptive *and* critical because it reveals the author's point of view.

Instructions

Prepare an annotated bibliography that contains two citations.

a. Select a bibliography topic that interests you (e.g., HIPAA privacy).
b. Locate two citations (e.g., journal articles) about your topic.
c. Review the citations to determine whether they contain useful information and ideas about your topic. Select two citations and read them thoroughly.
d. Prepare the annotated bibliography.
   - Cite each article using APA style.

   NOTE: The American Psychological Association (APA) established a style used in all of its published books and journals. Many authorities in the social and behavioral sciences adopted this style as their standard. The Modern Language Association (MLA) recommends its MLA style for the preparation of scholarly manuscripts and student research papers.

e. Summarize the article, incorporating at least four of the items below:
   - Description of article's content and/or focus
   - Consideration of whether the article's content is useful
   - Article's limitations (e.g., outdated)
   - Audience for which the article is intended
   - Evaluation of research methods used in the article
   - Author's background
   - Conclusions the author(s) make about the topic
   - Your reaction to the article

This informative, practical article by the project director of the Payment Error Prevention Support Peer Review Organization (PEPSPRO) in Texas discusses the issue of diagnosis-related group (DRG) billing as a major contributor to inaccurate Medicare payments and describes the negative consequences of undercoding and upcoding for the hospital. Recommendations are made and tools provided for completing a comprehensive assessment of records, staff qualifications, training, and use of coding resources, coding policies, and safeguards against upcoding. The author also discusses the various aspects of following up on a completed assessment, including implementing new policies, providing appropriate training, and monitoring compliance.

Fletcher, Robin. The importance of addressing inaccurate diagnosis related group assignment as a risk area. (2002). *Journal of Health Care Compliance, 45,* 40–46.

The author reports on the trend of hospitals using Internet-based automated compliance checking in place of more traditional billing methods in order to fulfill the requirements of the Medicare Correct Coding Initiative (CCI). Using Holy Cross Hospital in Ft. Lauderdale, Florida, as a case example, the author fully details the many benefits of using the automated system, including the reduction of billing errors, ease of use, evaluation of coding risk areas, and preventing noncompliance and the resulting penalty fees.

Moynihan, James J. Automated compliance checker helps ensure billing accuracy. (2000). *Healthcare Financial Management, 54,* 78.

Figure 1-2   Sample Annotated Bibliography Containing Two Citations

LAB ASSIGNMENT 1-3   Committee Minutes

OBJECTIVES

At the end of this assignment, the student should be able to:
- Observe the functioning of a committee meeting
- Take notes during the committee meeting
- Prepare minutes of the committee meeting and an agenda for the next meeting

Overview

Minutes document actions and discussions that occur during a committee meeting and should be recorded at each meeting. This assignment will familiarize the student with following a committee agenda, taking notes during meetings, preparing committee minutes, and creating an agenda for the next meeting.

Instructions

1. Select a committee meeting to attend. Upon arrival, be sure to request a copy of the committee agenda (Figure 1-3).

   NOTE: Committee meetings are routinely held at health care facilities (e.g., health information committee). Contact the health information department manager at a local facility to request permission to sit in on a meeting to take notes and prepare the minutes for a class assignment. If you are unable to attend a meeting at a health care facility, attend a meeting of your local American Red Cross office, school board, or the like.

2. Attend the meeting and take notes of topics discussed and actions taken (Figure 1-4). Be sure to include elements 3a–i below in your handwritten notes.

3. Prepare minutes of the meeting (Figure 1-5) based on notes recorded. Be sure to include the following elements:
   a. Date, place, and time of the meeting
   b. Members present
   c. Members absent
   d. Guests present
   e. Items discussed
   f. Actions taken
   g. Time meeting adjourned
   h. Location, time, and date of next meeting
   i. Closing

4. Prepare an agenda to be used at the next scheduled committee meeting.

Agenda

Health Information Committee

Chairperson:	David Lynn, M.D.	**Timekeeper:**	Thomas Kincaid
Facilitator:	Mary Jo Bowie, RHIA	**Note taker:**	Sally Brumley

Date/Time/Location: Wednesday, October 15th, Noon, Crandall Room

----- **Agenda Topics** -----

1. Ongoing record review
2. Revision of ICU/CCU nurses' notes
3. Transcription turnaround time
4. Conversion to electronic health record (EHR)
5. Health Information Technology Week

Figure 1-3   Sample Health Information Committee Agenda

Health Information Committee Meeting

Chairperson:	David Lynn, M.D.	**Timekeeper:**	Thomas Kincaid
Facilitator:	Mary Jo Bowie, RHIA	**Note taker:**	Sally Brumley

Date/Time/Location: Wednesday, October 15th, Noon, Crandall Room

Time Meeting Adjourned:

Date/Time/Location of Next Meeting:

Members Present:

Members Absent:

Guests Present:

----- **Agenda Topics** -----

1. Ongoing record review

    Discussion:

    Conclusions:

Action items:	Person responsible:	Deadline:

2. Revision of ICU/CCU nurses' notes

    Discussion:

    Conclusions:

Action items:	Person responsible:	Deadline:

Figure 1-4   Portion of Form Used to Record Minutes During a Committee Meeting

[NAME OF COMMITTEE]

Meeting Minutes

The meeting of the NAME OF COMMITTEE was called to order at [time] on [date] in [location] by [name of chairperson].

Present: [names and titles of members in attendance]
Absent: [names and titles of members not in attendance]
Guests Present: [names and titles of other individuals in attendance]

Approval of Minutes
The minutes of the previous meeting were unanimously approved as distributed.

Open Business
[Use paragraph format to summarize discussion, conclusions, and actions for each agenda item. Include the name of the person responsible for following through on any action and the deadline.]

New Business
[Use paragraph format to summarize discussion, conclusions, and actions for any new issues addressed during this meeting that were not included on the agenda. Include the name of the person responsible for following through on any action and the deadline.]

Agenda for Next Meeting
[List items to be discussed at the next meeting. These items serve as the basis for preparing the next meeting's agenda.]

Adjournment
The meeting was adjourned at [time] by [name of person]. The next meeting will be held at [time] on [date] in [location].

Respectfully submitted,   Approved,

[Name of recording secretary]   [Name of chairperson]
Recording Secretary   Chairperson

Figure 1-5   Format Used When Preparing Committee Minutes

Chapter 2

Health Information Management Professionals

🌹 INTRODUCTION

This chapter familiarizes students with locating professional association websites, interviewing a professional, creating a résumé and cover letter, interpreting professional codes of ethics, networking with other professionals via professional discussion forums, and interpreting (and understanding) information from professional journal articles.

LAB ASSIGNMENT 2-1   Interview of a Professional

OBJECTIVES

At the end of this assignment, the student should be able to:

- Delineate the responsibilities of a professional employed in the student's field of study
- Explain why the professional's position is one that the student would (or would not) be interested in obtaining

Overview

Health information management professionals often have similar educational backgrounds, but their job responsibilities and roles within organizations vary greatly. This assignment will familiarize students with the specific job responsibilities of a professional employed in their field of study.

Instructions

1. Prepare 10 questions that you would like to ask a professional employed in your field of study.

   NOTE: Your instructor might devote classroom time to brainstorming such questions (or use a discussion forum if you are an Internet-based student). This will allow you to share questions with other students in your course and to obtain additional questions to ask the professional.

2. Identify a credentialed professional in your field of study. Medical assistant students should interview a CMA or an RMA; coding students should interview a CCS or CPC; health information students should interview an RHIT or RHIA; and so on. Contact the professional to schedule an on-site interview. Conduct yourself in a professional manner and explain that you are a student completing a required assignment.

   NOTE: If it is not possible to schedule an on-site interview, check with your instructor to determine whether a telephone or email interview would be acceptable.

3. Prepare for the interview by reviewing and organizing the questions you will ask the professional.

4. Dress appropriately (as for a job interview), and arrive 10 minutes early for the interview.

5. Adopt a professional and respectful manner when asking interview questions, and be prepared to answer questions asked of you. Be sure to take notes as the professional responds to the interview questions. If you choose to record the interview, ask the professional for permission to do so.

6. After the interview, thank the professional for his or her time. Be sure to follow up the interview by mailing a handwritten thank-you note within 10 days.

7. Prepare a three-page paper summarizing the interview, as follows:
   a. Identify the professional's name, position, and facility.
   b. Writing in the third person, summarize the professional's responses to interview questions. Organize the interview content in logical paragraphs. (A paragraph consists of at least three sentences.) *Do **not** prepare this paper in a question/answer format.* If you have questions about how to write this paper, ask your instructor for clarification.
   c. In the last paragraph of the paper, summarize your reaction to the interview and whether you would be interested in having this professional's position (along with why or why not). Also, describe your future by writing about where you will be in 10 years (in terms of employment, family, etc.).

LAB ASSIGNMENT 2-2   Cover Letters and Résumés

OBJECTIVES

At the end of this assignment, the student should be able to:

- List the elements of a résumé and cover letter
- Demonstrate an understanding of the purpose of creating a résumé and cover letter that contain no errors
- Prepare a résumé and cover letter that can be submitted to a prospective professional practice site or for future employment opportunities
- Use the Internet to locate prospective job opportunities

Overview

Some facilities require students to submit a cover letter and résumé for consideration by the clinical supervisor prior to placement for professional practice. This assignment will result in the student creating a professional résumé and cover letter.

Instructions

1. Prepare a résumé and cover letter based on the examples in Figures 2-1 and 2-2, substituting your specific information. (Microsoft Word users can access the Résumé Wizard by clicking on File, New, then opening the résumé template.)
2. Consider having a rough draft of each professionally proofread by your school's career services department or someone at your local or state unemployment office.

SALLY S. STUDENT

5 Main Street   Alfred, NY 14802   (607) 555-1234

EDUCATION

STATE UNIVERSITY OF NEW YORK, COLLEGE OF TECHNOLOGY AT ALFRED, Alfred, New York.
Candidate for Associate in Science, Health Information Technology, May YYYY

Honors & Awards: Dean's List, Fall YYYY, Spring YYYY, and Fall YYYY. Member, Phi Theta Kappa National
Honor Society

CERTIFICATION

R.H.I.T. eligible, May YYYY

PROFESSIONAL ORGANIZATIONS

Student Member, American Health Information Management Association, New York Health Information
Management Association, and Rochester Regional Health Information Management Association.

Member, Health Information Management Club, Alfred State College.

PROFESSIONAL PRACTICE

Student Health Information Technician, Health Information Management Department, Alfred State Medical
Center, Alfred, New York. Summer YYYY. Assembled and analyzed discharged patient records, filed and
retrieved records, answered the telephone, processed release of information requests, attended health
information committee meetings, and coded inpatient, outpatient, and emergency department records
according to ICD-9-CM, CPT, and HCPCS Level II.

Student Health Information Technician, Quality Management Department, Alfred State Medical Center, Alfred,
New York. Spring YYYY. Performed quality management studies under the direction of the facility's quality
manager, and assisted with risk management, utilization management, and physician credentialing procedures.

Student Health Information Technician, Alfred Nursing Facility, Alfred, New York. Spring YYYY. Filed and
retrieved records, answered the telephone, processed discharged patient records, and attended committee meetings.

Student Health Information Technician, Alfred Health Insurance Company, Alfred, New York. Spring YYYY.
Verified the accuracy of ICD-9-CM, CPT, and HCPCS codes submitted on insurance claims, reviewed patient
records to determine medical necessity of procedures reported, and attended meetings.

WORK EXPERIENCE

Cashier, Burger King, Alfred, New York. Assisted customers, operated cash register, and opened/closed store.
August YYYY-Present.

Resident Assistant, Alfred State College, Alfred, New York. Responsible for supervising the housing of 250
student residents, planning student activities, enforcing disciplinary procedures, and scheduling student staff.

AVAILABILITY

June 1, YYYY

REFERENCES

Sally Supervisor, Alfred State Medical Center, Alfred, NY (607) 555-5626

Bob Boss, Burger King, Alfred, NY (607) 555-8956

Patty Professor, Alfred State College, Alfred, NY (607) 555-5434

Figure 2-1   Sample Résumé

10 Main St.
Alfred, NY 14802
April 15, YYYY

Edward Employer
Human Resources
Alfred State Medical Center
100 Main St.
Alfred, NY 14802

Dear Mr. Employer:

Please accept this letter of application for the position of Health Information Technician as advertised in the April 10, YYYY, edition of *The Buffalo News*.

I will be graduating from the State University of New York, College of Technology at Alfred in May YYYY with an Associate degree in Applied Science in Health Information Technology. In addition to taking formal course work, I also completed professional practices, which allowed me to apply the skills that I learned in the classroom. Please refer to the attached résumé for a detailed listing of my responsibilities at each practice site.

In June YYYY, I will be eligible to take the RHIT credentialing examination offered by the American Health Information Management Association. I am interested in interviewing for the above position and would appreciate your contacting me at (607) 555-1234 to schedule an interview.

Thank you for your consideration. I look forward to hearing from you soon.

Sincerely,

Sally S. Student

Enclosure

Figure 2-2   Sample Cover Letter

LAB ASSIGNMENT 2-3   Professional Discussion Forums (Listserv)

OBJECTIVES

At the end of this assignment, the student should be able to:

- Explain the value of joining professional discussion forums
- Join a professional discussion forum
- Review discussion forum contents to identify topics relevant to a particular field of study
- Demonstrate participation in a professional discussion forum

Overview

Networking, or sharing information among professionals, is a valuable professional activity. The Internet has made it much easier to network with other professionals by using web-based professional forums. This assignment will familiarize the student with the value of Internet professional discussion forums.

Instructions

1. Select a professional discussion forum from Table 2-1 and follow its instructions to access forums.
2. Access archived forum discussions and observe current discussions for the period designated by your instructor (e.g., 1–3 weeks), noting topics that are relevant to your field of study.
3. Post a discussion comment or question on the forum and observe responses from subscribers.
4. At the end of the period of observation and participation, determine whether the forum would be helpful to you on the job.

Table 2-1   Discussion Forums and Internet Sites for Professionals

Professional	Name of Forum	Internet Site
AHIMA Members	Communities of Practice	http://www.ahima.org In order to access the Communities of Practice Forum you must be a member of AHIMA.
Coders/Medical Transcriptionists	Forums, Blogs	http://health-infomation.advanceweb.com Click on COMMUNITY, Forums or click on COMMUNITY, Blogs
Other Professionals	Names of NIH forums vary. Medicaid Program Updates	https://list.nih.gov Next to the heading Browse, click on List of Lists. This will display a listing of all NIH LISTSERV titles. Discuss with your instructor those that apply to your field of study.

LAB ASSIGNMENT 2-4   Professional Code of Ethics

OBJECTIVES

At the end of this assignment, the student should be able to:

- State the reason a profession develops a code of ethics
- Discuss the importance of adhering to a professional code of ethics
- Identify situations in which a professional code of ethics has been breached
- Suggest ways to address situations in which a code of ethics is breached

Overview

A professional code of ethics provides guidelines for professional actions. This assignment will familiarize students with the code of ethics unique to their professional field of study and allow students to respond to case scenarios that require application of the code of ethics.

Instructions

1. Refer to the code of ethics for your field of study supplied to you by your instructor. The AHIMA Code of Ethics is found at http://library.ahima.org. Click on "Main". Below "Browse HIM Topics" expand the list below "AHIMA" by clicking on the plus sign. Click the link for "Code of Ethics." This will bring you to a list of search results. From here click on "AHIMA Code of Ethics" to view the document.
2. Carefully review each case scenario below and identify which code was breached.
3. Summarize how the breach could have been avoided, and explain how each situation should be handled once a breach occurs.

Case Scenarios

1. Her neighbor asks Chris Professional whether she should consult Dr. Smith. Chris Professional replies, "Heavens, no! He doesn't have many cases at the hospital and his patients have a lot of complications after surgery. Go to Dr. Jones; he's wonderful!"
2. The hospital planned to buy new transcription equipment and evaluated the products of several companies. Chris Professional believed that one product was the most suitable for the needs of the department and so informed her administrator when her opinion was sought. After the equipment had been purchased and installed, Chris Professional received an expensive-looking day planner from the salesperson, given in gratitude for her help in influencing the hospital's choice. Since she really thinks that the filing equipment is the best, Chris Professional accepts this unexpected gift.
3. Chris Professional is in charge of the professional practice for students placed by a local college. She instructs students in a variety of duties, and one day shows two students some new equipment. The subject of the health of another student in the program comes up. Chris Professional says, "Oh, just a minute, her emergency department record came into the department today; let's see what it says." She finds the record and shares its contents with the two students.
4. A record was subpoenaed for production in court. Chris Professional had not yet been placed on the stand and had the record in her possession when the noon recess was called. The attorney who had subpoenaed the record, and who had been unable to secure the patient's permission to review it, invites Chris Professional to lunch. During lunch, he asks her to let him see the record, explaining that he will get the information anyhow once she is placed on the witness stand. He says that it will save time and expedite justice if she will let him have this quick "preview." Chris Professional agrees and passes the record to him.
5. An inexperienced woman has been employed to manage patient records in a small, neighborhood home health agency. She asks Chris Professional for advice about what she should do. Chris Professional, believing that she has more than enough to do attending to her own work, tells her she cannot help.

6. Chris Professional agrees to supply a natural baby food service with the names and addresses of all mothers delivered of living infants in the hospital. For this service she will receive $5.00 per name.

7. When applying for a fellowship in the American College of Surgeons, Dr. Monroe uses, as examples of his own surgical work, the cases of several patients who were actually cared for by a senior surgeon on the staff. When his list of cases is sent to the hospital for verification, Chris Professional, knowing that the young surgeon is eager to obtain the qualification and not wanting to make trouble, verifies by her signature the statements that these were Dr. Monroe's patients.

8. Since doctors rarely use the disease index, and because she hopes to be married and gone by the time of the next visit from the Joint Commission surveyor, Chris Professional does not bother to make any entries in this index, believing that her other duties are more important.

9. Returning from a meeting of the Tissue Committee, where she took notes, Chris Professional excitedly informs the assistant department director, "You know Dr. Tardy, the one who's always so ugly about completing his records? Well, they said today that the big operation he did last month on Mary Jones wasn't necessary at all, and they're recommending that his surgical privileges be suspended!"

10. Chris Professional was sent to an educational institute by her hospital but decided to spend two of the four afternoons of the institute week shopping and sightseeing instead of attending the sessions.

11. Chris Professional notices a laboratory report that documents the patient as having a positive venereal disease research laboratory slide test, which screens for syphilis, so she adds the diagnosis of "syphilis" to the face sheet of the patient's record.

12. Chris Professional notices that the patient record of another hospital employee is to be reviewed as part of her job. As she reviews the documentation, she notices that it references human immunodeficiency virus (HIV, which causes AIDS). She shows the document to the employee sitting at the next desk and asks if he is aware of this information. Chris Professional then returns to her other tasks.

13. Chris Professional, a HIM professional at Sunny View Nursing Facility, is asked by her neighbor for the diagnoses of his mother's roommate. Chris replies by giving the neighbor the list of diagnoses.

14. Chris Professional was conducting an audit at a nursing facility on medication administration. She notices that her neighbor's father was late dosed three times the previous month. She shares this with her neighbor.

15. Chris Professional completed the coding on her ex-sister-in-law's record, which states alcohol addiction. She shares this information with the ex spouse, who is seeking custody of their two children.

LAB ASSIGNMENT 2-5   Journal Abstract

OBJECTIVES

At the end of this assignment, the student should be able to:

- Identify the journal of the professional association in the student's field of study
- Write a journal abstract of an article

Overview

Professional association journals communicate information about health care advancements, new technology, changing regulations, and so on. This assignment will familiarize students with the contents of their professional journal and require students to prepare a journal abstract (summary) of a selected article.

Instructions

1. Select your professional association's journal from Table 2-2.

2. Select an article from your professional association's journal. Locate a journal by:
   a. Going to its website (many journals are posted online)
   b. Borrowing a journal through interlibrary loan (e.g., college library, local library)
   c. Borrowing a journal from a professional in your field of study or your instructor

   NOTE: Borrowing a journal from a professional in your field of study is an excellent way to start the networking process that will lead to employment. However, if you borrow a journal, return it promptly and include a thank-you note.

   NOTE: Student members of professional associations receive professional journals. However, it usually takes eight weeks to receive your first journal.

3. Read an article published in a recent edition of your professional association's journal.

4. Prepare a one-page, double-spaced summary of the journal article, which includes the following information:
   a. Name of article
   b. Name of author
   c. Name of journal
   d. Date of journal
   e. Journal article summary (paragraph format, double-spaced), which summarizes the article's content. Do *not* include your opinion about content of the article.

Table 2-2 Professional Journals

Profession	Professional Journal	Professional Association
Cancer Registrar	*Journal of Registry Management*	National Cancer Registrars Association
Coding & Reimbursement Specialist	*Cutting Edge*	American Academy of Professional Coders
Health Information Technician or Administrator	*Journal of the American Health Information Management Association*	American Health Information Management Association
Medical Assistant	*CMA Today* *AMT Events Magazine*	American Association of Medical Assistants American Medical Technologists
Medical Staff Coordinator	*Synergy*	National Association of Medical Staff Services
Medical Transcriptionist	*Plexus*	Association for Healthcare Documentation Integrity (formerly the American Association of Medical Transcription)

Chapter 3

Health Care Settings

🦌 INTRODUCTION

This chapter focuses on familiarizing the student with a variety of health care settings, including acute care, ambulatory and outpatient care, behavioral health care facilities, home care and hospice, long-term care, managed care, and federal, state, and municipal health care.

LAB ASSIGNMENT 3-1   Health Care Facility Tour

OBJECTIVES

At the end of this assignment, the student should be able to:

- Discuss the health care services offered by a given facility
- Determine whether the facility would employ a professional in the student's field of study

Overview

A wide variety of health care facilities provide patients with appropriate levels of care based on patient medical needs. This assignment will familiarize the student with such facilities located in the community, along with professional positions available.

Instructions

1. Identify a health care facility in your community that you would like to tour.

   NOTE: If your instructor arranges for you to visit a facility with your class as a field trip, you won't need to complete this assignment.

2. Contact a professional in your field of study who is employed at the facility to arrange a tour.

   NOTE: Contact the facility and ask to be connected to the department that houses your field of study (e.g., health information department). Ask to speak with the department manager. Explain that as a student you are required to tour a facility to learn about your field of study. Schedule a specific date and time to tour the facility and the department.

3. Prepare for the tour by identifying questions you will ask to determine health care services offered by the hospital, types of patients treated, average length of stay, and so on.

4. Dress appropriately for the tour (as for a job interview), and arrive 10 minutes early.

5. Conduct yourself in a professional manner during the tour, and be sure to take notes of the responses you receive to questions you ask. During the tour, inquire about professional positions available in your field of study.

6. At the conclusion of the tour, thank the individual who conducted the tour. Follow up the tour with a hand-written thank-you note (no later than 10 days after the tour).

7. Prepare a brief summary of the tour, as follows:
    a. Identify the name and location (city, state) of the facility and department toured.
    b. Summarize information provided in response to questions asked during the tour.
    c. Comment on whether you would be interested in working for the facility.

LAB ASSIGNMENT 3-2   The Joint Commission

OBJECTIVES

At the end of this assignment, the student should be able to:

- Discuss the types of organizations accredited by The Joint Commission
- Identify the resources available on The Joint Commission website

Overview

The Joint Commission accredits numerous types of health care facilities. This assignment will familiarize the student with the types of facilities that are accredited by The Joint Commission.

Instructions

1. Log on The Joint Commission website at www.jointcommission.org.
2. Click on accreditation programs and review the types of facilities that are accredited. Select one of the types of facilities, that is, ambulatory care, behavioral health care, critical access hospitals, and so on and review the information that is available on the site.
3. Prepare a two-page typewritten paper that includes:
   a. The types of health care facilities accredited by The Joint Commission
   b. A summary of the information that is found relevant to the type of facility that you selected to review

LAB ASSIGNMENT 3-3   Health Care Facilities

OBJECTIVES

At the end of this assignment, the student should be able to:

- Recognize various types of health care facilities that treat specific patient populations

OVERVIEW

Patients are treated at various types of health care facilities based on the patients' specific health care needs. This assignment will familiarize the student with the various types of health care facilities.

Instructions

1. Review the following cases and identify one type of health care facility/service from the following list that would provide health care services to the patient described in the case.
   - Acute care hospital
   - Ambulatory surgery center
   - Chemical dependency inpatient program
   - Facility for the developmentally disabled
   - Home care services
   - Hospice care services
   - Pain management clinic
   - Respite care facility
2. Explain your rationale for choosing this type of health care facility.

Case 1

Asmer Natali is a 59-year-old male patient who has been diagnosed with an opioid addiction. He has been treated on an outpatient basis but currently has relapsed and needs to undergo detox and requires medically directed care management. His primary care outpatient addiction counselor feels he needs to have a more intensive level of service than outpatient care.

Case 2

Mr. Lamb, a 45-year-old patient, was diagnosed with severe kidney disease. He has been on dialysis for the last five years and has not been placed on a transplant list due to his many other health problems. At this time he has decided that he would like to receive palliative care rather than curative care services.

Case 3

Eileen Penna is a 27-year-old woman who suffered a cervical spine injury due to a motor vehicle accident three years ago. She has undergone surgery and is still experiencing pain that prevents her from performing daily activities. Eileen's primary care provider feels that her case should be evaluated through a multidisciplinary approach to attempt to provide her relief.

Case 4

Thomas is the primary caregiver for his 93-year-old father, Keith. Thomas and Keith live in the same house. Keith needs assistance with all of his activities of daily living and mealtime preparation due to his diagnosis of dementia. Thomas needs to go out of town for one week and does not feel that his father is able to stay at their residence alone.

Case 5

Mike James, an 84-year-old man, had open heart surgery three months ago. Following the surgery he was placed in a skilled nursing facility for intensive cardiac rehabilitation. He wants to be discharged but still needs assistance with daily living activities and the management of his illness.

Case 6

Tim, a 5-year-old boy, has a diagnosis of profound intellectual disability and also has numerous medical issues. His parents have kept him at home, but they are finding it more difficult to manage his care. They feel that he needs to be placed in a facility that can address his developmental and physical health concerns.

Case 7

Lisa, a 74-year-old woman, fell at home and was taken to the emergency department. The ED physician called an orthopedic surgeon to review the case. It was determined that she has a fracture of the left hip and needs surgery.

Case 8

Kayla is a 7-year-old girl who has had an ongoing sore throat and enlarged tonsils for the last six months. Her physician feels that she needs to have her tonsils removed. Kayla has no other health concerns that present a risk to her having a tonsillectomy.

Chapter 4

Introduction to the Patient Record

❦ INTRODUCTION

This chapter focuses on familiarizing the student with patient record content, formats, development and completion, and provider documentation requirements.

LAB ASSIGNMENT 4-1   Administrative and Clinical Data

OBJECTIVES

At the end of this assignment, the student should be able to:

- Differentiate between administrative and clinical data
- Critique a physician's office patient record form

Overview

Administrative and clinical data is captured from the time the patient initiates contact for medical care to the time of discharge. This assignment will familiarize the student with both administrative and clinical data that is collected on a registration form.

Instructions

1. Refer to Table 4-1 in Chapter 4 of your textbook to review examples of administrative and clinical data.
2. Review the registration form (Figure 4-1) used in a physician's office for the following information:
   a. Demographic
   b. Socioeconomic
   c. Financial
   d. Clinical
3. Create a table, as seen on the next page, and list all administrative and clinical items in column one, and enter the type of element in column two. (To get you started, the first four entries are included in the table.) The list of items should include:

Patient name	Admission date and time	Medication allergies/reactions
Patient address, city, state, and zip code	Primary insurance plan	Current medications
	Primary insurance plan ID#	BP, P, R, T, WT (vital signs)
Telephone	Secondary insurance plan	Chief compliant (CC)
Gender	Secondary insurance plan ID#	Past medical history (PMH)
Date of birth	Occupation	Note
Patient number	Name of employer	

Student Name _____

Administrative and Clinical Data Item	Type of Element
Patient name	Demographic
Address	Demographic
Primary insurance plan	Financial
Current medications	Clinical

Alfred State Medical Center
100 Main St, Alfred NY 14802
(607) 555-1234

PHYSICIAN OFFICE RECORD

EIN: 12-345678

PATIENT INFORMATION:

NAME:	DOE, John	**PATIENT NUMBER:**	123456
ADDRESS:	100 South Ave	**ADMISSION DATE & TIME:**	05-16-YYYY
CITY:	Alfred	**PRIMARY INSURANCE PLAN:**	BCBS of WNY
STATE:	NY	**PRIMARY INSURANCE PLAN ID #:**	12345678
ZIP CODE:	14802	**SECONDARY INSURANCE PLAN:**	N/A
TELEPHONE:	607-555-3264	**SECONDARY INSURANCE PLAN ID #:**	N/A
GENDER:	Male	**OCCUPATION:**	Accountant
DATE OF BIRTH:	07-07-1956	**NAME OF EMPLOYER:**	Alfred State College

NURSING DOCUMENTATION:

MEDICATIONS ALLERGIES/REACTIONS: None

CURRENT MEDICATIONS: Lithium 1,500 mg

BP: 130/80 **P:** 84 **R:** **T:** **WT:** 265

CC: Patient states he feels well today.

PMH: Bipolar disorder, manic type.

NOTES: Here for scheduled appointment. Voices no concerns.

SIGNATURE OF PRIMARY CARE NURSE: Jeanette Allen, R.N.

PHYSICIAN DOCUMENTATION:

Notes: HISTORY: Patient seen today for regular appointment. He appears relaxed, cooperative, and coherent. No evidence of recurrent manic behavior. He is a 46-year-old, divorced twice, Navy veteran, who served from 1971 to 1975 as an accountant in non-combat situation. He has been suffering from bipolar disorder, manic type, and takes medication, Lithium 1500 mg a day, which seems affective.

He has been employed at Alfred State College as an accountant for nine years, full time.

Mental Status Exam: He has been doing very well with the current medication. No evidence of memory loss or any psychotic behavior. He affect is appropriate, and mood is stable. Insight and judgment are good. He is not considered a danger to himself or others.

DIAGNOSIS: Bipolar disorder, manic type.

PLAN: Continue lithium 1500 mg a day.

SIGNATURE OF PROVIDER: Raymond E. Massey, M.D.
Raymond E. Massey, M.D

Figure 4-1 Sample Physician Office Record

LAB ASSIGNMENT 4-2   Provider Documentation Guidelines

OBJECTIVES

At the end of this assignment, the student should be able to:

- Explain provider documentation responsibilities
- Interpret provider documentation guidelines

Overview

Health care organizations are responsible for ensuring that health care services rendered to patients are documented according to federal and state regulations as well as accreditation, professional practice, and legal standards. This assignment will familiarize the student with patient record documentation standards.

Instructions

1. Refer to the *Provider Responsibilities* section in Chapter 4 of your textbook:
   a. Authentication of patient record entries
   b. Abbreviations used in the patient record
   c. Legibility of patient record entries
   d. Timeliness of patient record entries
   e. Amending the patient record
2. Use the chart format on the following page to summarize key concepts associated with provider documentation responsibilities.

Student Name _____

Provider Documentation Guidelines	
Provider Documentation Responsibilities	**Summary of Key Concepts**
Authentication of patient record entries	
Abbreviations used in the patient record	
Legibility of patient record entries	
Timeliness of patient record entries	
Amending the patient record	

LAB ASSIGNMENT 4-3   Flow of Patient Information

OBJECTIVES

At the end of this assignment, the student should be able to:

- Illustrate the flow of patient information from admission to discharge
- Identify the health care provider who is responsible for documenting patient record information

Overview

The inpatient record contains documents that are completed by various hospital personnel and providers. This assignment will familiarize the student with the inpatient record and the individuals responsible for the completion of the documents.

Instructions

1. The chart on the following page contains the flow of information developed for the patient record from the time of admission to discharge.
2. Enter the hospital staff member (e.g., ER nurse) or physician (e.g., attending physician) responsible for completing documentation listed.

Student Name _____

Flow of Patient Information	
Flow of Documentation	**Responsible Staff Member or Physician**
Face Sheet	
Admission Consent	
Nursing Assessment	
Physician Orders	
Admission History and Physical	
Laboratory Test Results	
Operative Note	
Physical Therapy Exam and Treatment	
Discharge Instructions	
Discharge Summary	

LAB ASSIGNMENT 4-4   Medicare Conditions of Participation

OBJECTIVES

At the end of this assignment, the student should be able to:

- Locate the Code of Federal Regulations (CFR) for public health and Medicare conditions of participation
- Interpret the Medicare Hospital Conditions of Participation: Medical Record Services

Overview

The Medicare Conditions of Participation (COP) are federal regulations that health care organizations must comply with in order to receive federal funds for services provided to patients. The COP are contained in the Code of Federal Regulations (CFR), which is the codification of general and permanent rules published in the *Federal Register* by executive departments and agencies of the federal government. It consists of 50 titles that represent broad areas subject to federal regulation, which are updated once each calendar year. Each title is divided into chapters (according to name of the issuing agency) and parts (covering specific regulatory areas). Large parts may be further subdivided into subparts.

NOTE: The searchable CFR database is available at www.federalregister.gov, where you can search the database.

EXAMPLE 1: Go to www.federalregister.gov, enter "conditions of participation: clinical records" in the Search box, and click on SUBMIT. Several citations are displayed. To view the content, click on the description of the information displayed.

Instructions

1. Review the conditions of participation for hospital medical record services (Subpart 482.24) (Figure 4-2).

2. Interpret medical record services conditions by summarizing the intent of each.

3. Enter the interpretation of each condition using the table format on the following page. Be sure to enter the condition from Figure 4-2 in column one and your interpretation in column two.

Code of Federal Regulations
Title 42
Part 482-Conditions of Participation For Hospitals
Subpart C-Basic Hospital Functions

TITLE 42-PUBLIC HEALTH
CHAPTER IV-HEALTH CARE
DEPARTMENT OF HEALTH AND HUMAN SERVICES

§482.24 CONDITION OF PARTICIPATION: MEDICAL RECORD SERVICES.

The hospital must have a medical record service that has administrative responsibility for medical records. A medical record must be maintained for every individual evaluated or treated in the hospital.

(a) *Standard: Organization and staffing.* The organization of the medical record service must be appropriate to the scope and complexity of the services performed. The hospital must employ adequate personnel to ensure prompt completion, filing, and retrieval of records.

(b) *Standard: Form and retention of record.* The hospital must maintain a medical record for each inpatient and outpatient. Medical records must be accurately written, promptly completed, properly filed and retained, and accessible. The hospital must use a system of author identification and record maintenance that ensures the integrity of the authentification and protects the security of all record entries.
   (1) Medical records must be retained in their original or legally reproduced form for a period of at least 5 years.
   (2) The hospital must have a system of coding and indexing medical records. The system must allow for timely retrieval by diagnosis and procedure, in order to support medical care evaluation studies.
   (3) The hospital must have a procedure for ensuring the confidentiality of patient records. Information from or copies of records may be released only to authorized individuals, and the hospital must ensure that unauthorized individuals cannot gain access to or alter patient records. Original medical records must be released by the hospital only in accordance with Federal or State laws, court orders, or subpoenas.

(c) *Standard: Content of record.* The medical record must contain information to justify admission and continued hospitalization, support the diagnosis, and describe the patient's progress and response to medications and services.
   (1) All patient medical record entries must be legible, complete, dated, timed, and authenticated in written or electronic form by the person responsible for providing or evaluating the service provided, consistent with hospital policies and procedures.
   (2) All orders, including verbal orders, must be dated, timed, and authenticated promptly by the ordering practitioner or by another practitioner who is responsible for the care of the patient only if such a practitioner is acting in accordance with State law, including scope-of-practice laws, hospital policies, and medical staff bylaws, rules, and regulations.
   (3) Hospitals may use pre-printed and electronic standing orders, order sets, and protocols for patient orders only if the hospital:
       (i) Establishes that such orders and protocols have been reviewed and approved by the medical staff and the hospital's nursing and pharmacy leadership;
       (ii) Demonstrates that such orders and protocols are consistent with nationally recognized and evidence-based guidelines;
       (iii) Ensures that the periodic and regular review of such orders and protocols is conducted by the medical staff and the hospital's nursing and pharmacy leadership to determine the continuing usefulness and safety of the orders and protocols; and
       (iv) Ensures that such orders and protocols are dated, timed, and authenticated promptly in the patient's medical record by the ordering practitioner or by another practitioner responsible for the care of the patient only if such a practitioner is acting in accordance with State law, including scope-of-practice laws, hospital policies, and medical staff bylaws, rules, and regulations.
   (4) All records must document the following, as appropriate:
       (i) Evidence of—
           (A) A medical history and physical examination completed and documented no more than 30 days before or 24 hours after admission or registration, but prior to surgery or a procedure requiring anesthesia services. The medical history and physical examination must be placed in the patient's medical record within 24 hours after admission or registration, but prior to surgery or a procedure requiring anesthesia services.
           (B) An updated examination of the patient, including any changes in the patient's condition, when the medical history and physical examination are completed within 30 days before admission or registration. Documentation of the updated examination must be placed in the patient's medical record within 24 hours after admission or registration, but prior to surgery or a procedure requiring anesthesia services.
       (ii) Admitting diagnosis.
       (iii) Results of all consultative evaluations of the patient and appropriate findings by clinical and other staff involved in the care of the patient.
       (iv) Documentation of complications, hospital acquired infections, and unfavorable reactions to drugs and anesthesia.
       (v) Properly executed informed consent forms for procedures and treatments specified by the medical staff, or by Federal or State law if applicable, to require written patient consent.
       (vi) All practitioners' orders, nursing notes, reports of treatment, medication records, radiology, and laboratory reports, and vital signs and other information necessary to monitor the patient's condition.
       (vii) Discharge summary with outcome of hospitalization, disposition of case, and provisions for follow-up care.
       (viii) Final diagnosis with completion of medical records within 30 days following discharge.

[51 FR 22042, June 17, 1986, as amended at 71 FR 68694, Nov. 27, 2006; 72 FR 66933, Nov. 27, 2007; 77 FR 29074, May 16, 2012]

Figure 4-2   Subpart 482.24-Hospital Medicare Conditions of Participation: Medical Record Services

Student Name _____

Condition of Participation: Medical Record Services (Hospital) (Subpart 482.24)	
Condition	**Interpretation**
(a) *Standard: Organization and staffing.* The organization of the medical record service must be appropriate to the scope and complexity of the services performed. The hospital must employ adequate personnel to ensure prompt completion, filing, and retrieval of records.	• Hospital must establish a medical record (or health information) department and provide appropriate physical space for it to perform its functions. • Hospital must hire enough qualified individuals to perform tasks necessary to maintain patient records for the facility.

LAB ASSIGNMENT 4-5   Amending the Patient Record

OBJECTIVES

At the end of this assignment, the student should be able to:

- Explain the procedure used to amend patient records
- Recognize appropriate and inappropriate amendments made to patient records

Overview

Laws, regulations, and standards that originally applied to the maintenance of paper-based records also apply to electronic (or computer-based) records that are properly created and maintained in the normal course of business. This assignment will require the student to recognize appropriate and inappropriate amendments made to patient records.

Instructions

1. Review the section entitled "Amending the Patient Record" found in chapter 4 of your textbook. For added information also review the following AHIMA website. Go to http://www.ahima.org. At the bottom of the page click on HIM Body of Knowledge, then click on Practice Briefs. Locate the following two practice briefs.
   - 10/2/13—Patient Access and Amendment to Health Records
   - 9/15/99—Correcting and Amending Entries in a Computerized Patient Record
2. Review the patient record entries in Figure 4-3, determine whether each is appropriately or inappropriately amended, and provide a justification for each.

Student Name _____

Instructions:	Review the amended patient record entries located in Figure 4-3. If correctly documented, enter an × in the Yes box. If not, enter an × in the No box.
	Write a justification for your selection indicating why the amended patient record entry was appropriately or inappropriately documented.

Case No.	Correctly documented?	Justification statement:
1	o Yes o No	
2	o Yes o No	
3	o Yes o No	
4	o Yes o No	
5	o Yes o No	
6	o Yes o No	
7	o Yes o No	
8	o Yes o No	
9	o Yes o No	
10	o Yes o No	

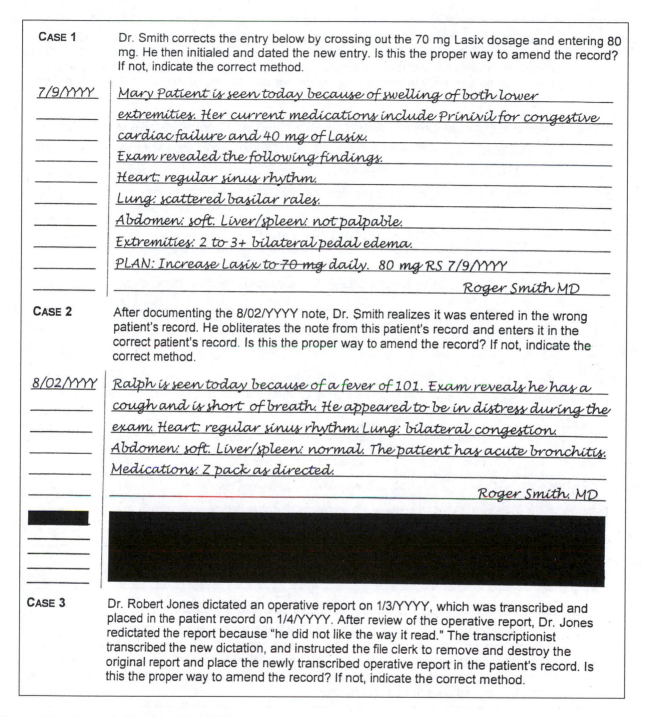

CASE 1 — Dr. Smith corrects the entry below by crossing out the 70 mg Lasix dosage and entering 80 mg. He then initialed and dated the new entry. Is this the proper way to amend the record? If not, indicate the correct method.

7/9/YYYY — Mary Patient is seen today because of swelling of both lower extremities. Her current medications include Prinivil for congestive cardiac failure and 40 mg of Lasix.
Exam revealed the following findings.
Heart: regular sinus rhythm.
Lung: scattered basilar rales.
Abdomen: soft. Liver/spleen: not palpable.
Extremities: 2 to 3+ bilateral pedal edema.
PLAN: Increase Lasix to ~~70 mg~~ daily. 80 mg RS 7/9/YYYY
Roger Smith MD

CASE 2 — After documenting the 8/02/YYYY note, Dr. Smith realizes it was entered in the wrong patient's record. He obliterates the note from this patient's record and enters it in the correct patient's record. Is this the proper way to amend the record? If not, indicate the correct method.

8/02/YYYY — Ralph is seen today because of a fever of 101. Exam reveals he has a cough and is short of breath. He appeared to be in distress during the exam. Heart: regular sinus rhythm. Lung: bilateral congestion. Abdomen: soft. Liver/spleen: normal. The patient has acute bronchitis. Medications: Z pack as directed.
Roger Smith. MD

CASE 3 — Dr. Robert Jones dictated an operative report on 1/3/YYYY, which was transcribed and placed in the patient record on 1/4/YYYY. After review of the operative report, Dr. Jones redictated the report because "he did not like the way it read." The transcriptionist transcribed the new dictation, and instructed the file clerk to remove and destroy the original report and place the newly transcribed operative report in the patient's record. Is this the proper way to amend the record? If not, indicate the correct method.

Figure 4-3   Amended Patient Record Entries

(Continues)

CASE 4	Alice Grey, RN, charted the following nurses' notes, including the one timed as 1030 in advance of the 0900 and 0945 entries. She contacted the health information department to determine how to correct this entry. She was instructed to cross out the first entry and re-enter it at the appropriate time. Is this the proper way to amend the record? If not, indicate the correct method.

2/3/YYYY	30-year-old gravida II para I admitted via ER in active labor. Called Dr. Patten's office. Has
0815	NKMA. EDC is 1/28/XX. Membranes are intact. Labor progressing as per noted on labor record and
	clinical observation sheets. Alice Grey RN
~~2/3/YYYY~~	~~Medications given as per physician orders. See medication administration record. Alice Grey RN~~
~~1030~~	
2/3/YYYY	Patient sleeping on and off for most of shift. Denies any discomfort. Frequency of contractions
0900	decreased. Alice Grey RN
2/3/YYYY	Contractions are becoming 8-10 minutes apart. See labor record. Alice Grey RN
0945	
2/3/YYYY	Medications given as per physician orders. See medication administration record. Alice Grey RN
1030	

CASE 5	When entering the APGAR score for Reflex Irritability below, the nurse made an error and corrected the entry. Is this the proper way to amend the record? If not, indicate the correct method.

	Score 0	Score 1	Score 2	1st Score	2nd Score	
Heart Rate	Absent	Slow Below 100	Over 100	2	2	
Respiratory Effort	Absent	Slow, Irregular	Good, Crying	2	2	
Muscle Tone	Limp	Same of Extremity	Active Motion	2	2	
Reflex Irritability	No response	Grimace	Cough or Sneeze	2	~~1~~	2
Color	Blue, Pale	Body, Pink Extremities, Blue	Completely Pink	1	2	
			Total	9	10	

CASE 6	Polly Tops, a former patient, comes to the HIM department with a handwritten list of amendments that she wants made to her medical record. She previously obtained a copy of her record with her physician's approval. The HIM clerk accepts the amendments from Polly and files them at the back of the patient's record. Is this the proper way to amend the record? If not, indicate the correct method.

Figure 4-3 (*Continued*) **Amended Patient Record Entries**

(Continues)

CASE 7	The progress note below was documented by Jane Smith, MD. Upon analysis of the record, the clerk realized the note was unsigned and indicated on the deficiency slip that Dr. Fog should authenticate it. Dr. Fog signed the note and handed the completed record to the HIM clerk for processing. Upon re-analysis, the clerk discovers the signature error and marks the deficiency slip for Dr. Smith to sign the note and make a notation that Dr. Fog signed in error.
1/3/YYYY	Mary has dementia, ischemic heart disease and she had an acute MI last month. According to nursing her vital signs have been stable. She is alert, conscious, and is able to speak to me. On exam her heart is in regular sinus rhythm. No additional cardiac findings at this time. Lungs are clear. Abdomen is soft. Continue orders as noted on 1/2/XX. Thomas Fog, MD
CASE 8	Alfred State Medical Center transcribes progress notes onto adhesive-backed blank paper forms that are placed on blank progress note pages in the medical record. A progress note dated 3/3/YYYY was transcribed and appropriately placed in the record. Upon review, the responsible physician notices transcription errors (e.g., typographical errors) and instructs the transcriptionist to rekey the note onto an adhesive-backed form and adhere the new note on top of the original note. Is this the proper way to amend the record? If not, indicate the correct method.
CASE 9	Nurse Anne Brown discovered that she had forgotten to document a 9:15 a.m. (0915 in military time) nurses' note in a patient's record. There was no room to squeeze the entry between the 0900 and 1000 notes, so she documented the 0915 entry below the 1000 entry, marking the 0915 entry as a late entry. Is this the proper way to amend the record? If not, indicate the correct method.
DATE/TIME	PROGRESS NOTE
4/15/YYYY 0900	55-year-old male admitted with chest pains by Dr. Jones. See initial nursing assessment. Bob Town, RN
4/15/YYYY 1000	Patient transferred to cardiac lab for testing. Bob Town, RN
LATE ENTRY 4/15/YYYY 0915	Physician orders received via phone, orders noted. Anne Brown RN
CASE 10	Nurse Mary Brown expanded on her original 5/13/YYYY note by entering an addendum two entries after the original. Is this the proper way to amend the record? If not, indicate the correct method.
5/13/YYYY 0500	Patient admitted via ambulance from possible domestic violence situation. See initial nursing intake report. Mary Brown, R.N.
5/13/YYYY 0515	Completed physical exam as noted on ER exam report Cynthia Lewis, R.N.
5/13/YYYY 0530	Addendum to note of 5/13/YYYY at 0500. Patient stated that police were called prior to ambulance coming to her home. She does not want to see her husband if he comes to the ER. Please call police. Mary Brown, R.N.

Figure 4-3 (*Continued*) Amended Patient Record Entries

Chapter 5

Electronic Health Records

♥ INTRODUCTION

This chapter focuses on the development and use of electronic health care records.

LAB ASSIGNMENT 5-1   Electronic Health Record Systems

OBJECTIVES

At the end of this assignment, the student should be able to:

- Identify an electronic health record (EHR) system and identify the types of facilities that would use the selected system
- Summarize the features of the electronic record system

Overview

Numerous electronic health record systems are used in health care. This assignment will allow the student to identify various systems and require the student to summarize the features of a system.

Instructions

1. Using an Internet browser (e.g., Microsoft Internet Explorer, Google Chrome), search for the term "electronic health record system."
2. Select a system located via the search.
3. Prepare a two-page summary of the system.
   a. List the name of the system and the website.
   b. Summarize the features of the system.
   c. Discuss the types of facilities that would benefit from installation of the system.

LAB ASSIGNMENT 5-2   Topics Relevant to E-HIM and EHR

OBJECTIVES

At the end of this assignment, the student should be able to:

- Identify the location of topics relevant to E-HIM and EHR on the website of the American Health Information Management Association
- Summarize information relevant to a topic in E-HIM and/or EHR

Overview

Electronic health records play an essential role in the documentation of patients' health experiences. This assignment will familiarize the student with electronic health records. Numerous topics are under discussion by health care professionals as the use of electronic health records becomes widespread.

Instructions

1. Using an Internet browser (e.g., Microsoft Internet Explorer, Google Chrome), go to www.ahima.org.
2. Click on HIM Body of Knowledge and then the folder entitled E-HIM/EHR. Topic headings relevant to E-HIM and electronic health records will appear within the folder. Select a topic heading. Various articles relevant to the topics will appear. Select one of the articles that have been written within the last two years.
3. Read through the article.
4. Prepare a one-page summary of the article, discussing how it is relevant to the health care industry today.

LAB ASSIGNMENT 5-3   AHIMA's myPHR

OBJECTIVES

At the end of this assignment, the student should be able to:

• Locate the AHIMA website, myPHR
• Discuss the benefits of patients developing personal health records

Overview

Personal health records benefit both patients and the health care community. This assignment will familiarize students with a website maintained by AHIMA that addresses the many benefits of personal health records. This website also discusses how to create a personal health record.

Instructions

1. Using an Internet browser (e.g., Microsoft Internet Explorer, Google Chrome), go to www.myphr.com.
2. Explore this site by reading some of the stories and viewing the videos.
3. Select a story or video and summarize the benefits of having a personal health record. Submit a one-page document to your instructor.

LAB ASSIGNMENT 5-4   Resistance to EHR

OBJECTIVES

At the end of this assignment, the student should be able to:

- Discuss how to address resistance to EHR
- Identify the benefits of EHR

Overview

Change is difficult for some individuals to accept. Many providers and staff members of health care facilities are resisting the implementation of electronic health record systems. This assignment will prepare students to address the resistance to EHR that can exist in health care.

Instructions

Assume that you are the HIM director at Sunny Valley Health Care. Sunny Valley Health Care is comprised of two acute care facilities, one long-term care facility, and 15 clinics that are within a 60-mile radius. It has been determined that the organization will be implementing an EHR system that will be used in all levels of care. Administration has determined that there is staff resistance to the implementation of the EHR system. You have been asked by the CEO to present a PowerPoint presentation on the benefits of implementing the system.

1. Research the benefits of EHR systems.
2. Prepare a 15-slide PowerPoint presentation on the benefits of EHR systems.

Chapter 6

Patient Record Documentation Guidelines: Inpatient, Outpatient, and Physician Office

❧ INTRODUCTION

This chapter will familiarize the student with aspects of inpatient, outpatient, and physician office records, including general documentation issues, administrative and clinical data, and forms control and design.

LAB ASSIGNMENT 6-1   Chart Assembly

OBJECTIVES

At the end of this assignment, the student should be able to:

- List the reports typically found in an acute care facility inpatient record
- Sequence acute care facility inpatient reports in a logical filing order

Overview

The acute care facility inpatient record contains numerous reports that are documented by various facility personnel and medical staff providers. Each facility establishes a filing order for inpatient and discharged patient reports to ensure that information can be easily located in the record. This assignment will familiarize the student with the content of an inpatient record and the typical order of reports filed in a discharged patient record.

NOTE: Some facilities adopt a *universal chart order*, which means the filing order of the inpatient and discharged patient record remains the same. This eliminates the task of assembling the discharged patient record.

Instructions

1. The chart below contains a list of acute care discharged patient reports.
2. Reorder the reports (1–15) according to the way they would be filed in a discharged patient record. (To get you started, numbers 1 and 15 have been entered.)

Student Name _____

Sequence	Reports
	Advanced Directives
	Anesthesia Record
	Ancillary Testing Reports
	Consent To Admission
	Consultation Reports
	Discharge Summary
1	Face Sheet
	History and Physical Examination
	Nursing Section
	Operative Report
	Pathology Report
15	Patient Property Form
	Physician Orders
	Physician Progress Notes
	Recovery Room Record

LAB ASSIGNMENT 6-2   Quantitative and Qualitative Analysis of Patient Records

OBJECTIVES

At the end of this assignment, the student should be able to:

- Analyze patient records to identify quantitative and qualitative documentation deficiencies
- Complete deficiency forms, indicating quantitative and qualitative documentation deficiencies

Overview

Quantitative and qualitative analyses of discharged patient records identify provider documentation deficiencies (e.g., missing authentication, incomplete diagnoses on face sheet). This assignment will require the student to analyze records to determine whether or not documentation is complete, and to complete a deficiency form (Figure 6-1) for each case.

NOTE: Some health care facilities perform concurrent analysis, which means records are analyzed while patients are still in the facility receiving care. The advantage to this is that the record is conveniently located on the nursing unit where providers routinely care for patients. The disadvantage is that more than one provider needs to access records at the same time, often making them unavailable for analysis and completion.

Instructions

1. Go to the Student Companion website and print one deficiency form for each patient record to be analyzed (10 total).

2. Refer to Appendix I, where Case01 through Case10 are located.

   NOTE: If you prefer, you may also access these cases at the Student Companion website and review online.

3. Refer to the Instructions for Completing the Deficiency Form (Table 6-1), and review the Guide for Quantitative Analysis of Acute Care Hospital Discharged Inpatient Records (Figure 6-2).

4. Review the Quantitative Analysis: Walkthrough of Case01 (Figure 6-3), which will familiarize you with completing the deficiency form for quantitative and qualitative analysis of discharged patient records.

5. Analyze Case01, and go to the Student Companion website to compare your completed deficiency form to the answer key. (Refer to Figure 6-3 for clarification of the answer key.)

NOTE: When performing quantitative and qualitative analysis, refer to the Guide for Quantitative Analysis of Acute Care Hospital Discharged Inpatient Records (Figure 6-2), and ask the following questions as you review each record:

- Is patient identification included on each report in the record?
- Are all necessary reports present, completely documented, and authenticated?

  EXAMPLE: Provider documents order for consultation in physician order. Was a consultation report dictated, transcribed, and filed in the record?

  EXAMPLE: A chest x-ray is missing the impression: the radiologist is responsible for documenting it.

- Are all entries authenticated (signed)?

  EXAMPLE: A resident documents the patient's history and physical examination, and authenticates it. Did the attending physician document additional information to support or dispute the resident's documentation? Did the attending physician also authenticate that entry?

- Are all diagnoses and procedures documented on the face sheet?

  EXAMPLE: Attending physician documents diabetes mellitus on the face sheet of discharged patient record. Does documentation in the patient record support adult-onset type and/or insulin dependency?

  EXAMPLE: Upon review of the discharged patient record, you notice that the responsible physician neglected to document several procedures that were performed during the stay.

  NOTE: On the job, follow your department's procedure for communicating questions to the responsible provider regarding incomplete or missing diagnoses and/or procedures.

6. Analyze Case02 through Case05, and go to the Student Companion website to compare your completed deficiency forms with the answer keys.

   NOTE: Re-analyze Case02 through Case05 for practice.

7. Analyze Case06 through Case10, and complete a deficiency form for each.

8. Submit completed deficiency forms to your instructor for evaluation.

Table 6-1   Instructions for Completing the Deficiency Form

1. Enter the patient name
2. Enter the case number (e.g., Case01 from the face sheet)
3. Enter the admission date from the face sheet. (This identifies the case analyzed in the event more than one record is stored in the same folder.)
4. Enter the attending doctor's name.
5. Enter the other doctor's name if a deficiency is present (e.g., emergency department physician).
6. Enter the other doctor's name if a deficiency is present (e.g., consultant, surgeon, anesthesiologist).
7–18. Review each report in the patient record, and compare to the Guide for Quantitative Analysis of Acute Care Hospital Discharged Inpatient Records (Figure 6-2):
   a. Circle **Authenticate** if the doctor needs to sign a report.
   b. Circle **Document** if the doctor needs to enter pertinent information to complete the report. On the line provided, enter specific information that needs to be documented (e.g., impression on physical examination).
   c. Circle **Dictate** if the doctor needs to dictate the entire report.
   d. Circle **Date** and/or **Time** if the doctor needs to date and/or time a report, progress note, physician order, or other document.

   NOTE: Shaded areas on the deficiency form are included to assist you in identifying the responsible doctor for each report.

   EXAMPLE 1: When reviewing the inpatient face sheet, if the attending physician documented abbreviations, circle **No Abbreviations.** The physician would then write out the meanings of abbreviations.

   EXAMPLE 2: When reviewing the record, if the discharge summary is missing, circle **Dictate** so that the physician is prompted to dictate the report. When the report is later transcribed and placed in the record, cross off **Dictate** and circle **Sign.** You won't be able to complete that aspect of analysis during this assignment.

   EXAMPLE 3: If the patient had a consultation ordered, and the report is present on the record but not signed, enter the consulting doctor's name after **Other Dr:** in column 3, and circle **Sign** for the **Consultation Report** entry.

Deficiency Form			
Patient Name:	**Patient Number:**		**Admission Date:**

NAME OF REPORT	Dr¹:	Dr²:	Dr²:
Inpatient Face Sheet	Sign No Abbreviations Complete _____		
Discharge Summary	Dictate Sign		
History & Physical	Dictate Sign		
Consultation Report		Dictate Sign	Dictate Sign
Admission Progress Note	Document Date Sign		
Daily Progress Notes	Document Date Sign	Document Date Sign	Document Date Sign
Discharge Progress Note	Document Date Sign		
Physician Orders	Document Date Sign	Document Date Sign	Document Date Sign
Discharge Order	Document Date Sign		
Anesthesia Report		Document Sign	Document Sign
Preanesthesia Evaluation		Document Sign	Document Sign
Postanesthesia Evaluation		Document Sign	Document Sign
Operative Report	Dictate Sign	Dictate Sign	Dictate Sign
Pathology Report		Dictate Sign	Dictate Sign
Recovery Room Record		Document Sign	Document Sign
Radiology Report		Document Sign	Document Sign
Other: _____ _____	Document Dictate Date Sign	Document Dictate Date Sign	Document Dictate Date Sign

Figure 6-1   Deficiency Form (also located at the Student Companion website)

Name of Inpatient Record Report	Quantitative Analysis Guidelines
Patient Identification	Review each report for: • Patient name • Patient record number • Hospital room number • Date of admission • Attending physician
Face Sheet	Review for presence of admission date/time, discharge date/time, and admission diagnosis. If dates/times are missing, enter them based on documentation in progress notes and physician orders. If admission diagnosis is missing, contact the Admission Department for information to be entered. Review for attending physician documentation of: • Principal diagnosis • Secondary diagnoses (e.g., comorbidities, complications) • Principal procedure • Secondary procedures • Condition at discharge • Authentication by attending physician **Note**: Abbreviations are not allowed when documenting diagnoses and/or procedures. If abbreviations are noted, instruct attending physician to write out full diagnosis/procedure.
Informed Consents for Admission/ Treatment, Release of Information, Advance Directives, and Surgery	Completed upon admission of patient to facility. (If not properly completed, contact your supervisor so Admission Department staff can receive in-service education.)
Discharge Summary	Review for documentation of: • Chief complaint (or reason for admission) • History of present illness • Significant findings during inpatient care, including preadmission testing (PAT) • Procedures performed/treatment rendered, and patient's response • Condition at discharge • Discharge instructions (e.g., physical activity, medications, diet, follow-up care) • Final diagnoses (principal diagnosis, comorbidities, and complications) • Authentication by attending physician **Note**: A discharge progress note (containing elements above) may be substituted for a discharge summary *if* the patient's stay is less than 48 hours, or for normal newborn infants and uncomplicated obstetrical deliveries.
Emergency Department (ED) Record[1]	Review for documentation of: • Arrival date, time, mode (including responsible party, such as ambulance co.) • History of present illness/injury • Physical findings (including vital signs) • Emergency care provided prior to arrival in ED • Treatment rendered in ED and results • Diagnosis • Inpatient admission order, if applicable • Referrals to other care providers • Authentication by ED physician [1]An emergency department record is included in the record only if the patient was admitted through the emergency department.

Figure 6-2   Guide for Quantitative Analysis of Acute Care Hospital Discharged Inpatient Records

(Continues)

History	Review for documentation of:
	• Admission date
	• Chief complaint
	• History of present illness
	• Past, family, and social history (PFSH)
	• Review of systems (ROS)
	• Authentication by attending physician
	Note: The history must be dictated and filed in the record within 24 hours of admission.
Physical Examination	Review for documentation of:
	• Findings for each body structure (e.g. neck, chest, abdomen)
	• Impression (or provisional diagnosis, admission diagnosis, tentative diagnosis)
	• Results of PAT
	• Inpatient hospital plan
	• Authentication by attending physician
	Note: The physical examination must be dictated within 24 hours of admission.

Note: If a *complete* history and physical examination was documented in the physician's office within 30 days prior to inpatient admission, a legible copy may be placed in the inpatient record instead of requiring the attending physician to document a new history and physical examination.

Interval History and Physical Examination[2]	Review for documentation of:
	• Chief complaint
	• History of present illness
	• Changes in patient's condition since previous admission
	• Changes in physical examination findings since previous admission
	• Impression
	• Authentication of attending physician
	[2]An Interval history and physical examination is documented only if patient is readmitted to hospital within 30 days for the same condition *and* the hospital utilizes a unit medical record. The previous inpatient history and physical examination report must be made available (e.g., copy filed in the current admission record). If the patient is scheduled for surgery during current inpatient admission, a complete physical examination is documented.
Consultation	Review for documentation of:
	• Date of consultation
	• Statement that patient was examined and record was reviewed
	• Findings
	• Opinion
	• Recommendations
	• Authentication by consulting physician
	Note: Be sure to review physician orders for documentation of consultation order by attending physician.
Progress Notes	Review each progress note for documentation of:
	• Date and time
	• Frequency dependent on patient's condition (e.g., intensive care unit patient record contains multiple daily progress notes)
	• Authentication by documenting physician
	In addition, review for documentation of:
	• Admission note
	• Discharge note
	Note: A discharge progress note (containing discharge summary elements) may be substituted for a discharge summary *if* the patient's stay is less than 48 hours, or for normal newborn infants and uncomplicated obstetrical deliveries.

Figure 6-2   (*Continued*) Guide for Quantitative Analysis of Acute Care Hospital Discharged Inpatient Records

(Continues)

Physician's Orders	Review each physician order for documentation of:

- Date and time
- Authentication by responsible physician

In addition, review for documentation of:

- Discharge order (except in the case of patient expiration)

Note: Verbal orders (e.g., telephone order or voice order) are documented by qualified personnel (nurse, pharmacist, and so on as determined by facility) and authenticated (countersigned) by responsible physician within 24 hours.

Anesthesia Record

Review for documentation of:

- Anesthetic dosages and fluids
- Techniques
- Unusual events
- Documentation of vital signs
- Status of patient at conclusion of anesthesia
- Date of surgery
- Name of procedure/surgeon/anesthesiologist
- Authentication of anesthesiologist

Preanesthesia Note

Review for documentation of:

- Note prior to surgery
- Patient's capacity to undergo anesthesia
- Physician's review of objective diagnostic data
- Interview with patient to discuss medications/anesthetics/drug history
- Patient's physical status
- Type of anesthesia to be administered
- Procedure to be performed
- Patient risks/complications
- Authentication by anesthesiologist

Postanesthesia Note

Review for documentation of:

- Note 3-24 hours after surgery
- Postoperative abnormalities or complications (if any)
- Vital signs and level of consciousness
- Presence or absence of swallowing reflex and/or cyanosis
- General condition of patient
- IV fluids and drugs administered
- Unusual events and postoperative complications (and management)
- Authentication by anesthesiologist

Operative Report

Review for documentation of:

- Dictation immediately following surgery (in progress notes)

Note: If operative report cannot be dictated by surgeon immediately following surgery, surgeon should document complete handwritten report in progress notes.

- Preoperative and postoperative diagnoses
- Name of operation/procedure performed
- Names of surgeon and assistants (if any)
- Description of operative findings
- Technical procedures utilized

Figure 6-2 (*Continued*) **Guide for Quantitative Analysis of Acute Care Hospital Discharged Inpatient Records**

(Continues)

	• Specimens removed
	• Authentication by surgeon
Recovery Room Record	Review for documentation of:
	• Vital signs
	• Level of consciousness upon transfer to and from recovery room
	• Order for patient to return to room (physician orders)
	• Authentication by nurse or anesthesiologist
Pathology Report	Review for documentation of:
	• Report within 24 hours of completion of tissue macroscopic/microscopic review
	• Gross (macroscopic) exam of tissue
	• Microscopic exam of tissue
	• Pathological diagnosis
	• Date of exam of tissue
	• Authentication by pathologist
Ancillary Service Reports	Review for documentation of:
	• Physician's order for ancillary service (e.g., ECG, laboratory)
	• Date
	• Name of exam
	• Results
	• Authentication by responsible provider
	Note: Laboratory reports are usually unauthenticated because they are computer-generated printouts. They may contain the printed name (or initials) of the laboratory technician.
Radiology Reports	Review for documentation of:
	• Physician's order for radiology service
	• Date
	• Name of exam
	• Results
	• Impression
	• Authentication by radiologist
Physical Rehabilitation	Review for documentation of:
	• Reason for referral (attending physician's progress note and/or physician order)
	• Date and time of physical rehabilitation progress note (e.g., physical therapy, occupational therapy, psychological services, recreational therapy, social work services, speech/language pathology, audiology services, vocational rehabilitative services)
	• Summary of patient's clinical condition
	• Goals of treatment
	• Treatment plan
	• Treatment and progress notes with ongoing assessments
	• Authentication by therapist
	Note: Responsible physician should document progress notes reflecting patient's response to therapy
Autopsy Report	Review for documentation of:
	• Provisional anatomic diagnosis (within 3 days after autopsy)
	• Complete protocol (within 60 days after autopsy)
	• Authentication by pathologist

Figure 6-2 (*Continued*) **Guide for Quantitative Analysis of Acute Care Hospital Discharged Inpatient Records**

Retrieve Case01 and a blank deficiency slip, and review this quantitative analysis "walkthrough." *To get started, enter the following information at the top of the deficiency slip:*

- *Marsha Dennis* (patient name)
- *Case01* (patient number)
- *4-27-YYYY* (admission date)
- *Thompson* (Dr[1]:) (He is the attending physician and, therefore, responsible for the majority of documentation.)

NOTE: As you review the case for deficiencies, if you notice documentation that seems out of place, it is likely that it is incorrectly documented in that patient's record (e.g., progress note written in wrong patient's record). Be sure to mark the deficiency slip so that the responsible physician corrects the entry. (To correct this type of entry, the responsible physician draws one line through the entry, writes the words "error; entry documented in wrong patient record," and dates and authenticates the entry.)

INPATIENT FACE SHEET

- Review the entire record to determine whether any diagnoses are missing from the inpatient face sheet.
- For Case01, the physician did not document all of the diagnoses; review the pathology report to see what I mean. *To determine if procedures are missing from the face sheet, review the operative report(s). Circle **Complete** in column 1 of the deficiency slip, and enter "dx" so the doctor knows to enter the complete diagnostic statement and additional diagnoses. (For other cases, review the inpatient face sheet to determine if it is missing diagnoses or procedures when compared to documentation in the record.)*
- The abbreviation D&C is used on the face sheet. Circle the words "No abbreviations." The words "No abbreviations" means that no abbreviations can be used on the face sheet.
- The "discharge instructions" are not documented. *You already circled **Complete** on the deficiency slip because the diagnoses are incompletely documented, so enter "disch instr" to alert the doctor to complete this section of the form.*
- There is no physician authentication (signature) at the bottom of the form. *Circle **Sign** in column 1 of the deficiency slip. In a facility, you would also flag this page with a paperclip, post-it note, etc. so the doctor can easily refer to the form to complete it.*
- Verify that **Discharge Date**, **Time**, and **Days** have been entered. If information is incomplete, refer to physician orders for discharge date and progress notes for discharge time, and calculate days by counting the day of admission in the total but **not** the date of discharge. *For Case01, the discharge date is 4-29-YYYY, the discharge time is 1:35 p.m. (1335 in military time) on the physician discharge order, and days are calculated as 2 (because you count the day of admission but not the day of discharge).*

CONSENT TO ADMISSION

- This form is completed by patient registration staff upon admission of the patient to the hospital.
- If incomplete at discharge, bring to your supervisor's attention so patient registration staff can receive in-service education as to proper completion of the form.
- *Case01 Consent to Admission is properly completed.*

ADVANCE DIRECTIVE

- This form is also completed by patient registration staff upon admission of the

Figure 6-3 Quantitative Analysis: Walkthrough of Case01

(Continues)

patient to the hospital. **Federal law requires completion of this type of form by each patient upon admission.**

- If incomplete at discharge, bring to your supervisor's attention so patient registration staff can receive in-service education as to proper completion of the form.
- *Case01 Advance Directive is properly completed.*

DISCHARGE SUMMARY

- The discharge summary must be placed on the record within 30 days after discharge. The attending physician usually dictates the discharge summary, and health information department medical transcriptionists transcribe the report and file it on the discharged inpatient record.
- *Case01 does not contain discharge summary, so circle **Dictate** in column 1 of the deficiency slip.*

HISTORY & PHYSICAL EXAM

- The history & physical exam must be placed on the record within 24 hours of admission.
- *Case01 contains no history & physical exam, so circle **Dictate** in column 1 of the deficiency slip.*

CONSULTATION REPORT

- Review the physician orders for an order for consultation.
- *Because Case01 does not contain an order for consultation, no consultation report is required; so, leave this blank on the deficiency slip.*

ADMISSION PROGRESS NOTE

- Review the progress notes for documentation of an admission progress note. Be sure it is authenticated.
- *Case01 does not contain an admission progress note, so circle **Document** in column 1 of the deficiency slip.*

DAILY PROGRESS NOTES

- Review the daily progress notes to be sure they are documented as warranted by the patient's condition. Usually there is at least one progress note document for each day the patient remains in the hospital. However, sometimes multiple progress notes are documented on a single day (e.g., critical patient). It would be unusual for a physician to not document a progress note for each day, but this occasionally happens. If the patient is stable, this might not be a deficiency that the physician would need to correct.
- *Case01 contains daily progress notes, but the 4/27/YYYY note is not authenticated. So, circle **Sign** in column 2 on the deficiency slip. Because this note was documented by the anesthesiologist, enter Galloway at the top of that column. He is the anesthesiologist. In order to determine that this note was documented by the anesthesiologist, you must read and understand the content of progress notes.*
- *The 4/28/YYYY and 4/29/YYYY progress notes documented by Dr. Thompson are unauthenticated. So, circle **Sign** in column 1 on the deficiency slip.*

DISCHARGE PROGRESS NOTE

- Review the final progress note to determine if it is the discharge progress note.
- *Case01 contains an incomplete discharge progress note because it doesn't include documentation of the patient's hospital outcome, condition on discharge (disposition), provisions for follow-up care including instructions,*

Figure 6-3 *(Continued)* **Quantitative Analysis: Walkthrough of Case01**

(Continues)

*and final diagnoses. So, circle **Document** in column 1 of the deficiency slip.*

PHYSICIAN ORDERS

- Review physician orders to make sure that entries are dated and authenticated.
- *For Case01, Dr. Thompson did not authenticate the 4/27/YYYY order, so circle **Sign** in column 1 of the deficiency slip.*

NOTE: On 4/27/YYYY, Dr. Townsend called the nursing unit to dictate physician orders to the nurse; this is called a telephone order (T.O.). L. Mosher, RN, documented the order and the abbreviation "RAV," which means "read and verified" – this means the nurse followed the hospital policy that requires any order called in by the physician to be dictated back to the doctor for verification of accuracy. She also authenticated the order as "T.O. Dr. Townsend/L Mosher, RN." Dr. Townsend then cosigns the order within 24 hours.

DISCHARGE ORDER

- The attending physician is responsible for documenting a discharge order (except when a patient dies). It can be as simple as "Discharge." However, it is best if the physician documents the discharge destination (e.g., home, home health care, nursing facility).
- *Case01 discharge order is documented and authenticated, so leave this blank on the deficiency slip.*

CONSENT FOR OPERATION(S) AND/OR PROCEDURE(S) AND ANESTHESIA

- This form is completed by the operating physician after discussion of the procedure, potential risks, and complications with the patient.
- If incomplete at discharge, bring to your supervisor's attention so surgeons can receive in-service education as to proper completion of the form.
- *Case01 Consent for Operation(s) and/or Procedure(s) and Anesthesia is properly completed.*

ANESTHESIA RECORD

- The anesthesia record is documented and authenticated by the circulating and scrub nurses, and it is also authenticated by either the anesthesiologist or certified registered nurse anesthetist (CRNA), whoever provided anesthesia services during surgery.
- *Case01 anesthesia record is properly documented and authenticated, so leave this blank on the deficiency slip.*

PREANESTHESIA AND POSTANESTHESIA RECORD

- This preanesthesia report is documented by the anesthesiologist 24 hours or more prior to the patient's surgery. The postanesthesia evaluation is documented by the anesthesiologist about 3 hours after surgery. **NOTE**: Some anesthesiologists document their pre- and postanesthesia evaluations in the progress notes instead of on this record.
- *Case01 preanesthesia and postanesthesia record is properly documented and authenticated, so leave this blank on the deficiency slip.* **NOTE**: Dr. Galloway documented progress notes in addition to the pre- and postanesthesia record.

OPERATIVE REPORT

- The operative report is to be dictated by the surgeon immediately following surgery, transcribed, and placed on the patient's record. This is important in case the patient develops complications and physicians need to refer to the operative report documentation shortly following treatment. If there is a medical transcription delay, the surgeon must document comprehensive progress notes describing the surgery.

Figure 6-3 *(Continued)* **Quantitative Analysis: Walkthrough of Case01**

(Continues)

- *Case01 operative report is present and authenticated by the surgeon, so leave this blank on the deficiency slip.*

PATHOLOGY REPORT

- The pathologist reviews tissue (and other items removed from patients) during and after surgery and dictates a pathology report, which is placed on the patient's record.
- *Case01 pathology report is present and authenticated by the pathologist, so leave this blank on the deficiency slip.* If the pathology report was missing or the pathologist's authentication was required, indicate this deficiency in column 3 of the deficiency slip (because neither the attending physician nor anesthesiologist is responsible for the pathology report).

RECOVERY ROOM RECORD

- The recovery room record is documented and authenticated by the recovery room nurse. Neither the anesthesiologist nor the surgeon authenticates this report.
- *Case01 recovery room report is present and authenticated, so leave this blank on the deficiency slip.*

LAB REPORTS

- Review the physician orders to make sure that any lab work ordered by the physician is present in the record. Do not mark the deficiency slip for completion if absent. Instead, find the reports and file them in the record.
- EXAMPLE: If the physician ordered a urinalysis, look for the results of urinalysis in the lab data section of the record.
- *On the job, you would locate the reports and place them in the record.*

RADIOLOGY REPORT

- Review the physician orders to make sure that the results of any x-rays ordered by the physician are present in the record.
- EXAMPLE: If the physician ordered a chest x-ray, look for a transcribed radiology report that is authenticated by the radiologist.
- *Case01 radiology report is present and authenticated, so leave this blank on the deficiency slip.*

Figure 6-3 (*Continued*) **Quantitative Analysis: Walkthrough of Case01**

LAB ASSIGNMENT 6-3   Forms Design

OBJECTIVES

At the end of this assignment, the student should be able to:
- Identify the functional characteristics of forms control and design
- Redesign an inpatient operative report

Overview

A paper-based record system requires that a single individual be responsible for the control and design of all forms adopted for use in the patient record. This assignment will familiarize the student with forms design processes.

Instructions

1. Review the Forms Control and Design section of Chapter 6 in your textbook.
2. Go to the section of Chapter 6 that discusses documentation requirements for an operative report. Compare those requirements to the operative report (Figure 6-4) used by Alfred State Medical Center in the 1950s. You will find that this operative report is out-of-date and contains elements that physicians now dictate (instead of handwriting on the report as was the practice in the 1950s). Keep this in mind as you redesign the form.
3. Redesign the operative report using MS Word or Excel, carefully considering the characteristics of forms control and design (from Chapter 6 of your textbook).

   NOTE: Be creative, and design your form to be visually appealing.
4. Be sure to include the following information on the form you design:
   a. Facility name, address, and phone number (at the bottom of the form)
   b. Patient identification area (e.g., addressograph box)
   c. Form number and revision date
5. *Remember!* You are redesigning the form, not transcribing a report. Therefore, it is unnecessary to include specific patient information or report results.

```
                                                          OPERATIVE RECORD

Name                              Ward
Date                              Hist #
Service                           Surgeon
Preoperative Dx:
Postoperative Dx:
Surgery Performed:
Postion                           Duration
Anesthetist
Duration
DESCRIPTION (Incision, Findings, Technique, Sutures, Drainage Culture, Specimen,
Clean, Borderline, Septic)




Condition:
Medication:
Drains:
F 550
LENOX HILL HOSPITAL, NEW YORK CITY
```

Figure 6-4   Operative Report Used by Alfred State Medical Center in the 1950s

Chapter 7

Numbering & Filing Systems and Record Storage & Circulation

🌹 INTRODUCTION

This chapter will focus on familiarizing the student with numbering and filing systems, filing equipment, file folders, filing controls, circulation systems, and the security of health information.

LAB ASSIGNMENT 7-1   Straight Numeric and Terminal-Digit Filing

OBJECTIVES

At the end of this assignment, the student should be able to:

- Sequence patient record numbers in straight numeric filing order
- Sequence patient record numbers in terminal-digit filing order

Overview

In straight numeric filing, records are filed in strict chronologic order according to patient number, from the lowest to the highest number. Terminal-digit filing is used in health care facilities that assign six-digit patient numbers because the number can be easily subdivided into three parts: primary, secondary, and tertiary digits. This assignment will familiarize the student with organizing patient numbers according to the straight numeric and terminal-digit filing order.

Instructions

1. Refer to the straight numeric and terminal-digit filing sections of Chapter 7 in your textbook.
2. Resequence patient record numbers in straight numeric order in column 2 and in terminal-digit order in column 3.
3. Then assign the next straight numeric and terminal-digit number in the sequence.
4. To get you started, the first two rows of each are completed.

Student Name _____

Straight Numeric and Terminal-Digit Order of Patient Record Numbers

PART I: Resequence patient record numbers in straight numeric order (column 2) and terminal-digit order (column 3).

	Straight Numeric Order	Terminal-Digit Order
031950	031950	878912
101075	061946	884325
212153		
651473		
451450		
901895		
608946		
516582		
878912		
061946		
990855		
894851		
619546		
625497		
884325		
606339		
129456		
213526		

PART II: State the next straight numeric and terminal-digit number for the sequencing of records in the file.

	Straight Numeric Order	Terminal-Digit Order
651430	651431	661430
845626	845627	855626
489225		
231027		
689212		
948312		
980855		
894851		
619546		
625497		
884325		
606339		
129456		
213526		

LAB ASSIGNMENT 7-2   Calculating Record Storage Needs

OBJECTIVES

At the end of this assignment, the student should be able to:

- Calculate record storage needs
- Determine the number of shelving units needed to store patient records

Overview

When purchasing filing equipment, the number of filing units for purchase must be predetermined. This assignment will familiarize the student with calculating record storage needs and determining the number of filing units needed.

Instructions

1.   Calculate the number of filing units to be purchased for each of the five cases below.

EXAMPLE: A 9-shelf unit contains 50 inches per shelf. There are 18,000 inches of current records to be housed, and it is projected that an additional 5,000 filing inches will be needed.

Step 1:   Calculate the total filing inches available per shelf unit.

$$9 \times 50 = 450 \text{ filing inches per unit}$$

Step 2:   Total the inches of current records and projected inches.

$$18,000 + 5,000 = 23,000 \text{ inches to be housed}$$

Step 3:   Divide inches to be housed by filing inches per unit, which determines the number of shelving units to be purchased.

$$23,000 \div 450 = 51.1 \text{ shelving units}$$

NOTE: Because ".1" (one-tenth) of a filing unit cannot be purchased, round to 52 filing units.

Student Name _____

Calculating Record Storage Needs

Case 1
10-shelf unit. 50 inches/shelf. 15,000 inches of current records. 8,000 projected inches needed for future.

Case 2
12-shelf unit. 150 inches/shelf. 21,000 inches of current records. 6,000 projected inches needed for future.

Case 3
20-shelf unit. 125 inches/shelf. 145,000 inches of current records. 20,000 projected inches needed for future.

Case 4
10-shelf unit. 135 inches/shelf. 27,000 inches of current records. 2,400 projected inches needed for future.

Case 5
15-shelf unit. 50 inches/shelf. 15,000 inches of current records. 10,000 projected inches needed for future.

LAB ASSIGNMENT 7-3   Guiding Terminal-Digit Files

OBJECTIVES

At the end of this assignment, the student should be able to:

- Calculate the number of file guides needed for a terminal-digit filing system
- Determine the number pattern for terminal-digit file guides

Overview

File guides are used to facilitate the filing and retrieval of patient records in a file system. This assignment will familiarize the student with identifying the number of file guides needed for file areas, as well as the pattern used to guide the files.

Instructions

1. Determine the number of file guides to be purchased as well as the pattern used to guide the terminal-digit files.

    EXAMPLE: The terminal-digit file area contains 125,000 records, and the standard rule of 50 records between file guides will be used. (Remember, there are 100 primary sections in a terminal-digit system, and there are 100 secondary sections in each primary section.)

    Step 1:   Calculate the number of file guides to be purchased.

    125,000 ÷ 50 = 2,500 file guides

    Step 2:   Determine the number of secondary guides for each primary section.

    2,500 ÷ 100 = 25 secondary guides for each primary section

    Step 3:   Determine the pattern to guide each primary section.

    100 ÷ 25 = 4

    Thus, for primary section 00, secondary guides will appear as:

    00 04 00
    00 08 00
    00 12 00
    00 16 00
    00 20 00
    etc.

Student Name _____

Guiding Terminal-Digit Files

1. Hospital XYZ has 60,000 records in its terminal-digit file area.

2. Hospital ABC has 80,000 records in its terminal-digit file area.

3. Hospital LMN has 100,000 records in its terminal-digit file area.

LAB ASSIGNMENT 7-4   Assigning Pseudonumbers

OBJECTIVES

At the end of this assignment, the student should be able to:

- Assign pseudonumbers to patients
- Explain the purpose of assigning pseudonumbers

Overview

Pseudonumbers are assigned to any patient who does not have a SSN when it is used as the patient record numbering system. This assignment will familiarize the student with assigning pseudonumbers.

Instructions

1. Assign a pseudonumber to each patient listed below. Refer to Chapter 7 in your textbook to review the purpose of assigning pseudonumbers.

   Pseudonumber

abc	1	jkl	4	stu	7
def	2	mno	5	vwx	8
ghi	3	pqr	6	yz	9

   NOTE: If the patient has no middle initial, assign 0.

   NOTE: The assigned pseudonumber uses the same format as the SSN (e.g., 000-00-0000).

   EXAMPLE: Mark R. Anderson. DOB 11/1/92. Pseudonumber: 561-11-0192.

Student Name _____

Assigning Pseudonumbers

Patient Name and DOB	Pseudonumber
Edward Francis Smart, 5/3/30	
Joseph Kenneth First, 9/18/37	
Eleanor Delores Comp, 7/4/45	
William David Love, 4/15/58	
Sherrie Rebecca Gage, 8/19/67	
Matthew David Brothers, 10/15/89	
Michelle Brittany Ash, 12/30/84	
Robert James Shumaker, 8/7/59	
Michaela Grace, 1/10/87	

LAB ASSIGNMENT 7-5   Assigning Soundex Codes

OBJECTIVES

At the end of this assignment, the student should be able to:

- Assign Soundex codes to patient names
- Explain the reason Soundex codes are assigned to patient names

Overview

The Soundex indexing system allows names that sound alike but are spelled differently to be indexed together. This means that surnames (last names) are indexed so they can be found regardless of spelling. This assignment will familiarize the student with assigning Soundex codes to patient names.

Instructions

1. Review the rules for assigning Soundex codes in Chapter 7 of your textbook.
2. Assign a Soundex code to each patient listed below.
3. To get you started, several codes have been assigned.

Student Name _____

Assigning Soundex Codes

EXAMPLE: To begin the process of assigning a phonetic code for patient Anderson, enter the first letter of the last name followed by a dash (A-). Then, disregarding that letter, assign a number to remaining letters according to the Soundex rules. Assign 5 to the n, 3 to the d, and 6 to the r. Do not assign numbers to vowels or the letters remaining after r (because the maximum length of the code is three numbers).

Anderson	A-536
Condor	
Senator	
Darlington	D-645
Goodyear	
Levy	
Shaw	
Abbott	
Farrell	
Mann	M-500
Jackson	
Biggs	
McCarthy	
Todt	
Gjeljuag	
Lloyd	
Schkolnick	
Skow	
Henman	

Chapter 8

Indexes, Registers, and Health Data Collection

🍀 INTRODUCTION

This chapter will familiarize the student with indexes, registers, case abstracting, and health data collection.

LAB ASSIGNMENT 8-1   Case Abstracting

OBJECTIVES

At the end of this assignment, the student should be able to:

- List core data elements for the Uniform Hospital Discharge Data Set (UHDDS)
- Abstract discharged acute care patient records for the purpose of generating indexes (e.g., disease index)

Overview

Case abstracting involves collecting patient information from records and entering data into a computerized abstracting program (or onto paper abstracts for data entry into a computerized abstracting program) to generate indexes (e.g., physician, diagnosis, and procedure) and report data to state and federal agencies. This assignment will familiarize the student with abstracting UHDDS core data elements from discharged acute care patient records.

Instructions

1. Go to the Student Companion Website and print one case abstracting form (Figure 8-1A, for use with ICD-9-CM codes, and Figure 8-1B, for use with ICD-10-CM codes.) for each patient record to be abstracted (10 total). Your instructor will advise you as to whether you should use Figure 8-1A or 8-1B.
2. Refer to Appendix I, where Case01 through Case10 are located.

   NOTE: If you prefer, you may also access these records at the Student Companion Website and review online.
3. Refer to the Overview of Case Abstracting (Figure 8-2), and review a sample completed abstract (Figure 8-3A, for use wtih ICD-9-CM codes, and Figure 8-3B, for use with ICD-10-CM codes).
4. Review the Case Abstracting: Walkthrough of Case01 (Figure 8-4).
5. Complete each abstracting form by entering data from Case01–Case10.
6. Submit completed abstracting forms to your instructor for evaluation.

ALFRED STATE MEDICAL CENTER ACUTE CARE (INPATIENT) CASE ABSTRACT

01 Hospital Number

02 Patient Date of Birth

Month   Day   Year (YYYY)

03 Patient Gender

1 Male
2 Female
3 Other
4 Unknown

04A Race

1 American Indian/Eskimo/Aleut
2 Asian or Pacific Islander
3 Black
4 White
5 Other
6 Unknown

04B Ethnicity

1 Spanish origin/Hispanic
2 Non-Spanish origin/Non-Hispanic
3 Unknown

05A Living Arrangement

1 Alone
2 With spouse
3 With children
4 With parent or guardian
5 With relative other than spouse
6 With nonrelatives
7 Unknown

05B Marital Status

1 Married
2 Single
3 Divorced
4 Separated
5 Unknown

06 Patient Number

07 Admission Date and Hour

Month   Day   Year (YYYY)

Military Time

08 Type of Admission

1 Scheduled
2 Unscheduled

09 Discharge Date and Time

Month   Day   Year (YYYY)

Military Time

10 Attending Physician Number

11 Operating Physician Number

12 Principal Diagnosis Code

ICD Code

16 Birth Weight of Neonate

Kilograms

Date Abstract Completed

Month   Day   Year (YYYY)

13 Other Diagnosis Code(s)

14 Qualifiers for Other Diagnoses

1 Onset preceded hospital admission
2 Onset followed hospital admission
3 Uncertain whether onset preceded or followed hospital
   admission

ICD Code

ICD Code

ICD Code

ICD Code

ICD Code

ICD Code

17 Procedures, Dates, and Operating Physician UPIN

Month   Day   Year (YYYY)   UPIN

Month   Day   Year (YYYY)   UPIN

Month   Day   Year (YYYY)   UPIN

Month   Day   Year (YYYY)   UPIN

Month   Day   Year (YYYY)   UPIN

Month   Day   Year (YYYY)   UPIN

Month   Day   Year (YYYY)   UPIN

15 External Cause of Injury Codes

ICD E-code

ICD E-code

ICD E-code

ICD E-code

ICD E-code

18 Disposition

1 Discharged to home
2 Discharged to acute care hospital
3 Discharged to nursing facility
4 Discharged home to be under the care of a home health
   service (including hospice)
5 Discharged to other health care facility
6 Left against medical advice (AMA)
7 Alive, other
8 Died

19 Patient's Expected Payment Source

1 Blue Cross/Blue Shield
2 Other commercial insurance
3 Other liability insurance
4 Medicare
5 Medicaid
6 Workers' Compensation
7 Self-insured employer plan
8 Health maintenance
   organization (HMO)

9 TRICARE
10 CHAMPVA
11 Other government payer
12 Self-pay
13 No charge (e.g., charity,
    special research, teaching)
14 Other

20 Total Charges

$

Figure 8-1A   Case Abstracting Form for Use with ICD-9-CM Codes (Based on California Office of Statewide Health Planning and Development.)

ALFRED STATE MEDICAL CENTER ACUTE CARE (INPATIENT) CASE ABSTRACT

01 Hospital Number

02 Patient Date of Birth

Month   Day   Year (YYYY)

03 Patient Gender

1 Male
2 Female
3 Other
4 Unknown

04A Race

1 American Indian/Eskimo/Aleut
2 Asian or Pacific Islander
3 Black
4 White
5 Other
6 Unknown

04B Ethnicity

1 Spanish origin/Hispanic
2 Non-Spanish origin/Non-Hispanic
3 Unknown

05A Living Arrangement

1 Alone
2 With spouse
3 With children
4 With parent or guardian
5 With relative other than spouse
6 With nonrelatives
7 Unknown

05B Marital Status

1 Married
2 Single
3 Divorced
4 Separated
5 Unknown

06 Patient Number

07 Admission Date and Hour

Month   Day   Year (YYYY)

Military Time

08 Type of Admission

1 Scheduled
2 Unscheduled

09 Discharge Date and Time

Month   Day   Year (YYYY)

Military Time

10 Attending Physician Number

11 Operating Physician Number

12 Principal Diagnosis Code

ICD Code

16 Birth Weight of Neonate

Kilograms

Date Abstract Completed

Month   Day   Year (YYYY)

13 Other Diagnosis Code(s)

14 Qualifiers for Other Diagnoses

1 Onset preceded hospital admission
2 Onset followed hospital admission
3 Uncertain whether onset preceded or followed hospital
  admission

ICD Code

ICD Code

ICD Code

ICD Code

ICD Code

ICD Code

17 Procedures, Dates, and Operating Physician UPIN

Month   Day   Year (YYYY)   UPIN

Month   Day   Year (YYYY)   UPIN

Month   Day   Year (YYYY)   UPIN

Month   Day   Year (YYYY)   UPIN

Month   Day   Year (YYYY)   UPIN

Month   Day   Year (YYYY)   UPIN

Month   Day   Year (YYYY)   UPIN

15 External Cause of Injury Codes

18 Disposition

1 Discharged to home
2 Discharged to acute care hospital
3 Discharged to nursing facility
4 Discharged home to be under the care of a home health
  service (including hospice)
5 Discharged to other health care facility
6 Left against medical advice (AMA)
7 Alive, other
8 Died

19 Patient's Expected Payment Source

1 Blue Cross/Blue Shield
2 Other commercial insurance
3 Other liability insurance
4 Medicare
5 Medicaid
6 Workers' Compensation
7 Self-insured employer plan
8 Health maintenance
  organization (HMO)

9 TRICARE
10 CHAMPVA
11 Other government payer
12 Self-pay
13 No charge (e.g., charity,
   special research, teaching)
14 Other

20 Total Charges

$

Figure 8-1B   Case Abstracting Form for Use with ICD-10-CM Codes (Based on California Office of Statewide Health Planning and Development.)

Abstracting involves transferring information from the patient record onto a data entry source document called the case abstract or discharge data abstract. Two methods are typically used:

- *Paper abstract:* prepared for each discharged patient, batched, and sent to the facility's computer center or mailed to a commercial service

- *Online data entry:* abstracted data is entered into a computer and processed by the facility or data is transferred onto a disk and mailed to a commercial service, or data is transmitted to the commercial service using a modem

Advantages of facility-based abstracting systems include:

- Ready access to information from in-house data-processing department

- Less costly than a commercial service

Disadvantages of facility-based abstracting systems include:

- No access to national comparison statistical reports (e.g., comparison of one hospital's infection rate to another's)

- Other departments (e.g., payroll) may take priority when reports are being run

Advantages of a commercial abstracting service include:

- Comparative reports on national and areawide statistics are available

- Such services are in business to serve the health information management department

Disadvantages of a commercial abstracting service include:

- Can be costly (e.g., charge per discharged patient)

- Comparative reports can cost extra

Figure 8-2   Overview of Case Abstracting

ALFRED STATE MEDICAL CENTER ACUTE CARE (INPATIENT) CASE ABSTRACT

01 Hospital Number

| 0 | 0 | 0 | 9 | 9 | 9 |

02 Patient Date of Birth

| 0 | 5 | 3 | 0 | Y | Y | Y | Y |

Month　Day　Year (YYYY)

03 Patient Gender

1 Male
2 Female
3 Other
4 Unknown

| 2 |

04A Race

1 American Indian/Eskimo/Aleut
2 Asian or Pacific Islander
3 Black
4 White
5 Other
6 Unknown

| 3 |

04B Ethnicity

1 Spanish origin/Hispanic
2 Non-Spanish origin/Non-Hispanic
3 Unknown

| 2 |

05A Living Arrangement

1 Alone
2 With spouse
3 With children
4 With parent or guardian
5 With relative other than spouse
6 With nonrelatives
7 Unknown

| 2 |

05B Marital Status

1 Married
2 Single
3 Divorced
4 Separated
5 Unknown

| 1 |

06 Patient Number

| 1 | 2 | 3 | 4 | 5 | 6 |

07 Admission Date and Hour

| 1 | 0 | 1 | 0 | Y | Y | Y | Y |

Month　Day　Year (YYYY)

| 1 | 1 | 0 | 0 |

Military Time

08 Type of Admission

1 Scheduled
2 Unscheduled

| 1 |

09 Discharge Date and Time

| 1 | 0 | 1 | 3 | Y | Y | Y | Y |

Month　Day　Year (YYYY)

| 0 | 9 | 0 | 0 |

Military Time

10 Attending Physician Number

| 0 | 0 | 0 | 1 | 4 | 1 |

11 Operating Physician Number

| | | | | | |

12 Principal Diagnosis Code

| 4 | 1 | 0 | . | 0 | 1 |

ICD Code

16 Birth Weight of Neonate

| | | | | |

Kilograms

Date Abstract Completed

| 1 | 0 | 1 | 3 | Y | Y | Y | Y |

Month　Day　Year (YYYY)

13 Other Diagnosis Code(s)

14 Qualifiers for Other Diagnoses

1 Onset preceded hospital admission
2 Onset followed hospital admission
3 Uncertain whether onset preceded or followed hospital admission

| 4 | 1 | 3 | . | 9 |　　| |
ICD Code

| 4 | 0 | 1 | . | 9 |　　| |
ICD Code

| | | | . | |　　| |
ICD Code

| | | | | . |　　| |
ICD Code

| | | | | . |　　| |
ICD Code

| | | | | . |　　| |
ICD Code

17 Procedures, Dates, and Operating Physician UPIN

| 3 | 7 | . | 2 | 3 | | 1 | 0 | 1 | 0 | Y | Y | Y | Y | | 4 | 5 | B | 6 | 8 | 0 |
| | | | | | | Month　Day　Year (YYYY) | | | | | | | | | UPIN |

| 8 | 8 | . | 5 | 5 | | 1 | 0 | 1 | 0 | Y | Y | Y | Y | | 4 | 5 | B | 6 | 8 | 0 |
| | | | | | | Month　Day　Year (YYYY) | | | | | | | | | UPIN |

(remaining procedure, Month/Day/Year, and UPIN rows blank)

15 External Cause of Injury Codes

| | | | . | |
ICD E-code

| | | | . | |
ICD E-code

| | | | . | |
ICD E-code

| | | | . | |
ICD E-code

| | | | . | |
ICD E-code

18 Disposition

1 Discharged to home
2 Discharged to acute care hospital
3 Discharged to nursing facility
4 Discharged home to be under the care of a home health service (including hospice)
5 Discharged to other health care facility
6 Left against medical advice (AMA)
7 Alive, other
8 Died

| 1 |

19 Patient's Expected Payment Source

| 1 |

1 Blue Cross/Blue Shield
2 Other commercial insurance
3 Other liability insurance
4 Medicare
5 Medicaid
6 Workers' Compensation
7 Self-insured employer plan
8 Health maintenance organization (HMO)

9 TRICARE
10 CHAMPVA
11 Other government payer
12 Self-pay
13 No charge (e.g., charity, special research, teaching)
14 Other

20 Total Charges

| $ | | 2 | 8 | , | 9 | 4 | 5 | . | 5 | 9 |

Figure 8-3A   Sample Completed Acute Care (Inpatient) Case Abstract (Note: This form is designed for use with ICD-9-CM codes.)

ALFRED STATE MEDICAL CENTER ACUTE CARE (INPATIENT) CASE ABSTRACT

01 Hospital Number

| 0 | 0 | 0 | 9 | 9 | 9 |

02 Patient Date of Birth

| 0 | 5 | 3 | 0 | Y | Y | Y | Y |
| Month | | Day | | Year (YYYY) | | | |

03 Patient Gender

1 Male
2 Female
3 Other
4 Unknown

2

04A Race

1 American Indian/Eskimo/Aleut
2 Asian or Pacific Islander
3 Black
4 White
5 Other
6 Unknown

3

04B Ethnicity

1 Spanish origin/Hispanic
2 Non-Spanish origin/Non-Hispanic
3 Unknown

2

05A Living Arrangement

1 Alone
2 With spouse
3 With children
4 With parent or guardian
5 With relative other than spouse
6 With nonrelatives
7 Unknown

2

05B Marital Status

1 Married
2 Single
3 Divorced
4 Separated
5 Unknown

1

06 Patient Number

| 1 | 2 | 3 | 4 | 5 | 6 |

07 Admission Date and Hour

| 1 | 0 | 1 | 0 | Y | Y | Y | Y |
| Month | | Day | | Year (YYYY) | | | |

| 1 | 1 | 0 | 0 |
Military Time

08 Type of Admission

1 Scheduled
2 Unscheduled

1

09 Discharge Date and Time

| 1 | 0 | 1 | 3 | Y | Y | Y | Y |
| Month | | Day | | Year (YYYY) | | | |

| 0 | 9 | 0 | 0 |
Military Time

10 Attending Physician Number

| 0 | 0 | 0 | 1 | 4 | 1 |

11 Operating Physician Number

| | | | | | |

12 Principal Diagnosis Code

| I | 2 | 1 | . | 0 | 9 | |
ICD Code

16 Birth Weight of Neonate

| | | | |
Kilograms

Date Abstract Completed

| 1 | 0 | 1 | 3 | Y | Y | Y | Y |
| Month | | Day | | Year (YYYY) | | | |

13 Other Diagnosis Code(s)

14 Qualifiers for Other Diagnoses

1 Onset preceded hospital admission
2 Onset followed hospital admission
3 Uncertain whether onset preceded or followed hospital admission

| I | 2 | 0 | . | 8 | | |
ICD Code

| I | 1 | 0 | . | | | |
ICD Code

| | | | . | | | |
ICD Code

| | | | . | | | |
ICD Code

| | | | . | | | |
ICD Code

| | | | . | | | |
ICD Code

17 Procedures, Dates, and Operating Physician UPIN

| 4 | A | 0 | 2 | 0 | N | 8 | | 1 | 0 | 1 | 0 | Y | Y | Y | Y | | 4 | 5 | B | 6 | 8 | 0 |
| | | | | | | | | Month | | Day | | Year (YYYY) | | | | | UPIN | | | | | |

| B | 2 | 0 | 1 | 0 | Z | Z | | 1 | 0 | 1 | 0 | Y | Y | Y | Y | | 4 | 5 | B | 6 | 8 | 0 |
| | | | | | | | | Month | | Day | | Year (YYYY) | | | | | UPIN | | | | | |

(Month / Day / Year (YYYY) / UPIN rows continue blank below)

15 External Cause of Injury Codes

| | | | . | | |

| | | | . | | |

| | | | . | | |

| | | | . | | |

| | | | . | | |

18 Disposition

1 Discharged to home
2 Discharged to acute care hospital
3 Discharged to nursing facility
4 Discharged home to be under the care of a home health service (including hospice)
5 Discharged to other health care facility
6 Left against medical advice (AMA)
7 Alive, other
8 Died

1

19 Patient's Expected Payment Source

1 Blue Cross/Blue Shield
2 Other commercial insurance
3 Other liability insurance
4 Medicare
5 Medicaid
6 Workers' Compensation
7 Self-insured employer plan
8 Health maintenance organization (HMO)
9 TRICARE
10 CHAMPVA
11 Other government payer
12 Self-pay
13 No charge (e.g., charity, special research, teaching)
14 Other

1

20 Total Charges

| $ | | 2 | 8 | , | 9 | 4 | 5 | . | 5 | 9 |

Figure 8-3B   Sample Completed Acute Care (Inpatient) Case Abstract (Note: This form is designed for use with ICD-10-CM and ICD-10-PCS codes.)

BLOCK 01:	Enter 000999 as the hospital number.
Block 02:	Enter patient's date of birth in MMDDYYYY format. **EXAMPLE**: 08021957
Block 03:	Enter 1-digit code for the patient's gender.
Block 04A: Block 04B:	Enter 1-digit code for the patient's race. Enter 1-digit code for the patient's ethnicity. **NOTE**: If race and ethnicity are not located on face sheet, review patient record.
Block 05A: Block 05B:	Enter 1-digit code for patient's living arrangement. **NOTE**: Review patient record to locate living arrangement. Enter 1-digit code for patient's marital status.
Block 06:	Enter 6-digit patient number. **EXAMPLE**: CASE01 Block 07: Enter patient's date of admission as MMDDYYYY. **EXAMPLE**: 01012004 Enter time of admission as military time. **EXAMPLE**: 1300 (1 p.m.)
Block 09:	Enter patient's date of discharge as MMDDYYYY. **EXAMPLE**: 01012004 Enter time of discharge as military time. **EXAMPLE**: 1300 (1 p.m.)
Block 10:	Enter attending physician's facility-assigned number. **NOTE**: For this assignment, 999 is pre-entered. Block 11: Enter operating physician's facility-assigned number, if applicable. **NOTE**: If the patient underwent surgery, enter 001 as the operating physician's number.
Block 12: Block 13: Block 14: Block 15:	Enter principal diagnosis code. Enter secondary diagnosis code(s). Enter the 1-digit number to indicate onset of condition. **NOTE**: Review admission progress note to determine onset. Enter external cause of injury code, if applicable. Otherwise, leave blank.
Block 16:	If newborn, enter birth weight in kilograms. Otherwise, leave blank.
Block 17:	Enter principal procedure code.
Block 18:	Enter 1-digit number to indicate patient's disposition. **NOTE**: Review discharge progress note or discharge summary to locate disposition.
Block 19:	Enter 1- or 2-digit code to indicate patient's expected payment source. **NOTE**: Expected payment source is primary third-party payer (e.g., BCBS).
Block 20:	Enter charges. **NOTE**: Total charges are not documented in acute care inpatient records. This data will be input by the billing office.

Figure 8-4   Case Abstracting: Walkthrough of Case01

LAB ASSIGNMENT 8-2   Master Patient Index Data Entry

OBJECTIVES

At the end of this assignment, the student should be able to:

- Enter complete and accurate data onto a master patient index card
- Explain the purpose of maintaining a master patient index

Overview

Complete and accurate data is entered into an automated master patient index (MPI) or onto MPI cards so that patient information can be easily retrieved. This assignment will familiarize the student with completion of an MPI card.

Instructions

1. Go to the Student Companion Website and print the Master Patient Index Form (Figure 8-5).

2. Refer to Appendix I, where Case01 through Case10 are located.

   NOTE: If you prefer, you may also access these records at the Student Companion Website and review online.

3. Review the sample completed MPI (Figure 8-6).

4. Complete each MPI form for Case01 through Case10 by entering information from each record onto each form.

5. Submit completed MPI forms to your instructor for evaluation.

1. LAST NAME	2. FIRST NAME	3. MIDDLE NAME	4. GENDER	5. AGE	6. RACE	7. PATIENT NUMBER

8. ADDRESS			9. DATE OF BIRTH			10. THIRD PARTY PAYERS
			a. MONTH	b. DAY	c. YEAR	

11. MAIDEN NAME	12. PLACE OF BIRTH	13. SOCIAL SECURITY NUMBER (SSN)

14. ADMISSION DATE	15. DISCHARGE DATE	15. PROVIDER	17. TYPE	18. DISCHARGE STATUS

Figure 8-5   Sample Blank Master Patient Index Card

1. LAST NAME	2. FIRST NAME	3. MIDDLE NAME	4. GENDER	5. AGE	6. RACE	7. PATIENT NUMBER
LAMBERT	PATRICIA	ANN	F	48	BLACK	123456

8. ADDRESS			9. DATE OF BIRTH			10. THIRD PARTY PAYERS
101 MAIN ST			a. MONTH	b. DAY	c. YEAR	BCBS
ALFRED NY 14802			05	30	YYYY	AETNA

11. MAIDEN NAME	12. PLACE OF BIRTH	13. SOCIAL SECURITY NUMBER (SSN)
SANFORD	ELMIRA, N.Y.	123-56-6789

14. ADMISSION DATE	15. DISCHARGE DATE	15. PROVIDER	17. TYPE	18. DISCHARGE STATUS
1010YYYY	1013YYYY	GRIFFITH	IP	HOME
0304YYYY	0306YYYY	GRIFFITH	ED	HOME

Figure 8-6   Sample Completed Master Patient Index Card

LAB ASSIGNMENT 8-3 Disease, Procedure, and Physician Indexes

OBJECTIVES

At the end of this assignment, the student should be able to:

- Analyze data located on disease, procedure, and physician indexes
- Interpret data from disease, procedure, and physician indexes

Overview

Disease, procedure, and physician indexes (Figures 8-7, 8-8, and 8-9) contain data abstracted from patient records and entered into a computerized database, from which the respective index is generated. This lab assignment will allow students to analyze and interpret data found in disease, procedure, and physician indexes.

Instructions

1. Answer each question by reviewing information in the appropriate index.
   a. What is the primary arrangement of the disease index?
   b. What is the primary arrangement of the procedure index?
   c. What is the primary arrangement of the physician index?
   d. How many different attending physicians treated patients listed on the disease index?
   e. How many different attending physicians treated patients listed on the procedure index?
   f. What is the average patient age treated by Dr. James Smith on the physician index?

2. The quality management committee has requested the following information. Determine the correct answer, and identify the index used to locate the information.
   a. Age of the youngest and oldest patient who underwent craniotomy surgery.
   b. Secondary diagnoses codes for patients treated for acute poliomyelitis.
   c. Medical record numbers for patients treated by Dr. Jane Thompson.
   d. Medical record numbers of patients treated with HIV as primary diagnosis.
   e. Age of the oldest patient treated for acute poliomyelitis by Dr. Jane Thompson.

Alfred State Medical Center

Disease Index

Reporting Period   0801YYYYó0801YYYY   Date Prepared   08-02-YYYY

                                                                              Page   1 of 5

Principal Diagnosis	Secondary Diagnoses	Attending Physician	Age	Gender	Payer	Patient Number
HUMAN IMMUNODEFICIENCY VIRUS [HIV] DISEASE						
042	112.0	138	24	M	BC	236248
042	136.3	024	35	M	BC	123456
042	176.0	036	42	F	BC	213654
ACUTE POLIOMYELITIS						
045.00	250.00	236	80	M	MC	236954
045.00	401.9	235	60	F	MD	562159
045.00	496	138	34	F	WC	236268

Figure 8-7   Disease Index

Alfred State Medical Center

Procedure Index

Reporting Period   0301YYYYñ0301YYYY   Date Prepared   03-02-YYYY

                                                                              Page   1 of 5

Principal Procedure	Secondary Procedures	Attending Physician	Age	Gender	Payer	Patient Number
CLOSED BIOPSY OF BRAIN						
01.13		248	42	F	01	562359
CRANIOTOMY NOS						
01.24		235	56	F	03	231587
01.24		326	27	M	02	239854
01.24		236	08	F	05	562198
01.24		236	88	M	05	615789
DEBRIDEMENT OF SKULL NOS						
01.25		326	43	M	03	653218

Figure 8-8   Procedure Index

```
                    Alfred State Medical Center

                         Physician Index

Reporting Period     0101YYYY60101YYYY              Date Prepared   01-02-YYYY

                                                        Page   1 of 5


 Attending      Patient    Age   Gender   Payer   Admission   Discharge   LOS   Principal
 Physician      Number                             Date        Date              Diagnosis

JAMES SMITH, M.D.
    024         123456     35     M        BC      1228YYYY    0101YYYY    4     042

    024         213654     42     F        BC      1229YYYY    0101YYYY    3     042

    024         236248     24     M        BC      1229YYYY    0101YYYY    3     042


JANE THOMSON, M.D.
    025         236268     34     F        WC      1229YYYY    0101YYYY    3     045.00

    025         562159     60     F        MD      1230YYYY    0101YYYY    2     045.00

    025         236954     80     M        MC      1231YYYY    0101YYYY    1     045.00
```

Figure 8-9   Physician Index

Chapter 9

Legal Aspects of Health Information Management

🍄 INTRODUCTION

This chapter will familiarize the student with legal aspects of documentation, legislation that impacts health information management, and release of protected health information (PHI).

LAB ASSIGNMENT 9-1   Notice of Privacy Practices

OBJECTIVES

At the end of this assignment, the student should be able to:

- Explain the standards for privacy of health information as established by the HIPAA Privacy Rule
- Analyze the contents of a Privacy Notice

Overview

Patients have a right to the privacy of their health information, and they must be provided with written notice of this right (e.g., Notice of Privacy Practices) when they receive services from health care facilities and providers. This assignment will familiarize the student with the HIPAA Privacy Rule and require the student to analyze a Notice of Privacy Practices.

Instructions

1. Using an Internet browser (e.g., Microsoft Internet Explorer, Google Chrome), go to www.ahima.org.
2. Click on HIM BODY OF KNOWLEDGE.
3. On the left, click the "PRACTICE BRIEFS" folder. Search for the Practice Brief entitled "Notice of Privacy Practices (Updated) 10/2/13."
4. Review the practice brief, paying close attention to the section on federal requirements.
5. Review Figure 9-1, Notice of Privacy Practices, and determine whether the notice is complete as compared with the requirements listed in the AHIMA Practice Brief.
6. Prepare a brief summary of the deficiencies you found upon review of the Notice of Privacy Practices found in Figure 9-1.

Alfred State Medical Center

NOTICE OF PRIVACY PRACTICES

Effective Date: October 1, 2013

We are required by law to protect the privacy of health information and to provide you with a written copy of this notice outlining the health information privacy practices of our medical center. We are also required to abide by the terms of the notice currently in effect. We have the right to change the terms of this notice and will provide you with this revised notice upon your receiving health care services. The revised notice will be effective for all protected health information. You can also obtain your own copy by calling our office at 607-555-1234. *If you have any questions about this notice or would like further information, please contact: Ima Secret, Privacy Officer, Alfred State Medical Center, 101 Main St, Alfred NY 14802, 607-555-1234.*

PERMITTED DISCLOSURES:

The following is a list of disclosures that will be made without authorization.

Treatment, Payment and Healthcare Operations.

We will only obtain written consent one time to use and disclose your health information for treatment, payment, and business operations. Your health information may be released to your insurance company in the processing of your bill.

Patient Directory and Disclosure to Family and Friends.

You will be asked if you have any objection to including information about yourself in our Patient Directory. You will also be asked if you have any objection to sharing information about your health with your family and friends regarding your care.

Emergencies or Public Need.

We may use or disclose your health information in an emergency or for important public needs.

DISCLOSURES THAT REQUIRE AUTHORIZATION

All other uses and disclosures require authorization and will be made only with your written authorization. You also have the right to revoke the authorization at any time. To revoke a written authorization, please contact the Privacy Officer in writing.

PRIVACY RIGHTS

You have the right to:

- Request restrictions on certain uses and disclosures of information.

- Inspect and copy your health information.

- Receive a paper copy of this notice.

- Special privacy of HIV-related information, alcohol and substance abuse treatment information, mental health information, and genetic information.

Filing a Complaint

If you believe your privacy rights have been violated, you may file a complaint with our Privacy Officer. There will be no retaliation or action taken against you for filing a complaint.

Figure 9-1 Privacy Notice

LAB ASSIGNMENT 9-2 Release of Patient Information

OBJECTIVES

At the end of this assignment, the student should be able to:

- Determine circumstances for which it is appropriate to release patient information
- Communicate a suitable response to the requestor when it has been established that release of patient information is inappropriate

Overview

Facilities must obtain appropriate authorization prior to disclosing patient information; however, HIPAA delineates certain exceptions. This assignment will familiarize the student with the proper release of patient information.

Instructions

1. Review the case scenarios in Figure 9-2, and determine whether patient information should be released.
2. If the patient information should *not* be released, enter a response that would be communicated to the requestor.

1.	The local sheriff enters the medical record department and asks to see the patient record of a recently discharged patient. The patient was involved in a traffic accident and had left the scene. The identification of the agent appears to be in order. Do you release the information? Why or why not?
2.	You are the correspondence secretary and receive an authorization signed by the patient to release medical records to the Aetna Insurance Company. The authorization was signed and dated by the patient on January 27 of this year. According to your records, the patient was admitted to the hospital on January 30 of this year. Do you release the information? Why or why not?
3.	A medical student who is working on her master's degree research project needs to review the medical records of patients who have been diagnosed with myocardial infarction. The facility's policy is that students can review patient information under the supervision of a health information department staff member if the student provides a letter from their instructor indicating that such review is required. The student supplies the letter and agrees to be supervised during the review. Do you allow the student to review the records? Why or why not?
4.	You are served a properly executed *subpoena duces tecum* on a patient discharged last year with the diagnosis of pneumonia. The document states that a copy of the record can be submitted in lieu of your personal appearance in court. Your department routinely uses a record copy service to process requests for information, including *subpoena duces tecum* documents that allow for copies to be sent instead of a court appearance. Do you allow the record copy service to process the release of information to comply with this *subpoena duces tecum*? Why or why not?
5.	The minister of a patient who was recently discharged enters the health information department and states that he needs to view the medical record of a patient who is a member of his congregation. He explains that the patient is in a desperate situation, and he needs to understand the patient's medical situation so he can properly counsel the patient. (The minister also serves as hospital chaplain.) Do you release the information? Why or why not?
6.	Two police detectives arrive in the health information department and properly identify themselves. They inform you that the lab drew blood on an ED patient last night, and the blood vial was properly given to the transporter for the coroner's office. Unfortunately, the vial broke in transport. The detectives are requesting that you make a copy of the blood alcohol level that was documented in the patient's record so they can use it to make the case against the patient that he was driving while under the influence of alcohol. Do you release the information? Why or why not?
7.	The local district attorney arrives in the department with an authorization for release of information that is appropriately completed, signed, and dated by the patient. He is requesting access to the patient's records so he can review them. Do you release the information? Why or why not?
8.	The city police department desk sergeant calls the health information department and requests information of a medical nature on a patient who has been injured in a fight. Do you release the information? Why or why not?
9.	A physician from a neighboring city enters the health information department to review the record of a patient he is now treating. The physician is not on your hospital's medical staff. Do you allow him to review the information? Why or why not?
10.	You receive a telephone call from a hospital emergency department (ED) located in another state. The ED physician states that this is an emergency situation, and he needs to obtain pertinent medical information about a patient currently under treatment. Do you release the information? Why or why not?

Figure 9-2   Release of Information Case Scenarios

LAB ASSIGNMENT 9-3   Release of Information Correspondence Log

OBJECTIVES

At the end of this assignment, the student should be able to:
- Appropriately respond to correspondence requests for release of patient information
- Complete the entries in a correspondence log

Overview

Health information professionals are responsible for releasing patient information. To ensure proper release of patient information, an authorization must be obtained from the patient, and facilities must document information released to fulfill such requests. This assignment will familiarize the student with reviewing correspondence requests for information and entry of released patient information into a correspondence log.

Instructions

1. Go to the Student Companion Website and print one copy of the release of information correspondence log form (Figure 9-3).
2. Refer to Appendix I, where Case01 through Case10 are located.

   NOTE: If you prefer, you may also access these records at the Student Companion Website at and review online.

3. Review the requests for patient information (Figures 9-4A through 9-4J) to be used for Case01 through Case10.
4. Determine the following, and enter your responses on the correspondence log:
   a. Type of request
   b. Whether request was appropriately completed
   c. Response form letter to be used
   d. Information released and cost

   NOTE: Specific instructions for processing release of information requests and completing the correspondence log are found in Table 9-1.

5. Submit the completed correspondence log to your instructor for evaluation.

Table 9-1   Instructions for Processing Release of Information Requests and Completing the Correspondence Log

Step 1:   Review each request for information (Figures 9-4A through 9-4J) to determine the "type of request," and enter the type in column 1 of the correspondence log. Types of requests include:
  • Attorney
  • Blue Cross
  • Commercial Insurance
  • Court Order
  • Hospital
  • Physician
  • *Subpoena Duces Tecum*

Step 2:   Determine whether copies of records can be released in response to the request. Enter "Yes" or "No" in column 2 of the correspondence log.

  NOTE: If you enter "No" on the correspondence log, indicate why records cannot be released. Reasons include:
  • Authorization is not HIPAA compliant.
  • Authorization is outdated. (This means the date the request was received in the department was more than 90 days after the patient signed/dated the authorization.)
  • Authorization predates dates of service.

Step 3:   Refer to the response form letter (Figure 9-5) and determine the number(s) that should be marked with an X.
  • Select "A" if you are mailing copies of records and will charge for them.
  • Select "B" if you are mailing copies of records and no payment is required.
  • Select "C" if the patient's authorization for release of information was dated 90 days prior to the health information department receiving it for processing.
  • Select "D" if the requestor did not include a HIPAA-compliant authorization signed by the patient or his/her representative.
  • Select "E" if the patient's authorization to release information was dated prior to treatment provided.

Step 4:   Enter the information released from the record in response to the request.
  • Enter "entire record" if every page in the record would be copied.
  • Enter the abbreviation for reports copied if the entire record was not copied. Abbreviations include the following:
    • Face sheet (FS)
    • Discharge summary (DS)
    • History & physical examination (HP)
    • Consultation (CON)
    • Progress notes (PN)
    • Doctors orders (DO)
    • Operative report (OP)
    • Laboratory tests (LAB)
    • Radiology reports (XRAY)
    • Nurses notes (NN)
  • Enter "none" if you determined that records would not be sent in response to the request.

Step 5:   Enter the charge for copies, if applicable.
  • Enter "n/c" (no charge) for physician and hospital requests.
  • Charge .75 cents per copy for requests from insurance companies and attorneys. To calculate the number of copies, refer to the patient record (because some reports are multiple pages).

  NOTE: Pay attention to requests received from insurance companies as they sometimes specify what they will pay for copies of records. In that case, enter the amount specified (and not the 75 cents/page calculation).

CORRESPONDENCE LOG				
CASE	TYPE OF REQUEST	IS REQUEST APPROPRIATE? (IF NO, WHY NOT?)	RESPONSE FORM LETTER SENT	REPORTS RELEASED AND COST
1	Physician	Yes	B	Entire record $0.00
2				
3				
4				
5				
6				
7				
8				
9				
10				

Figure 9-3   Release of Information Correspondence Log

Case01 – Request for Information

Received in Health Information Department for processing on June 1, (this year).

AUTHORIZATION FOR DISCLOSURE OF PROTECTED HEALTH INFORMATION (PHI)

(1) I hereby authorize Alfred State Medical Center to disclose/obtain information from the health records of:

Marsha Dennis	02/09/YYYY	(607) 555-7771
Patient Name	Date of Birth (mmddyyyy)	Telephone (w/ area code)
344 Maple Avenue, Alfred NY 14802		Case01
Patient Address		Medical Record Number

(2) Covering the period(s) of health care:

04/27/YYYY	04/29/YYYY		
From (mmddyyyy)	To (mmddyyyy)	From (mmddyyyy)	To (mmddyyyy)

(3) I authorize the following information to be released by Alfred State Medical Center (check applicable reports):

❑ Face Sheet	❑ Progress Notes	❑ Pathology Report	❑ Drug Abuse Care
❑ Discharge Summary	❑ Lab Results	❑ Nurses Notes	☒ Other: Entire record
❑ History & Physical Exam	❑ X-ray Reports	❑ HIV Testing Results	
❑ Consultation	❑ Scan Results	❑ Mental Health Care	
❑ Doctors Orders	❑ Operative Report	❑ Alcohol Abuse Care	

This information is to be disclosed to ~~or obtained from~~:

Dr. Raymond Beecher	9 Langston Dr, St. Petersburg, FL 00000	(800) 555-5698
Name of Organization	Address of Organization	Telephone Number

for the purpose of: follow-up treatment by Dr. Beecher.

Statement that information used or disclosed may be subject to re-disclosure by the recipient and may no longer be protected by this rule.

(4) I understand that I have a right to revoke this authorization at any time. I understand that if I revoke this authorization I must do so in writing and present my written revocation to the Heath Information Management Department. I understand that the revocation will not apply to information that has already been released in response to this authorization. I understand that the revocation will not apply to my insurance company when the law provides my insurer with the right to contest a claim under my policy. Unless otherwise revoked, this authorization will expire on the following date, event, or condition.

5/25/(next year)			
Expiration Date		Expiration Event	Expiration Condition

If I fail to specify an expiration date, event or condition, this authorization will expire within six (6) months.

Signature of individual and date.

(5) I understand that authorizing the disclosure of this health information is voluntary. I can refuse to sign this authorization. I need not sign this form in order to assure treatment. I understand that I may inspect or copy the information to be used or disclosed, provided in CFR 164.534. I understand that any disclosure of information carries with it the potential for an unauthorized redisclosure and may not be protected by federal confidentiality rules. If I have questions about disclosure of my health information, I can contact the Privacy Officer at Alfred State Medical Center.

Signed:

Marsha Dennis	May 25, (this year)
Signature of Patient or Legal Representative	Date

Figure 9-4A   Case01 Request for Information

Case02 – Request for Information
Received in Health Information Department for processing on July 30, (this year).

EMPIRE BLUE CROSS AND BLUE SHIELD of Central New York
344 South Warren Street, Box 4809
Syracuse, New York 13221
315/424-3700

July 15, (this year)

ATTENTION: Health Information Department

                Alfred State Medical Center

Patient: Dilbert Hunter

Service Date: 4/26/YYYY – 4/29/YYYY

Group #:   52656388

Claim #:   02216

Copies of the following provider records are requested for the adjudication of the above-mentioned claim. Under terms of our subscriber contract, the patient has given prior authorization for the release of this information. Please send the following reports:

[X] Final Diagnosis (Face Sheet)

[X] History & Physical Examination

[ ] Progress Notes

[ ] Physician's Orders

[ ] Operative Report

[ ] Ancillary Reports

Please return a copy of this letter with a copy of the records to:

Medical Review

Blue Cross Claims Department

Patient #: 1104272

Thank you.

Sincerely,

Mary Ann Jones

Mary Ann Jones, Claims Reviewer

Figure 9-4B   Case02 Request for Information

Case03 – Request for Information

Received in Health Information Department for processing on May 30, (this year).

AUTHORIZATION FOR DISCLOSURE OF PROTECTED HEALTH INFORMATION (PHI)

(1) I hereby authorize Alfred State Medical Center to disclose/obtain information from the health records of:

Erica P. Stanley	04/05/YYYY	(607)555-8818
Patient Name	Date of Birth (mmddyyyy)	Telephone (w/ area code)

23 Langley Drive, Alfred NY 14802	Case03
Patient Address	Medical Record Number

(2) Covering the period(s) of health care:

04/28/YYYY	04/29/YYYY		
From (mmddyyyy)	To (mmddyyyy)	From (mmddyyyy)	To (mmddyyyy)

(3) I authorize the following information to be released by Alfred State Medical Center (check applicable reports):

☒ Face Sheet	☐ Progress Notes	☐ Pathology Report	☐ Drug Abuse Care
☐ Discharge Summary	☒ Lab Results	☐ Nurses Notes	☐ Other:
☒ History & Physical Exam	☒ X-ray Reports	☐ HIV Testing Results	
☐ Consultation	☐ Scan Results	☐ Mental Health Care	
☐ Doctors Orders	☐ Operative Report	☐ Alcohol Abuse Care	

This information is to be disclosed to or obtained from:

Abdul Raish,M.D.	1421 Lincoln Avenue New York, NY 10035	(800) 555-8951
Name of Organization	Address of Organization	Telephone Number

for the purpose of: treatment by Dr. Raish.

Statement that information used or disclosed may be subject to re-disclosure by the recipient and may no longer be protected by this rule.

(4) I understand that I have a right to revoke this authorization at any time. I understand that if I revoke this authorization I must do so in writing and present my written revocation to the Heath Information Management Department. I understand that the revocation will not apply to information that has already been released in response to this authorization. I understand that the revocation will not apply to my insurance company when the law provides my insurer with the right to contest a claim under my policy. Unless otherwise revoked, this authorization will expire on the following date, event, or condition.

5/1/(next year)		
Expiration Date	Expiration Event	Expiration Condition

If I fail to specify an expiration date, event or condition, this authorization will expire within six (6) months.

Signature of individual and date.

(5) I understand that authorizing the disclosure of this health information is voluntary. I can refuse to sign this authorization. I need not sign this form in order to assure treatment. I understand that I may inspect or copy the information to be used or disclosed, provided in CFR 164.534. I understand that any disclosure of information carries with it the potential for an unauthorized redisclosure and may not be protected by federal confidentiality rules. If I have questions about disclosure of my health information, I can contact the Privacy Officer at Alfred State Medical Center.

Signed:

Erica P. Stanley	May 1, (this year)
Signature of Patient or Legal Representative	Date

Figure 9-4C   Case03 Request for Information

Case04 – Request for Information

Received in Health Information Department for processing on August 30, (this year).

DWYER & DWYER, P.C.

ATTORNEYS AT LAW

PARK PLACE PROFESSIONAL BUILDING

OLEAN, NY 14760

716/373-1920

Joseph C. Dwyer & Elaine N. Dwyer   **Practice Limited to Civil Trial Law**
Barbara L. Laferty, Legal Assistant

August 16, (this year)

Alfred State Medical Center
Alfred, NY 14802
ATTN: Records Room

RE: Our Client: Mary C. Howe

Date of Injury: 04/29/YYYY

Gentlemen:

We have been retained by the above to represent the above-named with regard to an injury which occurred on the above date, resulting in personal injuries. It is our understanding that our client was treated at your institution either as an outpatient or inpatient. We respectfully request that you forward to us copies of the hospital records, excluding only TPR, fluid, and laboratory reports. <u>We specifically need the nurse's notes.</u>

Would you please have your billing office send us an original bill as to hospital services rendered but not indicating on it what, if anything, has been paid to date. Please enclose any statement for your customary charges in providing these records. Thank you kindly for your cooperation and assistance.

Yours very truly,

DWYER & DWYER, P.C.

By:

Joseph C. Dwyer

JCD:cd

Figure 9-4D   Case04 Request for Information

Case05 – Request for Information
Received in Health Information Department for processing on August 9, (this year).

HOSPITAL FOR JOINT DISEASES & MEDICAL CENTER (HJD&MC), 1919 MADISON AVENUE, NEW YORK 10035

DATE July 14, (this year)   NAME GIBBON, Andrew   PATIENT # Case05

TO ALFRED STATE MEDICAL CENTER, ALFRED NY

DEAR SIRS:

We have been informed that the above-named patient was treated in your institution on or about 1/1/YYYY. May we obtain from you a resume of your findings, including the radiology reports, operations or other treatment provided?

Very truly yours,
MEDICAL RECORD DEPARTMENT

AUTHORIZATION FOR DISCLOSURE OF PROTECTED HEALTH INFORMATION (PHI)

(1) I hereby authorize Alfred State Medical Center to disclose/obtain information from the health records of:

Andrew Gibbon	08/19/YYYY	(607) 555-4500
Patient Name	Date of Birth (mmddyyyy)	Telephone (w/ area code)
22 Market Street, Alfred NY 14802		Case05
Patient Address		Medical Record Number

(2) Covering the period(s) of health care:

January YYYY			
From (mmddyyyy)	To (mmddyyyy)	From (mmddyyyy)	To (mmddyyyy)

(3) I authorize the following information to be released by Alfred State Medical Center (check applicable reports):

☒ Face Sheet	☐ Progress Notes	☐ Pathology Report	☐ Drug Abuse Care
☐ Discharge Summary	☒ Lab Results	☐ Nurses Notes	☐ Other:
☒ History & Physical Exam	☒ X-ray Reports	☐ HIV Testing Results	
☐ Consultation	☐ Scan Results	☐ Mental Health Care	
☐ Doctors Orders	☐ Operative Report	☐ Alcohol Abuse Care	

This information is to be disclosed to ~~or obtained from~~:

HJD&MC	1919 Madison Avenue, New York, NY 10035	(800) 555-9567
Name of Organization	Address of Organization	Telephone Number

for the purpose of: treatment by Dr. HJD&MC.

Statement that information used or disclosed may be subject to re-disclosure by the recipient and may no longer be protected by this rule.

(4) I understand that I have a right to revoke this authorization at any time. I understand that if I revoke this authorization I must do so in writing and present my written revocation to the Heath Information Management Department. I understand that the revocation will not apply to information that has already been released in response to this authorization. I understand that the revocation will not apply to my insurance company when the law provides my insurer with the right to contest a claim under my policy. Unless otherwise revoked, this authorization will expire on the following date, event, or condition.

5/1/(next year)		
Expiration Date	Expiration Event	Expiration Condition

If I fail to specify an expiration date, event or condition, this authorization will expire within six (6) months.

Signature of individual and date.

(5) I understand that authorizing the disclosure of this health information is voluntary. I can refuse to sign this authorization. I need not sign this form in order to assure treatment. I understand that I may inspect or copy the information to be used or disclosed, provided in CFR 164.534. I understand that any disclosure of information carries with it the potential for an unauthorized redisclosure and may not be protected by federal confidentiality rules. If I have questions about disclosure of my health information, I can contact the Privacy Officer at Alfred State Medical Center.

Signed:

Andrew Gibbon	*May 1, (this year)*
Signature of Patient or Legal Representative	Date

Figure 9-4E   Case05 Request for Information

Case06 – Request for Information

Received in Health Information Department for processing on October 15, (this year).

PRUDENTIAL

The Prudential Insurance Company of America

August 15, (this year)

AUTHORIZATION TO RELEASE INFORMATION

TO: Alfred State Medical Center, Alfred NY

For purposes of evaluating a claim, you are authorized to permit the Prudential Insurance Company of America and its authorized representatives to view or obtain a copy of ALL EXISTING RECORDS (including those of psychiatric, drug, or alcohol treatment) pertaining to the examination, medical and dental treatment, history, prescriptions, employment, and insurance coverage of Charles Benson.

This authorization specifically covers a period of hospitalization or medical care and treatment during 4/24/YYYY through 4/29/YYYY. This information is for the sole use of Prudential's representatives or the group policy holder or contract holder involved in processing the claim and will not be furnished in an identifiable form to any other persons without my written consent unless expressly permitted or required by law.

I understand that this authorization may be revoked by written notice to Prudential, but this will not apply to information already released. If not revoked, this authorization will be valid while the claim is pending or a maximum of one year from the date it is signed.

I have been furnished a copy of this authorization and acknowledge receipt. I also agree that a photographic copy shall be as valid as the original.

Limitations, if any:

DATE August 15, (this year)

SIGNED: _Charles Benson_

Figure 9-4F   Case06 Request for Information

Case07 – Request for Information
Received in Health Information Department for processing on May 5, (this year).

BLUE CROSS & BLUE SHIELD   **A MEDICARE CARRIER**

UTICA, NEW YORK 13502

DATE: April 30, (this year)

TO: Alfred State Medical Center, Alfred NY

ATTN: Health Information Department

PATIENT: Holley E. Hoover

DOB: 01/15/YYYY

ADMISSION: 04/30/YYYY

We request the following information to process the above patient's claim:

1. Face sheet
2. Surgical procedures performed
3. History of condition
4. Discharge summary

Please send a statement for clerical services with this information, and we will be glad to promptly send you a check. Thank you for your prompt cooperation.

Jean Lewis

Claims Examiner

Figure 9-4G   Case07 Request for Information

Case08 – Request for Information

Received in Health Information Department for processing on November 1, (this year).

ADAM ATTORNEY
15 MAIN STREET
ALBANY NY 00000
PHONE: (518) 555-1234

JOHN DOE, Petitioner,	)) *SUBPOENA DUCES TECUM*)
vs.	))
RICHARD ROE, M.D. Respondent.	)) Case No. _____ NY-895623591 _____)

TO: Alfred State Medical Center
         100 Main St
         Alfred NY 14802

RE: Molly P. Mason
DOB: 3/1/YYYY

YOU ARE COMMANDED to produce at the <u>County Courthouse, 15 Main Street, Room 14A, Alfred NY 14802</u> on November 15, (this year) at 9 A.M., a complete copy of your medical records, pertaining to the above-referenced individual who has requested the Division of Professional Licensing to conduct a prelitigation panel review of a claim of medical malpractice. **Attendance is not required if records are timely forwarded to the indicated address.**

DATED this <u>twenty-fifth</u> day of <u>October</u> (this year).

By: *Petra Lyons*
                                             Clerk of the Court

Figure 9-4H   Case08 Request for Information

Case 09 – Request for Information

Received in Health Information Department for processing on November 15, (this year).

ADAM ATTORNEY
15 MAIN STREET
ALBANY NY 00000
PHONE: (518) 555-1234

DAVID LUCK, Petitioner, vs. ALAN GHANN, M.D. Respondent.	)) ***COURT ORDERED SUBPOENA***) ***DUCES TECUM***)))) Case No. _____ NY-895623591))

TO: Alfred State Medical Center
        100 Main St
        Alfred NY 14802

RE: David Luck
DOB: 11/21/YYYY

YOU ARE COMMANDED to produce at the <u>County Courthouse, 15 Main Street, Room 14A, Alfred NY 14802</u> on November 25, (this year) at 9 A.M., a complete copy of your medical records, pertaining to the above-referenced individual who has requested the Division of Professional Licensing to conduct a prelitigation panel review of a claim of medical malpractice. **Attendance is not required if records are timely forwarded to the indicated address.**

DATED this <u>fifth</u> day of <u>November</u> (this year).

By: *Petra Lyons*
                                                    Clerk of the Court

Figure 9-4I   Case09 Request for Information

Case10 – Request for Information

Received in Health Information Department for processing on October 5, (this year).

Authorization for Release of Confidential HIV-Related Information

Name and address of facility/provider obtaining release:

Alfred State Medical Center, 100 Main Street, Alfred NY 14802

Name of person whose HIV-related information will be released:

Paula P. Paulson

Name(s) and address(es) of person(s) signing this form (if other than above):

Relationship to person whose HIV information will be released (if other than above):

Name(s) and address(es) of person(s) who will be given HIV-related information:

Michael Diamond, M.D., 1423 Main Street, Wellsville NY 14895

Reason for release of HIV-related information:

To provide historical perspective of HIV status for physician's office record.

Time during which release is authorized: From: 4/26/YYYY   To: 5/1/YYYY

The Facility/Provider obtaining this release must complete the following:

Exceptions, if any, to the right to revoke consent for disclosure: (for example cannot revoke if disclosure has already been made.) N/A

Description of the consequences, if any, of failing to consent to disclosure upon treatment, payment, enrollment, or eligibility for benefits: N/A

(Note: Federal privacy regulations may restrict some consequences.)

My questions about this form have been answered. I know that I do not have to allow release of HIV-related information, and that I can change my mind at any time and revoke my authorization by writing the facility/provider obtaining this release.

Oct 1, (this year)   Paula P. Paulson
_____   _____
Date   Signature

Figure 9-4J   Case10 Request for Information

ALFRED STATE MEDICAL CENTER
ALFRED, NEW YORK 14802
Health Information Department
(607) 555-1234

RE: _____

Your request for copies of patient records on the above-named patient has been received.

Please comply with the following checked items:

A. _____ Please consider this an invoice in the amount of $____.
Copies of requested patient records are enclosed.

B. _____ Copies of requested patient records are enclosed; no payment is required.

C. _____ Authorizations for release of information must be dated within 90 days of receipt. Attached is a HIPAA-compliant form. Please have the patient complete and sign, and return in the enclosed self-addressed stamped envelope (SASE).

D. _____ To process the request for information, we must have a HIPAA-compliant authorization signed by the patient or his/her representative. Attached is a HIPAA-compliant form. Please have the patient complete and sign, and return in the SASE.

E. _____ The patient's authorization to release information was dated prior to treatment. It is against policy to release such patient information. Attached is a HIPAA-compliant form. Please have the patient complete and sign, and return in the SASE.

Sincerely,

Debra Director, RHIA

Health Information Department

Figure 9-5   Response Form Letter

LAB ASSIGNMENT 9-4   Telephone Calls for Release of Information Processing

OBJECTIVES

At the end of this assignment, the student should be able to:

- Explain the release of information processing protocol for responding to telephone requests for patient information
- Appropriately respond to verbal requests for patient information

Overview

Health information professionals receive numerous telephone requests for patient information. This assignment will familiarize students with the appropriate response to a verbal request for patient information.

Instructions

1. Carefully read the telephone simulations in Figure 9-6.
2. Respond to the following questions about each telephone simulation.

Simulation #1:

- How would you rate the RHIT's greeting?
- Did the RHIT respond appropriately to the patient's request?
- Do you agree with the RHIT's reason for not releasing records immediately to the new physician? Why or why not?
- What is the significance of the RHIT using the patient's name during the conversation?
- What would you have said differently?

Simulation #2:

- How would you rate the MA's phone response?
- Did the MA respond appropriately to the request?
- What would you have said differently?

Simulation #3:

- Critique Barbara's greeting.
- Determine how you would handle this situation if you were Barbara. What would you have done differently, if anything, from the onset? Given the situation, what would you do next?

Simulation #4:

- What information can be released over the telephone?

SIMULATION #1: The caller is a patient who requests that the health records from her recent hospitalization be forwarded to her new physician in Billings, Montana. The patient, Janice McDonald, has relocated to a suburb of Billings, Montana.

THE TELEPHONE IN THE HEALTH INFORMATION DEPARTMENT RINGS THREE TIMES AND THE REGISTERED HEALTH INFORMATION TECHNICIAN (RHIT) ANSWERS THE PHONE.

RHIT: [professional tone of voice] "Good afternoon (morning). Health information department. May I help you?"

JANICE: [questioning tone of voice] "Hi! Ummm, this is Janice McDonald. I've moved to Montana and want to get my latest inpatient records sent to my new doctor. Can you do that?"

RHIT: [friendly tone of voice] "Sure, Ms. McDonald. I'll just need to send you a release of information authorization form. You'll need to complete it, sign it, and date it. Then, return it in the envelope provided."

JANICE: [confused tone of voice] "Oh. I'm seeing the new doctor next week. Do you think that you can just send the records to him?"

RHIT: [polite tone of voice] "I'm sorry, Ms. McDonald. Your health records are confidential and we cannot release copies without your written authorization."

JANICE: [resigned tone of voice] "Oh, okay. I guess that will have to do."

RHIT: [reassuring tone of voice] "Ms. McDonald, the department is really just trying to maintain privacy of your records. If you like, I can fax the authorization form to you. Then, you could overnight express it to the department. We can't accept a fax of the completed form because we need your original signature. That's hospital policy."

JANICE: [pleased tone of voice] "Oh! That would be great. I'll call my new doctor and get his fax number and give you a call back with it. Okay?"

RHIT: [friendly tone of voice] "That would be just fine, Ms. McDonald."

THE CONVERSATION IS ENDED. THE RHIT HANGS UP THE PHONE.

Figure 9-6   Telephone Simulations

(Continues)

SIMULATION #2: Joe Turner from the State Farm Insurance Company is an angry insurance agent who calls to inform the medical assistant (MA) at the physician's office that the company had mailed a proper authorization three weeks ago for release of records on a recently discharged patient.

THE TELEPHONE RINGS SIX TIMES BEFORE THE MEDICAL ASSISTANT (MA) ANSWERS THE PHONE.

MA: [quick, professional tone of voice] "Good afternoon (morning). Doctor's office."

TURNER: [brusk tone of voice] "Hello. I'm calling to find out why the records I requested three weeks ago have not been sent to me yet. Oh. This is Joe Turner from State Farm Insurance Company."

MA: [courteous tone of voice — recognizes an impatient person] "Could you tell me the name of the patient, please?"

TURNER: [brusk tone of voice] "Mary Jones. Her birth date is 10/02/55. She was discharged on September 1 of this year. I need copies of the doctor's notes in order to get the claim paid. She has called me several times this past couple of weeks. I guess the office keeps sending bills for her to pay and she is as disgusted as I am about this situation!"

MA: [courteous tone of voice] "Mr. Turner, would you like to hold while I check this or could I call you back?"

TURNER: [brusk tone of voice] "No way am I going to let you off the hook. I'll hold!"

MA: [courteous tone of voice — but showing signs of wear] "No problem, Mr. Turner. I'll be with you in a couple of minutes."

ONE MINUTE PASSES AND THE MA TAKES MR. TURNER OFF HOLD.

MA: [pleasant tone of voice] "Mr. Turner, I checked our correspondence log and found that copies of Mary Jones' records were forwarded to your attention last week. You should have them."

TURNER: [impatient tone of voice] "Well, I don't! Oh . . . I guess they were placed on my desk while I wasn't looking. Here they are. Sorry about that. Goodbye."

THE CALLER HANGS UP.

Figure 9-6 (*Continued*) **Telephone Simulations**

(Continues)

SIMULATION #3: Barbara Allen is a new health information technology graduate hired by the medical center's health information management department. This is her first day on the job.

THE TELEPHONE RINGS TWICE, IS ANSWERED BY THE DEPARTMENT SECRETARY, AND THE CALL IS FORWARDED TO BARBARA ALLEN, CORRESPONDENCE TECHNICIAN.

BARBARA: "Correspondence section. May I help you?"

DOCTOR: "Hello, this is Dr. Ahbibe from Breyne's Clinic in Columbia, New Mexico. We have a patient here by the name of Garrick Tanner who was admitted for status epilepticus. We need a past history for this patient and all pertinent documents sent to us immediately. The seizure activity is progressing in frequency and the patient is unable to provide information about drug allergies."

BARBARA: "Would you hold while I pull the patient's record?"

DOCTOR: "Certainly."

Several minutes pass as Barbara searches by checking the MPI and retrieving the record. Upon inspection of the record, she realizes that this is a "sealed file" because of a pending lawsuit. She also notes that Garrick Tanner has an extensive history of cocaine abuse that has been the main cause of his seizures. She closes the record, confused as to how she should handle this situation.

SIMULATION #4: Susie Sits is answering the telephone for the correspondence technician who is on break. Susie usually works in the discharge analysis section of the health information department.

THE TELEPHONE RINGS TWICE, AND SUSIE PICKS UP.

SUSIE: "Good morning, health information management department. Susie Sits speaking."

DOCTOR: "This is Dr. Jones' office calling from Phoenix, Arizona. Could you please give me the final diagnosis for Alfred Peoples, who was recently discharged from your facility?"

SUSIE: "Well, just hold a minute and I will get everything you need."

The doctor is on hold for three minutes while Susie pulls the health record.

SUSIE: "Hello, I think I have everything you need. Mr. Peoples was a patient in our alcohol rehab unit last month. . . ."

Figure 9-6 (*Continued*) **Telephone Simulations**

LAB ASSIGNMENT 9-5   Statement of Confidentiality

OBJECTIVES

At the end of this assignment, the student should be able to:

- Explain the purpose of a confidentiality statement
- Sign a statement of confidentiality

Overview

Health information students will have access to protected health information when completing professional practice experiences and course assignments. It is essential that patient confidentiality be maintained at all times. In this assignment the student will review and sign a statement of confidentiality.

Instructions

1. Go to the Student Companion website and print the statement of confidentiality form (Figure 9-7).
2. Review the statement of confidentiality.
3. Sign and date the statement of confidentiality, and have a witness (e.g., proctor, supervisor) sign and date the form.
4. Submit the completed form to your instructor.

PERSONAL HEALTH INFORMATION PLEDGE OF CONFIDENTIALITY

In consideration of my status as a student at _____ and/or association with health care facilities that provide professional practice experiences, and as an integral part of the terms and conditions of association, I hereby agree, pledge and undertake that I will not at any time access or use personal health information, or reveal or disclose to any persons within or outside the provider organization, any personal health information except as may be required in the course of my duties and responsibilities and in accordance with applicable legislation, and corporate and departmental policies governing proper release of information.

I understand that my obligations outlined above will continue after my association with the School and/or facility ends.

I further understand that my obligations concerning the protection of the confidentiality of personal health information relate to all personal health information whether I acquired the information through my association with the School and/or facility.

I also understand that unauthorized use or disclosure of such information will result in a disciplinary action up to and including involuntary expulsion from the School, the imposition of fines pursuant to relevant state and federal legislation, and a report to my professional regulatory body.

_____   _____
Date Signed   Signature of Student

                                         _____
                                         Student's Printed Name

_____   _____
Date Signed   Signature of Witness

Figure 9-7   Confidentiality Statement

Chapter 10

Introduction to Coding and Reimbursement

❦ INTRODUCTION

This chapter will familiarize the student with classification systems, third-party payers, and reimbursement systems.

LAB ASSIGNMENT 10-1   Hospital Financial Reports

OBJECTIVES

At the end of this assignment, the student should be able to:

- Interpret the information in a hospital financial report
- Analyze a hospital financial report to calculate reimbursement amounts

Overview

Software is used to assign each inpatient to a diagnosis-related group (DRG) according to principal diagnosis code, patient's discharge status, and so on. For this assignment, the student will review a hospital financial report and calculate the total payment that the facility will receive based on DRG assignment.

Instructions

1. Review Table 10-1 (Base Payment Amount per DRG) and Figure 10-1 (Alfred State Medical Center Financial Report).
2. Complete the financial report in Figure 10-1 by using information from Table 10-1 to:
   a. Determine the base rate for each DRG listed
   b. Calculate the total reimbursement rate (base rate times the number of cases equals reimbursement amount)

Table 10-1   Base Payment Amount per DRG

DRG	Base Payment Amount
368	$ 3,421.55
372	$ 2,730.16
423	$ 4,730.28
467	$ 1,349.05

Alfred State Medical Center Financial Report – June YYYY				
Date	DRG Assignment	Base Payment	Number of Cases	Reimbursement
June 1	423	$	25	$
June 4	368	$	32	$
June 5	372	$	15	$
June 10	372	$	41	$
June 15	372	$	11	$
June 19	372	$	27	$
June 25	467	$	31	$
			Total for June YYYY	$

Figure 10-1   Alfred State Medical Center Financial Report

LAB ASSIGNMENT 10-2 Updating Clinic Encounter Form

OBJECTIVES

At the end of this assignment, the student should be able to:

- Analyze the contents of a clinic encounter form
- Revise a clinic encounter form with up-to-date information

Overview

ICD-9-CM or ICD-10-CM/PCS, CPT, and HCPCS codes are updated annually, which means that providers must review and revise encounter forms on an annual basis. This assignment will require students to review a clinic encounter form to update and revise the codes.

Instructions

1. Review the encounter form (Figure 10-2) currently in use.
2. Using current editions of the ICD-9-CM/ICD-10-CM, CPT, and HCPCS Level II coding manuals, verify each code, and edit those that have changed. Get directions from your instructor to determine if you are to assign ICD-9-CM or ICD-10-CM codes for this assignment.

Appendix I

Case 01 through Case 10

This appendix contains 10 inpatient medical records, which students will use to complete assignments in Chapters 6, 8, and 9.

 NOTE: Case 01 through Case 10 are also located online at www.CengageBrain.com, so students can review records in an online format.

Case 01

ALFRED STATE MEDICAL CENTER 100 MAIN ST, ALFRED NY 14802 (607) 555-1234 HOSPITAL #: 000999				INPATIENT FACE SHEET			

PATIENT NAME AND ADDRESS				GENDER	RACE	MARITAL STATUS	PATIENT NO.
DENNIS, Marsha 344 Maple Avenue Alfred, NY 14802				F	W	M	Case01
				DATE OF BIRTH	MAIDEN NAME	OCCUPATION	
				02/09/YYYY	Taylor	Unemployed	

ADMISSION DATE	TIME	DISCHARGE DATE	TIME	LENGTH OF STAY	TELEPHONE NUMBER	
04/27/YYYY	0800	04/29/YYYY	1335	02 DAYS	(607)555-7771	

GUARANTOR NAME AND ADDRESS		NEXT OF KIN NAME AND ADDRESS	
DENNIS, Dennis 344 Maple Avenue Alfred, NY 14802		DENNIS, Dennis 344 Maple Avenue Alfred, NY 14802	

GUARANTOR TELEPHONE NO.	RELATIONSHIP TO PATIENT	NEXT OF KIN TELEPHONE NUMBER	RELATIONSHIP TO PATIENT
(607)555-7771	Husband	(607)555-7771	Husband

ADMITTING PHYSICIAN	SERVICE	ADMIT TYPE	ROOM NUMBER/BED
Donald Thompson, MD	Surgical	3	0603/01

ATTENDING PHYSICIAN	ATTENDING PHYSICIAN UPIN	ADMITTING DIAGNOSIS	
Donald Thompson, MD	100B01	Abnormal Pap Smear	

PRIMARY INSURER	POLICY AND GROUP NUMBER	SECONDARY INSURER	POLICY AND GROUP NUMBER
BC/BS of WNY	6350088		

DIAGNOSES AND PROCEDURES	ICD-9-CM	ICD-10-CM/PCS
PRINCIPAL DIAGNOSIS		
Acute and chronic cervicitis with squamous metaplasia	616.0	N72 N87.1
SECONDARY DIAGNOSES		
PRINCIPAL PROCEDURE		
D & C	69.09	0UDB7ZZ
SECONDARY PROCEDURE(S)		
Cold Cone	67.2	0UBC7ZZ
TOTAL CHARGES: $ 4,954.40		

DISCHARGE INSTRUCTIONS					
ACTIVITY:	☐ Bedrest	☐ Light	☐ Usual	☐ Unlimited	☐ Other:
DIET:	☐ Regular	☐ Low Cholesterol	☐ Low Salt	☐ ADA	☐ _____ Calorie
FOLLOW-UP:	☐ Call for appointment	☐ Office appointment on _____		☐ Other:	
SPECIAL INSTRUCTIONS:					
ATTENDING PHYSICIAN AUTHENTICATION:					

DENNIS, Marsha
Case01
Dr. Thompson

Admission: 04-27-YYYY
DOB: 02/09/YYYY
Room: 0603

CONSENT TO ADMISSION

I, *Marsha Dennis* hereby consent to admission to the Alfred State Medical Center (ASMC), and I further consent to such routine hospital care, diagnostic procedures, and medical treatment that the medical and professional staff of ASMC may deem necessary or advisable. I authorize the use of medical information obtained about me as specified above and the disclosure of such information to my referring physician(s). This form has been fully explained to me, and I understand its contents. I further understand that no guarantees have been made to me as to the results of treatments or examinations done at the ASMC.

Marsha Dennis
_____
Signature of Patient

4-27-YYYY
_____
Date

_____
Signature of Parent/Legal Guardian for Minor

_____
Date

_____
Relationship to Minor

Mary M Adams
_____
WITNESS: Alfred State Medical Center Staff Member

4-27-YYYY
_____
Date

CONSENT TO RELEASE INFORMATION FOR REIMBURSEMENT PURPOSES

In order to permit reimbursement, upon request, the Alfred State Medical Center (ASMC) may disclose such treatment information pertaining to my hospitalization to any corporation, organization, or agent thereof, which is, or may be liable under contract to the ASMC or to me, or to any of my family members or other person, for payment of all or part of the ASMC's charges for services rendered to me (e.g., the patient's health insurance carrier). I understand that the purpose of any release of information is to facilitate reimbursement for services rendered. In addition, in the event that my health insurance program includes utilization review of services provided during this admission, I authorize ASMC to release information as is necessary to permit the review. This authorization will expire once the reimbursement for services rendered is complete.

Marsha Dennis
_____
Signature of Patient

4-27-YYYY
_____
Date

_____
Signature of Parent/Legal Guardian for Minor

_____
Date

_____
Relationship to Minor

Mary M Adams
_____
WITNESS: Alfred State Medical Center Staff Member

4-27-YYYY
_____
Date

ALFRED STATE MEDICAL CENTER ■ 100 MAIN ST, ALFRED, NY 14802 ■ (607) 555-1234

DENNIS, Marsha	Admission: 04-27-YYYY	ADVANCE DIRECTIVE
Case01	DOB: 02/09/YYYY	
Dr. Thompson	Room: 0603	

Your answers to the following questions will assist your Physician and the Hospital to respect your wishes regarding your medical care. This information will become a part of your medical record.

	YES	NO	PATIENT'S INITIALS
1. Have you been provided with a copy of the information called "Patient Rights Regarding Health Care Decision?"	X		MD
2. Have you prepared a "Living Will?" If yes, please provide the Hospital with a copy for your medical record.		X	MD
3. Have you prepared a Durable Power of Attorney for Health Care? If yes, please provide the Hospital with a copy for your medical record.		X	MD
4. Have you provided this facility with an Advance Directive on a prior admission and is it still in effect? If yes, Admitting Office to contact Medical Records to obtain a copy for the medical record.		X	MD
5. Do you desire to execute a Living Will/Durable Power of Attorney? If yes, refer to in order: a. Physician b. Social Service c. Volunteer Service		X	MD

HOSPITAL STAFF DIRECTIONS: Check when each step is completed.

1. ___✓___ Verify the above questions where answered and actions taken where required.

2. ___✓___ If the "Patient Rights" information was provided to someone other than the patient, state reason:

_____

_____   _____

Name of Individual Receiving Information   Relationship to Patient

3. ___✓___ If information was provided in a language other than English, specify language and method.

4. ___✓___ Verify patient was advised on how to obtain additional information on Advance Directives.

5. ___✓___ Verify the Patient/Family Member/Legal Representative was asked to provide the Hospital with a copy of the Advance Directive which will be retained in the medical record.

File this form in the medical record and give a copy to the patient.

_____

Name of Patient (Name of Individual giving information if different from Patient)

Marsha Dennis   *April 27, YYYY*

Signature of Patient   Date

Mary M Adams   *April 27, YYYY*

Signature of Hospital Representative   Date

ALFRED STATE MEDICAL CENTER ■ 100 MAIN ST, ALFRED, NY 14802 ■ (607) 555-1234

DENNIS, Marsha Case01 Dr. Thompson	Admission: 04-27-YYYY DOB: 02/09/YYYY Room: 0603	PROGRESS NOTES

Date	(Please skip one line between days)
04-27-YYYY 1328	Pre-Anes: Patient cleared for general anesthesia. D. Galloway, MD
04-27-YYYY 1430	Post-Anes: No apparent anesthesia complications. No N + V. Awake. Satisfactory condition.
04 - 27 - YYYY 1200	Under general anesthesia a D&C and cone was done without anesthetic or operative complications. Patient has oxycel packing, vag. gauze pack & foley catheter. D. Thompson, MD
04 - 28 - YYYY 0900	Patient is doing fine. Packing & cath in until tomorrow. Please discharge tomorrow. Incidentally DRG note says discharge is anticipated for today. During precertification it was necessary for me to get doctor approval, which I did for surgery the day of admission, one day in hospital, the day after surgery, and discharge the following day, which is the plan.
04 - 29 - YYYY 1000	Packing & Foley out. May go home today. Shall call with Path report.

DENNIS, Marsha		Admission: 04-27-YYYY
Case01		DOB: 02/09/YYYY
Dr. Thompson		Room: 0603

DOCTORS ORDERS

Date	Time	Physician's signature required for each order. (Please skip one line between dates.)
4/22/YYYY	0830	1. For AM admit 04 -27 -YYYY
		2. Pre Cert # 139-129-62143
		3. Urinalysis
		4. Urine preg test
		5. Chest x-ray done 04-22-YYYY
		6. EKG done
		7. NPO after MN 04-26-YYYY
		Donald Thompson
04-27 -YYYY	0830	Admit to Surgical Unit. N.P.O. Perineal shave prep
		Start IV w / 5 % gluc. In Ringers Lactate @ 125 ML/hr
		Premeds by Anesthesia
		To O.R. about 1000 AM. For d & C and Cone
		T.O. Dr. Thompson/L. Mosher LPN *Donald Thompson*
04-27 -YYYY	1515	Diet as tol.
		Bed rest today. Up tomorrow.
		Tylenol w/ cod. PRN.
		Connect foley to straight drainage.
		Discharge from RR @ 1455
		Donald Thompson
04-27 -YYYY	1525	DC IV when finished
04-29 -YYYY	1335	DC Foley. Discharge home.
		Donald Thompson

DENNIS, Marsha	Admission: 04-27-YYYY	Consent for Operation(s) and/or
Case01	DOB: 02/09/YYYY	Procedure(s) and Anesthesia
Dr. Thompson	Room: 0603	

PERMISSION. I hereby authorize Dr. _Thompson_ , or associates of his/her choice at the

Alfred State Medical Center (the "Hospital") to perform upon _Marsha Dennis_

the following operation(s) and/or procedure(s): _Remove conical section of cervix & D&C_

including such photography, videotaping, televising or other observation of the operation(s)/procedure(s) as may be purposeful for the advance of medical knowledge and/or education, with the understanding that the patient's identity will remain anonymous.

EXPLANATION OF PROCEDURE, RISKS, BENEFITS, ALTERNATIVES. Dr. _Thompson_

has fully explained to me the nature and purposes of the operation(s)/procedures named above and has also informed me of expected benefits and complications, attendant discomforts and risks that may arise, as well as possible alternatives to the proposed treatment. I have been given an opportunity to ask questions and all my questions have been answered fully and satisfactorily.

UNFORESEEN CONDITIONS. I understand that during the course of the operation(s) or procedure(s), unforeseen conditions may arise which necessitate procedures in addition to or different from those contemplated. I, therefore, consent to the performance of additional operations and procedures which the above-named physician or his/her associates or assistants may consider necessary.

ANESTHESIA. I further consent to the administration of such anesthesia as may be considered necessary by the above-named physician or his/her associates or assistants. I recognize that there are always risks to life and health associated with anesthesia. Such risks have been fully explained to me and I have been given an opportunity to ask questions and all my questions have been answered fully and satisfactorily.

SPECIMENS. Any organs or tissues surgically removed may be examined and retained by the Hospital for medical, scientific or educational purposes and such tissues or parts may be disposed of in accordance with accustomed practice and applicable State laws and/or regulations.

NO GUARANTEES. I acknowledge that no guarantees or assurances have been made to me concerning the operation(s) or procedure(s) described above.

MEDICAL DEVICE TRACKING. I hereby authorize the release of my Social Security number to the manufacturer of the medical device(s) I receive, if applicable, in accordance with federal law and regulations which may be used to help locate me if a need arises with regard to this medical device. I release the Alfred State Medical Center from any liability that might result from the release of this information.*

UNDERSTANDING OF THIS FORM. I confirm that I have read this form, fully understand its contents, and that all blank spaces above have been completed prior to my signing. I have crossed out any paragraphs above that do not pertain to me.

Patient/Relative/Guardian*

Marsha Dennis   Marsha Dennis
Signature   Print Name

Relationship, if other than patient signed: _____

Witness:

William Preston   William Preston
Signature   Print Name

Date: _4/27/YYYY_

*The signature of the patient must be obtained unless the patient is an unemancipated minor under the age of 18 or is otherwise incompetent to sign.

PHYSICIAN'S CERTIFICATION. I hereby certify that I have explained the nature, purpose, benefits, risks of and alternatives to the operation(s)/procedure(s), have offered to answer any questions and have fully answered all such questions. I believe that the patient (relative/guardian) fully understands what I have explained and answered.

PHYSICIAN: _Donald Thompson, MD_   _4/27/YYYY_
Signature   Date

ALFRED STATE MEDICAL CENTER ■ 100 MAIN ST, ALFRED, NY 14802 ■ (607) 555-1234

DENNIS, Marsha	Admission: 04-27-YYYY		ANESTHESIA RECORD		
Case01	DOB: 02/09/YYYY				
Dr. Thompson	Room: 0603				

PROCEDURE(S):	D&C. Cold cone.			START	STOP
		ANESTHESIA		1322	1415
SURGEON(S):	Thompson	PROCEDURE		1325	1340
DATE OF SURGERY:	4/27/YYYY	ROOM TIME		IN: 1300	OUT: 1420

PRE-PROCEDURE

- ☑ Patient Identified ☑ ID band verified
- ☑ Patient questioned ☑ Chart reviewed
- ☑ Consent form signed
- ☑ Patient reassessed prior to anesthesia (ready to proceed)
- ☑ Peri-operative pain management discussed with patient/guardian (plan of care completed)
- Pre-Anesthetic State:
- ☐ Awake ☑ Anxious ☐ Calm
- ☐ Lethargic ☐ Uncooperative
- ☐ Unresponsive
- ☐ Other: _____
- ☑ Anesthesia machine #5626984 checked
- ☑ Secured with safety belt
- ☑ Arm secured on board ☑ Left ☐ Right

MONITORS/EQUIPMENT

- ☑ Stethoscope ☐ Precordial
- ☐ Suprasternal ☐ Esoph
- ☑ Non-invasive B/P ☐ V-lead ECG
- ☑ Continuous ECG ☐ ST Analysis
- ☑ Pulse oximeter ☐ End tidal CO_2
- ☐ Nerve stimulator: ☐ Ulnar ☐ Tibial ☐ Facial
- ☑ Oxygen monitor ☐ Cell Saver
- ☐ ET agent analyzer ☐ B/S ☐ TEE
- ☐ Fluid/Blood warmer ☐ Temp:
- ☐ BIS ☐ ICS
- ☑ NG/OG tube ☐ FHT monitor
- ☐ Foley catheter ☐ EEG
- ☐ Airway humidifier
- ☐ Evoked potential: ☐ SSEP ☐ BAEP ☐ MEP
- ☐ Arterial line _____ ☐ CVP _____

ANESTHETIC TECHNIQUES

- GA Induction: ☑ IV ☐ Pre-O_2 ☐ RSI ☐ PR
- ☐ Cricoid pressure ☐ Inhalation ☐ IM
- GA Maintenance: ☐ TIVA ☐ Inhalation
- ☑ Inhalation/IV ☐ GA/Regional Comb.
- Regional:
- Epidural : ☑ Thoracic ☐ Lumbar ☐ Caudal
- ☐ Femoral ☐ Auxiliary ☐ Interscalene
- ☐ CSE ☐ Bier ☐ SAB ☐ Ankle
- ☐ Continuous Spinal ☐ Cervical Plexus
- Regional Techniques: ☐ See Remarks
- ☐ Position _____ ☐ Prep _____
- ☐ Site _____ ☐ Needle _____
- ☐ LA _____ ☐ Narcotic _____
- ☐ Additive _____ ☐ Test dose Rx ___

AIRWAY MANAGEMENT

- ☑ Oral ETT ☐ LTA ☐ RAE
- ☐ Nasal ETT ☐ LMA #
- ☐ Stylet ☐ LMA Fastrach # ___
- ☐ DVL ☐ LMA ProSeal # ___
- ☐ EMG ETT ☐ Bougie
- ☐ Armored ETT ☐ LIS
- ☑ Breath sounds = bilateral
- ☐ Cuffed – min occ pres with ☑ air ☐ NS
- ☐ Uncuffed – leaks at _____ cm H_2O
- ☑ Oral airway ☐ Nasal airway ☐ Bite block
- Circuit: ☐ Circle system ☐ NRB ☐ Bain
- ☐ Via tracheotomy/stoma ☐ Mask case
- ☐ Nasal cannula ☑ Simple O_2 mask
- Nebulizer: _____
- Nerve Block(s): _____

AGENTS	TIME:	15	30	45		15	30	45		15	30	45		15	30	45		15	30	45	TOTALS
☐ Des ☐ Iso ☐ Sevo ☐ Halo (%)																					
☑ Air (L/min)			2.5	2.5	X																
☑ Oxygen (L/min)		66	2	2	66																
☑ N_2O (L/min)			2.5	2.5	X																
☑ Forane (%)			1/5	2/5	2/0	X															
☑ Anectine (mg)																					
☑ Pentothal (mg)			100	100	100	X															226

FLUIDS																					
Urine																					
EBL																					
Gastric																					

SYMBOLS

∨∧ BP cuff pressure

⊥ Arterial line pressure

× Mean arterial pressure

● Pulse

○ Spontaneous Respirations

∅ Assisted Respirations

T Tourniquet

MONITORS																					
☑ ECG																					
☑ % Oxygen Inspired (FIO_2)			98	98	98	98															
☑ End Tidal CO_2				44	44	44															
☑ Temp: ☐ C ☑ F			98			98															
☑ BP Monitor																					

PERI-OP MEDS																					
200																					
180																					
160																					
140		∨	∨	∨																	
120				∨	∨																
100			•	•	•																
80		•	•	∧	∧																
60		∧	∧			∧															
40																					
20		○	○	○	○	○															
10																					

Time of Delivery: _____

Gender: ☐ M ☐ F

Apgars: ___/___

VENT																					
Tidal Volume (ml)																					
Respiratory Rate			SA	SA	SA	SA															
Peak Pressure (cm H_2O)																					
☐ PEEP ☐ CPAP (cm H_2O)																					

Position: Lithotomy

Mask. S32 Nasal airway, rt nostril. S20 Oral tubing. Intake D5LR 1000. Total 650 cc. S18 gu, left.

Surgeon	Thompson
Assistant	
Scrub Nurse	Mary Marks, RN
Circulating Nurse	Cynthie Lewis, RN
Signature of Anesthesiologist or C.R.N.A.	Don Galloway, M.D.

DENNIS, Marsha Case01 Dr. Thompson	Admission: 04-27-YYYY DOB: 02/09/YYYY Room: 0603	PRE-ANESTHESIA AND POST-ANESTHESIA RECORD

PRE-ANESTHESIA EVALUATION

HISTORY TAKEN FROM: ☑ Patient ☐ Parent/ Guardian ☐ Significant Other ☑ Chart ☐ Poor Historian ☐ Language Barrier

PROPOSED PROCEDURE: *D&C. Cold cone.* **DATE OF SURGERY:** *4/27/YYYY*

AGE	GENDER	HEIGHT	WEIGHT	BLOOD PRESSURE	PULSE	RESPIRATIONS	TEMPERATURE	O2 SAT%
54	☐ Male ☑ Female	5'5"	145	130/80	75	22	98.6	96

PREVIOUS ANESTHESIA: ☑ None

PREVIOUS SURGERY: ☑ None

CURRENT MEDICATIONS: ☑ None

FAMILY HX – ANES. PROBLEMS: ☑ None

ALLERGIES ☑ None

AIRWAY ☐ MP1 ☐ MP2 ☐ MP3 ☐ MP4 ☐ Unrestricted neck ROM ☐ T-M distance = _____

(Enter ✗ in appropriate boxes.) ☐ Obesity ☐ ↓ neck ROM ☐ History of difficult airway ☐ Short muscular neck

☐ Teeth poor repair ☐ Teeth chipped/loose ☐ Edentulous ☐ Facial hair

BODY SYSTEM	COMMENTS	DIAGNOSTIC STUDIES
RESPIRATORY ☑ WNL	Tobacco Use: ☐ Yes ☑ No ☐ Quit _____ Packs/Day for _____ Years	ECG CHEST X-RAY *Negative* PULMONARY STUDIES
CARDIOVASCULAR ☑ WNL	Pre-procedure Cardiac Assessment:	**LABORATORY STUDIES** PT/PTT/INR: T&S / T&C:
GASTROINTESTINAL ☑ WNL	Ethanol Use: ☐ Yes ☑ No ☐ Quit Frequency _____ ☐ History of Ethanol abuse	HCG: *13.2* UA
Abnormal pap smear		**OTHER DIAGNOSTIC TESTS** *Hct 38.4*
MUSCULOSKELETAL ☑ WNL		**PLANNED ANESTHESIA/MONITORS** *ECG. ETCO2. O2. Temp.*
GENITOURINARY ☐ WNL		*O2 Sat. BP monitor.*
OTHER ☐ WNL *ASA risk classification I*		**PRE-ANESTHESIA MEDICATION**
PREGNANCY ☐ WNL	☐ AROM ☐ SROM ☐ Pitocin Drip ☐ Induction ☐ MgDrip EDC: _____ Weeks Gestation: _____ G: _____ P: _____	
		SIGNATURE OF ANESTHESIOLOGIST OR C.R.N.A. *Don Galloway, M.D.*

POST-ANESTHESIA EVALUATION

Location	Time	B/P	O2Sat	Pulse	Respirations	Temperature
Room	1630	142/84	96	90	14	98.6

☑ Awake ☐ Mask O₂ ☐ Somnolent ☐ Unarousable ☐ Oral/nasal airway

☑ Stable ☐ NC O₂ ☐ Unstable ☐ T-Piece ☐ Intubated ☐ Ventilator

☐ Regional – dermatome level: ☐ Continuous epidural analgesia

☐ Direct admit to hospital room ☑ No anesthesia related complications noted

☐ See progress notes for anesthesia related concerns ☑ Satisfactory postanesthesia/analgesia recovery

CONTROLLED MEDICATIONS

Medication	Used	Destroyed	Returned

SIGNATURE OF ANESTHESIOLOGIST OR C.R.N.A.

Don Galloway, M.D.

ALFRED STATE MEDICAL CENTER ■ 100 MAIN ST, ALFRED, NY 14802 ■ (607) 555-1234

DENNIS, Marsha   Admission: 04-27-YYYY   OPERATIVE REPORT
Case01   DOB: 02/09/YYYY
Dr. Thompson   Room: 0603

DATE OF SURGERY: 4-27-YYYY

PREOPERATIVE DIAGNOSIS: Abnormal Papanicolaou smear

POSTOPERATIVE DIAGNOSIS: Squamous dysplasia
                                Acute and chronic cervicitis with squamous metaplasia

OPERATION PERFORMED: Dilatation and curettage and conization

SURGEON: Dr. Thompson

ANESTHETIC: General

COMPLICATIONS: None

OPERATIVE NOTE: The patient was anesthetized, placed in lithotomy position and prepped and draped in the usual manner for vaginal surgery. The cervix was painted with Schiller's stain delineating the iodine negative Schiller positive area. The cervix was then grasped with a single toothed tenaculum at 3 and 9 o'clock outside of the unstained area of the cervix and an area of excisional cone biopsy was done in such a way as to incl 1.rle all the iodine negative areas. The conization specimen was labeled with suture at 12 o'clock and sent to Pathology in saline for processing. The uterine cavity was then sounded to a depth of 4+ inches and the endometrial cavity curetted with a sharp curette. A very scanty amount of endometrium was obtained and sent to Pathology as specimen ®2. Oxycel pack was then placed in the defect left by the cone and because of the size of the cone it was necessary to close the angles with interrupted sutures of 1 chromic catgut. A vaginal packing was placed in the vagina to hold the Oxycel pack. A Foley catheter was placed in the bladder. There was no significant bleeding. The patient withstood the procedure well and was returned to the Recovery Room in good condition. No anesthetic or operative complications.

DD: 04-28-YYYY   *Donald Thompson, MD*

DT: 04-29-YYYY   Donald Thompson, M.D.

PATHOLOGY REPORT

DENNIS, Marsha
Case01
Dr. Thompson

Admission: 04-27-YYYY
DOB: 02/09/YYYY
Room: 0603

Date of Surgery: 4/27/YYYY

OPERATION: Cold cone cervix. D&C.

SPECIMEN: #1. Cone cervix suture @ 1200
#2. Uterus curettements

GROSS

Number one consists of a cervical cone which measures 3.4 cm in diameter x 2.5 cm in greatest thickness. The mucosal surface is reddened and slightly irregular noted especially involving the inferior portion of the mucosa. The specimen is cut into thin parallel sections and entirely submitted as indicated on the diagram below labeled as "A," "B," "C," and "D." A portion of suture is attached to the specimen which is designated as "1200." Number two submitted as "uterine curettings" consists of approximately .5 grams of fragmented pink-tan and purple-tan tissue which is entirely submitted as "E."

MICROSCOPIC

Sections "A," "B," "C," and "D" are all similar showing portions of cervix including the squamocolumnar junction. There is acute and chronic cervicitis and focal squamous metaplasia of the endocervix including squamous metaplasia effecting some endocervical glands. In the region of the squamocolumnar junction, the squamous epithelium shows some cells with enlarged hyperchromatic nuclei and there is a mild decrease in maturation with some mild disorganization. In some regions, the upper levels or even the entire epithelium is absent. This seems to extend out on the ectocervical side of the squamocolumnar junction and is not obviously in the margin, however, in some regions the margins are incomplete. Multiple levels are examined. The dysplasia is most advanced in the sections labeled "C." Section "E" shows fragments of endometrium containing convoluted nonsecretory glands. The stroma consists of spindle- and polygonal-type cells.

DIAGNOSIS

#1. "CONE CERVIX:" MILD TO MODERATE SQUAMOUS DYSPLASIA. ACUTE AND CHRONIC CERVICITIS WITH SQUAMOUS METAPLASIA.

#2."UTERINE CURETTEMENTS:" FRAGMENTS OF NONSECRETORY PHASE ENDOMETRIUM.

DD: 04-29-YYYY
DT: 04-30-YYYY

Albert Gardner, M.D.
Albert Gardner, M.D.

RECOVERY ROOM RECORD

DENNIS, Marsha
Case01
Dr. Thompson

Admission: 04-27-YYYY
DOB: 02/09/YYYY
Room: 0603

DATE: 4/27/YYYY **TIME:** 1420

OPERATION: D&C. Cold cone.

ANESTHESIA: General

AIRWAY: N/A

O₂ USED: ☒ YES ☐ NO

ROUTE: Mask @ 6L/min.

TIME	MEDICATIONS	SITE

INTAKE	AMOUNT
300 D5L R Left hand	
IV site w/o redness or edema	
250 D5L. R on discharge	
TOTAL	50 cc

OUTPUT		AMOUNT
CATHETER	Clear light yellow	10 cc
LEVINE	N/A	
HEMOVAC	N/A	
TOTAL		10 cc

DISCHARGE STATUS

ROOM: 0603 **TIME:** 1455

CONDITION: Satisfactory

TRANSFERRED BY: Stretcher

R.R. NURSE: Sally James, RN

PREOP VISIT:

POSTOP VISIT: Report given to Dr.
Galloway at 1500 by S. James, R.N.

↑ hermoscan probe. Oral mode q9 adm.

POSTANESTHESIA RECOVERY SCORE		Adm	30 min	1 hr	2 hr	Disch
Moves 4 extremities voluntarily or on command (2) Moves 2 extremities voluntarily or on command (1) Moves 0 extremities voluntarily or on command (0)	Activity	2	2	2	2	2
Able to deep breathe and cough freely (2) Dyspnea or limited breathing (1) Apneic (0)	Respiration	2	2	2	2	2
BP ± 20% of preanesthetic level BP ± 20% of preanesthetic level BP + 50% of preanesthetic level	Circulation	2	2	2	2	2
Fully awake (2) Arouseable on calling (1) Not responding (0)	Consciousness	2	2	2	2	2
Pink (2) Pale, dusky, blotchy, jaundiced, other (1) Cyanotic (0)	Color	2	2	2	2	2

COMMENTS & OBSERVATIONS:

Dinamap BP monitor R arm q5min.

Pt awake on arrival to RR with respirations deep, easy and regular.

2" vaginal packing in place as reported by circulating nurse.

Foley draining small amount yellow urine.

Mary Crawford, RN
SIGNATURE OF RECOVERY ROOM NURSE

ALFRED STATE MEDICAL CENTER ■ 100 MAIN ST, ALFRED, NY 14802 ■ (607) 555-1234

DENNIS, Marsha   Admission: 04-27-YYYY

Case01   DOB: 02/09/YYYY

Dr. Thompson   Room: 0603

LABORATORY DATA

SPECIMEN COLLECTED: 04-22-YYYY   SPECIMEN RECEIVED: 04-22-YYYY

TEST	RESULT	FLAG	REFERENCE
URINALYSIS			
DIPSTICK ONLY			
COLOR	CLOUDY YELLOW		
SP GRAVITY	1.025		≤ 1.030
GLUCOSE	110		≤ 125 mg/dl
BILIRUBIN	NEG		≤ 0.8 mg/dl
KETONE	TRACE		≤ 10 mg/dl
BLOOD	0.03		0.06 mg/dl hgb
PH	5.0		5-8.0
PROTEIN	NORMAL		≤ 30 mg/dl
UROBILINOGEN	NORMAL		≤ -1 mg/dl
NITRITES	NEG		NEG
LEUKOCYTE	NEG		≤ 15 WBC/hpf
W.B.C.	5-10		≤ 5/hpf
R.B.C.	RARE		≤ 5/hpf
BACT.	4f		1+ (≤ 20/hpf)
URINE PREGNANCY TEST			
	NEG		

End of Report

DENNIS, Marsha   Admission: 04-27-YYYY   RADIOLOGY REPORT
Case01   DOB: 02/09/YYYY
Dr. Thompson   Room: 0603

Date Requested: 04-22-YYYY
Pre-op: 04-27-YYYY

CHEST: PA and lateral views show that the heart, lungs, thorax, and mediastinum are normal.

DD: 04-22-YYYY

Philip Rogers
_____
DT: 04-22-YYYY   Philip Rogers, M.D., Radiologist

EKG REPORT

DENNIS, Marsha
Case01
Dr. Thompson

Admission: 04-27-YYYY
DOB: 02/09/YYYY
Room: 0603

Date of EKG: *04-22-YYYY*

Time of EKG: *10:56:20*

Rate	*66*
PR	*184*
QRSD	*60*
QT	*363*
QTC	*380*
-- Axis --	
P	*76*
QRS	*79*
T	*71*

Normal.

Bella Kaplan
Bella Kaplan, M.D.

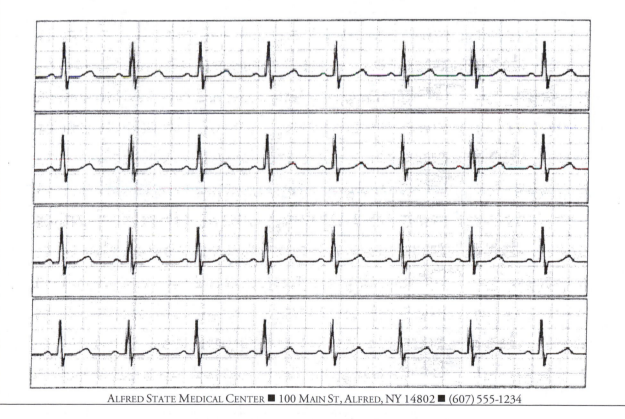

Case 02

ALFRED STATE MEDICAL CENTER 100 MAIN ST, ALFRED NY 14802 (607) 555-1234 HOSPITAL #: 000999				INPATIENT FACE SHEET			

PATIENT NAME AND ADDRESS				GENDER	RACE	MARITAL STATUS	PATIENT NO.
HUNTER, Dilbert 543 Yukon Trail Alfred, NY 14802				M	W	M	Case02
				DATE OF BIRTH	MAIDEN NAME		OCCUPATION
				09-22-YYYY	N/A		Unemployed

ADMISSION DATE	TIME	DISCHARGE DATE	TIME	LENGTH OF STAY	TELEPHONE NUMBER	
04-26-YYYY	15:20	04-29-YYYY	10:10	03 DAYS	(607) 555-6632	

GUARANTOR NAME AND ADDRESS		NEXT OF KIN NAME AND ADDRESS	
Hunter, Anita 543 Yukon Trail Alfred, NY 14802		Hunter, Anita 543 Yukon Trail Alfred, NY 14802	

GUARANTOR TELEPHONE NO.	RELATIONSHIP TO PATIENT	NEXT OF KIN TELEPHONE NUMBER	RELATIONSHIP TO PATIENT
(607) 555-6632	Wife	(607) 555-6632	Wife

ADMITTING PHYSICIAN	SERVICE	ADMIT TYPE	ROOM NUMBER/BED
William Ruddy, MD	Medical	2	0366/01

ATTENDING PHYSICIAN	ATTENDING PHYSICIAN UPIN	ADMITTING DIAGNOSIS	
William Ruddy, MD	100T32	Rule out pneumonia.	

PRIMARY INSURER	POLICY AND GROUP NUMBER	SECONDARY INSURER	POLICY AND GROUP NUMBER
Empire Plan	352656388		

DIAGNOSES AND PROCEDURES	ICD-9-CM	ICD-10-CM/PCS
PRINCIPAL DIAGNOSIS		
Acute Bronchitis	491.22	J44.0
SECONDARY DIAGNOSES		
Asthma	493.20	J44.9
COPD	401.9	I10
↑ B.P.		
PRINCIPAL PROCEDURE		
SECONDARY PROCEDURES		
TOTAL CHARGES: $ 2,692.74		

ACTIVITY:	☐ Bedrest	☑ Light	☐ Usual	☐ Unlimited	☐ Other:	
DIET:	☐ Regular	☐ Low Cholesterol	☑ Low Salt	☐ ADA	☐ _____ Calorie	
FOLLOW-UP:	☐ Call for appointment	☐ Office appointment on ____	☐ Other:			

SPECIAL INSTRUCTIONS:

Signature of Attending Physician: William Ruddy, MD

HUNTER, Dilbert	Admission: 04-26-YYYY	CONSENT TO ADMISSION
Case 02	DOB: 09-22-YYYY	
Dr. Ruddy	ROOM: 0366	

I, _Dilbert Hunter_ hereby consent to admission to the Alfred State Medical Center (ASMC), and I further consent to such routine hospital care, diagnostic procedures, and medical treatment that the medical and professional staff of ASMC may deem necessary or advisable. I authorize the use of medical information obtained about me as specified above and the disclosure of such information to my referring physician(s). This form has been fully explained to me, and I understand its contents. I further understand that no guarantees have been made to me as to the results of treatments or examinations done at the ASMC.

Dilbert Hunter   _April 26, YYYY_
Signature of Patient   Date

Signature of Parent/Legal Guardian for Minor   Date

Relationship to Minor

Andrea Witteman   _April 26, YYYY_
WITNESS: Alfred State Medical Center Staff Member   Date

CONSENT TO RELEASE INFORMATION FOR REIMBURSEMENT PURPOSES

In order to permit reimbursement, upon request, the Alfred State Medical Center (ASMC) may disclose such treatment information pertaining to my hospitalization to any corporation, organization, or agent thereof, which is, or may be liable under contract to the ASMC or to me, or to any of my family members or other person, for payment of all or part of the ASMC's charges for services rendered to me (e.g., the patient's health insurance carrier). I understand that the purpose of any release of information is to facilitate reimbursement for services rendered. In addition, in the event that my health insurance program includes utilization review of services provided during this admission, I authorize ASMC to release information as is necessary to permit the review. This authorization will expire once the reimbursement for services rendered is complete.

Dilbert Hunter   _April 26, YYYY_
Signature of Patient   Date

Signature of Parent/Legal Guardian for Minor   Date

Relationship to Minor

Andrea Witteman   _April 26, YYYY_
WITNESS: Alfred State Medical Center Staff Member   Date

HUNTER, Dilbert	Admission: 04-26-YYYY	ADVANCE DIRECTIVE
Case02	DOB: 09-22-YYYY	
Dr. Ruddy	ROOM: 0366	

Your answers to the following questions will assist your Physician and the Hospital to respect your wishes regarding your medical care. This information will become a part of your medical record.

	YES	NO	PATIENT'S INITIALS
1. Have you been provided with a copy of the information called "Patient Rights Regarding Health Care Decision?"	X		DH
2. Have you prepared a "Living Will?" If yes, please provide the Hospital with a copy for your medical record.		X	DH
3. Have you prepared a Durable Power of Attorney for Health Care? If yes, please provide the Hospital with a copy for your medical record.		X	DH
4. Have you provided this facility with an Advance Directive on a prior admission and is it still in effect? If yes, Admitting Office to contact Medical Records to obtain a copy for the medical record.		X	DH
5. Do you desire to execute a Living Will/Durable Power of Attorney? If yes, refer to in order: a. Physician b. Social Service c. Volunteer Service		X	DH

HOSPITAL STAFF DIRECTIONS: Check when each step is completed.

1. ___✓___ Verify the above questions where answered and actions taken where required.

2. ___✓___ If the "Patient Rights" information was provided to someone other than the patient, state reason:

_____

_____   _____
Name of Individual Receiving Information   Relationship to Patient

3. ___✓___ If information was provided in a language other than English, specify language and method.

4. ___✓___ Verify patient was advised on how to obtain additional information on Advance Directives.

5. ___✓___ Verify the Patient/Family Member/Legal Representative was asked to provide the Hospital with a copy of the Advance Directive which will be retained in the medical record.

File this form in the medical record and give a copy to the patient.

_____
Name of Patient (Name of Individual giving information if different from Patient)

Dilbert Hunter   April 26, YYYY
_____   _____
Signature of Patient   Date

Andrea Wittleman   April 26, yyyy
_____   _____
Signature of Hospital Representative   Date

```
HUNTER, Dilbert          Admission: 04-26-YYYY
Case 02                  DOB: 09-22-YYYY
Dr. Ruddy                ROOM: 0366
```

HISTORY & PHYSICAL EXAM

CHIEF COMPLAINT: Shortness of breath.

HISTORY OF PRESENT ILLNESS: The patient is a 55 yr. old gentleman with severe COPD with asthma and hypertension, who had developed an acute bronchitis about a week ago and five days ago was started on Ampicillin taking his usual 500 mg. t.i.d. This did not help, and he was started on a Medrol Dose-Pak but he had already been taking Prednisone. The patient had increasing shortness of breath the last 24 hours and came in. He had to stop four times to walk from the parking lot into the office due to increasing shortness of breath. He has some orthopnea, paroxysmal nocturnal dyspnea with it, which is typical for a flare up of his COPD with asthma and especially if infected. The patient has severe allergies to nonsteroidals causing him almost an anaphylactic type of reaction and with severe shortness of breath and had one respiratory arrest requiring intubation for that particular problem.

PAST MEDICAL HISTORY: General health has been good when he is in between his breathing attacks. Childhood diseases-no rheumatic or scarlet fever. Adult diseases-no TB or diabetes. Has had recurrent pneumonias. Operations: hemorrhoidectomy.

MEDICATIONS: At this time include Lasix 40 mg. daily. Calan 80 mg. t.i.d. Prednisone 10 mg. daily. Vasotec 10 mg. daily. Theolair 250 b.i.d. Allopurinol 300 mg. daily. Proventil and Azmacort 2 puffs q. i .d.

ALLERGIES: Nonsteroidal antiinflammatory drugs, including aspirin.

SOCIAL HISTORY: Does not smoke or drink.

FAMILY HISTORY: Noncontributory.

REVIEW OF SYSTEMS: Head: no headaches, seizures or convulsions. EENT reveals rhinorrhea and allergies, particularly with sinusitis. Chest and heart: see HPI. GI: no nausea, diarrhea, constipation. GU: no dysuria, hematuria, nocturia. Extremities: no edema. Has a lot of arthritic problems getting along with Tylenol at this time.

GENERAL APPEARANCE: The patient is a middle-aged gentleman who is short of breath at rest.

VITAL SIGNS: Temperature is 97, pulse is 60, respirations 24, blood pressure 146/68. Weight 254 lbs.

SKIN: Normal color and texture. No petechiae or ecchymoses.

HEENT: Normal cephalic. No mastoid or cranial tenderness. Eyes, pupils equal and reactive to light and accommodation. Extra-ocular muscle function intact. Funduscopic examination within normal limits. Ears: no inflammation or bulging of the drums. Nose: no inflammation, though there is same clear rhinorrhea. Mouth: no inflammation or exudate.

NECK: Supple. No adenopathy. Trachea in the midline. Thyroid normal. Carotids 2/4 with no bruits.

CHEST: Symmetrical.

LUNGS: There are wheezes heard throughout the lung fields with rhonchi and rales at the right base.

HEART: Regular rhythm. Sl 2/4, S2 2/4, with no S3, S4 or murmurs.

BACK: No CVA or spinal tenderness.

ABDOMEN: Soft. No organomegaly, masses, or tenderness to palpation or percussion. Normal bowel sounds.

GENITALIA: Normal external genitalia.

RECTAL: Good sphincter tone. No mucosal masses. Stool hemoccult negative. Prostate 2+ with no nodules.

EXTREMITIES: Peripheral pulses 2+. No edema, cyanosis or clubbing.

NEUROLOGIC: Within normal limits.

IMPRESSION: 1) Asthma with acute bronchitis and bronchospasm.

           2) Hypertension.

DD: 04-26-YYYY

DT: 04-27-YYYY

William Ruddy, MD
William Ruddy, MD

HUNTER, Dilbert	Admission: 04-26-YYYY	PROGRESS NOTES
Case02	DOB: 09-22-YYYY	
Dr. Ruddy	ROOM: 0366	

Date	(Please skip one line between dates.)
4/26/YYYY	Chief Complaint: Shortness of breath.
	Dx: COPD, asthma, acute brohchitis.
	Plan of Treatment: See physician orders.
	Discharge Plan: Home. William Ruddy, MD
4/27/YYYY	Pt. is less SOB today but still has considerable wheezing. Will cont same meds
	until I get results of culture and sensitivity. William Ruddy, MD

HUNTER, Dilbert	Admission: 04-26-YYYY	
Case 02	DOB: 09-22-YYYY	**DOCTORS ORDERS**
Dr. Ruddy	ROOM: 0366	

Date	Time	Physician's signature required for each order. (Please skip one line between dates.)		
4/26/YYYY	1525	Sputum C & S. CBC, UA, ABG Rx and call CXR; NAS diet; Saline Lock		
		Ancef 1 gm q 8°		
		Solumedrol 125mg q 6° IV		
		Calan 80mg Tid		
		Vasotic 10mg daily		
		Theodur 300mg Bid (q 12°)		
		Allopurinol 300mg daily		
		Proventil and Azmacort puffs qid – do own Rx		*William Ruddy, MD*
			R.A.V.	V.O. Dr. Ruddy/J.Anderson, RN
4/26/YYYY	1720	D/C ABC. Do RA oximetry.	R.A.V.	T.O. Dr. Ruddy/E. Blossom RN
4/26/YYYY	1720	O2 2L/Ne	R.A.V.	T.O. Dr. Ruddy/E. Blossom RN
4/27/YYYY	1320	*Tylenol 650mg po q 4° prn pain* *R.A.V.* *T.O. Dr. Ruddy/H. Figgs RN*		
4/28/YYYY	1020	1) D/C IV		
		2) Ceftin 250mg P.O. BID		
		3) Prednisone 20mg P.O.		*William Ruddy, MD*
		4) Walk hall as tolerated	R.A.V.	T.O. Dr. Ruddy/E. Blossom RN
				William Ruddy, MD
4/28/YYYY	0900	*DC O2*	R.A.V.	*T.O. Dr. Ruddy/H. Figgs RN*
4/29/YYYY	1200	*Discharge – dict later*		*William Ruddy, MD*

ALFRED STATE MEDICAL CENTER ■ 100 MAIN ST, ALFRED, NY 14802 ■ (607) 555-1234

HUNTER, Dilbert	Admission: 04-26-YYYY		LABORATORY DATA
Case02	DOB: 09-22-YYYY		
Dr. Ruddy	ROOM: 0366		

SPECIMEN COLLECTED: 04-26-YYYY   **SPECIMEN RECEIVED:** 04-26-YYYY

URINALYSIS

URINE DIPSTICK

COLOR	STRAW	
SP GRAVITY	1.010	1.001-1.030
GLUCOSE	NEGATIVE	< 125 mg/dl
BILIRUBIN	NEGATIVE	NEG
KETONE	NEGATIVE	NEG mg/dl
BLOOD	NEGATIVE	NEG
PH	7.5	4.5-8.0
PROTEIN	NEGATIVE	NEG mg/dl
UROBILINOGEN	NORMAL	NORMAL-1.0 mg/dl
NITRITES	NEGATIVE	NEG
LEUKOCYTES	NEGATIVE	NEG
WBC	RARE	0-5 /HPF
RBC	--	0-5 /HPF
EPI CELLS	RARE	/HPF
BACTERIA	--	/HPF
CASTS.	--	< 1 HYALINE/HPF

End of Report

HUNTER, Dilbert   Admission: 04-26-YYYY   **LABORATORY DATA**
Case 02   DOB: 09-22-YYYY
Dr. Ruddy   ROOM: 0366

SPECIMEN COLLECTED: 04-26-YYYY   **SPECIMEN RECEIVED:** 04-26-YYYY

CBC c̄ DIFF

TEST	RESULT	FLAG	REFERENCE
WBC	7.4		4.5-11.0 thous/UL
RBC	5.02	**L**	5.2-5.4 mill/UL
HGB	15.0		11.7-16.1 g/dl
HCT	45.8		35.0-47.0 %
MCV	91.2		85-99 fL.
MCHC	32.8	**L**	33-37
RDW	15.2	**H**	11.4-14.5
Platelets	165		130-400 thous/UL
MPV	8.4		7.4-10.4
LYMPH %	21.1		20.5-51.1
MONO %	7.8		1.7-9.3
GRAN %	71.1		42.2-75.2
LYMPH x 10^3	1.6		1.2-3.4
MONO x 10^3	.6	**H**	0.11-0.59
GRAN x 10^3	5.3		1.4-6.5
EOS x 10^3	< .7		0.0-0.7
BASO x 10^3	< .2		0.0-0.2
ANISO	SLIGHT		

End of Report

HUNTER, Dilbert	Admission: 04-26-YYYY	RADIOLOGY REPORT
Case02	DOB: 09-22-YYYY	
Dr. Ruddy	ROOM: 0366	

Initial Diagnosis/History: COPD

Date Requested: 04-26-YYYY

Transport: ☑ Wheelchair   ☐ Stretcher   ☐ O_2 ☐ IV
             ☑ IP   ☐ OP   ☐ ER
             ☐ PRE OP   ☐ OR/RR   ☐ Portable

CHEST: PA and lateral views reveals the heart and mediastinum to be normal. The lungs are hyperinflated with flattening of the diaphragms and disorganization of the interstitial markings secondary to chronic disease. There is also some old pleural thickening at the left base laterally. Since our previous study of 4-30-YYYY, an area of atelectasis has developed in the middle lobe. I do not know if this is of any current significance. No areas of consolidation or any pleural effusions are visible.

DD: 04-26-YYYY

DT: 04-27-YYYY

Philip Rogers

_____

Philip Rogers

MEDICATION (dose and route)	DATE: 04-26 TIME	INITIALS	DATE: 04-27 TIME	INITIALS	DATE: 04-28 TIME	INITIALS	DATE: 04-29 TIME	INITIALS
ANCEF 1GM Q 8°	0800	VT	0800	VT	0800	HF		
	1600	JD	1600	OR	D/c			
	2400	P.S.	2400	P.S.	D/c			
SOLUMEDROL 125 MG IV 1 6°	0600	GPW	0600	GPW	0600	GPW		
	1200	GPW	1200	VT	D/c			
	1800	JD	1800	OR	D/c			
	2400	GPW	2400	GPW	D/c			
CALAN 80 MG TID	0800	VT	0800	VT	0800	HF	0800	HF
	1300	VT	1300	VT	1300	HF	D/c	
	1800	JD	1800	JD	1800	OR	1800	JD
VASOTEC 10MG DAILY	0800	JD	0800	JD	0800	HF	0800	HF
THEODUR 300MG Q 12°	0800	JD	0800	JD	0800	HF	0800	HF
	2000	JD	2000	JD	2000	OR	2000	JD
ALLOPURINOL 300MG DAILY	0800	JD	0800	JD	0800	HF	0800	HF
SALINE FLUSH P EACH USE	0800	JD	0800	JD	D/c			
CEFTIN 250 mg PO BID	0800	HF	0800	HF	0800	HF	0800	HF
	1600	JD	1600	JD	1600	JD	D/c	

INITIALS	SIGNATURE AND TITLE	INITIALS	SIGNATURE AND TITLE	INITIALS	SIGNATURE AND TITLE
VT	VERA SOUTH, EN	GPW	G. P. WELL, RCP		
OR	ORA RICHARDS, RN	P.S.	P. SMALL, RN		
JD	JANE DOBBS, RN				
HF	H. Figgs RN				

HUNTER, Dilbert · Case02 · Dr. Ruddy · Admission: 04-26-YYYY · DOB: 09-22-YYYY · ROOM: 0366 · MEDICATION ADMINISTRATION RECORD · ALFRED STATE MEDICAL CENTER 100 MAIN ST, ALFRED, NY 14802 (607) 555-1234

HUNTER, Dilbert	Admission: 04-26-YYYY	PATIENT PROPERTY RECORD
Case02	DOB: 09-22-YYYY	
Dr. Ruddy	ROOM: 0366	

I understand that while the facility will be responsible for items deposited in the safe, I must be responsible for all items retained by me at the bedside. (Dentures kept at the bedside will be labeled, but the facility cannot assure responsibility for them.) I also recognize that the hospital cannot be held responsible for items brought in to me after this form has been completed and signed.

Dilbert Hunter   *April 26, YYYY*
_____   _____
Signature of Patient   Date

Andrea Witteman   *April 26, yyyy*
_____   _____
Signature of Witness   Date

- -

I have no money or valuables that I wish to deposit for safekeeping. I do not hold the facility responsible for any other money or valuables that I am retaining or will have brought in to me.

I have been advised that it is recommended that I retain no more than $5.00 at the bedside.

Dilbert Hunter   *April 26, YYYY*
_____   _____
Signature of Patient   Date

Andrea Witteman   *April 26, yyyy*
_____   _____
Signature of Witness   Date

- -

I have deposited valuables in the facility safe. The envelope number is _____.

_____   _____
Signature of Patient   Date

_____   _____
Signature of Person Accepting Property   Date

- -

I understand that medications I have brought to the facility will be handled as recommended by my physician. This may include storage, disposal, or administration.

_____   _____
Signature of Patient   Date

_____   _____
Signature of Witness   Date

Case 03

ALFRED STATE MEDICAL CENTER 100 MAIN ST, ALFRED, NY 14802 (607) 555-1234 HOSPITAL #: 000999			INPATIENT FACE SHEET		

PATIENT NAME AND ADDRESS		GENDER	RACE	MARITAL STATUS	PATIENT NO.
STANLEY, Erica P. 23 Langley Drive Alfred, NY 14802		F	W	M	Case03
		DATE OF BIRTH	MAIDEN NAME		OCCUPATION
		04-05-YYYY	Holland		Homemaker

ADMISSION DATE	TIME	DISCHARGE DATE	TIME	LENGTH OF STAY	TELEPHONE NUMBER
04-28-YYYY	06:20	04-29-YYYY	10:20	01 DAY	(607)555-8818

GUARANTOR NAME AND ADDRESS	NEXT OF KIN NAME AND ADDRESS
Stanley, Robert 23 Langley Drive Alfred, NY 14802	Stanley, Robert 23 Langley Drive Alfred, NY 14802

GUARANTOR TELEPHONE NO.	RELATIONSHIP TO PATIENT	NEXT OF KIN TELEPHONE NUMBER	RELATIONSHIP TO PATIENT
(607)555-8818	Husband	(607)555-8818	Husband

ADMITTING PHYSICIAN	SERVICE	ADMIT TYPE	ROOM NUMBER/BED
E.W. Wylie, MD	Surgical	03	0255/01

ATTENDING PHYSICIAN	ATTENDING PHYSICIAN UPIN	ADMITTING DIAGNOSIS	
E.W. Wylie, MD	100D43	Gallbladder disease	

PRIMARY INSURER	POLICY AND GROUP NUMBER	SECONDARY INSURER	POLICY AND GROUP NUMBER
Medicaid	329130095		

DIAGNOSES AND PROCEDURES	ICD-9-CM	ICD-10-CM/PCS
PRINCIPAL DIAGNOSIS		
chronic acalculus cholecystitis	575.11	K81.1
SECONDARY DIAGNOSES		
PRINCIPAL PROCEDURE		
Laparoscopic cholecystectomy	51.23	0FT44ZZ
SECONDARY PROCEDURES		
TOTAL CHARGES: $ 3,500.50		

ACTIVITY:	☐ Bedrest	☑ Light	☐ Usual	☐ Unlimited	☑ Other: Don't lift heavy or stairs

DIET:	☑ Regular	☐ Low Cholesterol	☐ Low Salt	☐ ADA	☐ _____ Calorie

FOLLOW-UP:	☐ Call for appointment	☑ Office appointment in 2 wks	☑ Other: Dr. Winslow in One wk

SPECIAL INSTRUCTIONS: May shower.

SIGNATURE OF ATTENDING PHYSICIAN: E Wylie, M.D.

STANLEY, Erica P.
Case 03
Dr. Wylie

Admission: 04-28-YYYY
DOB: 04-05-YYYY
ROOM: 0255

CONSENT TO ADMISSION

I, _Erica P. Stanley_ hereby consent to admission to the Alfred State Medical Center (ASMC) , and I further consent to such routine hospital care, diagnostic procedures, and medical treatment that the medical and professional staff of ASMC may deem necessary or advisable. I authorize the use of medical information obtained about me as specified above and the disclosure of such information to my referring physician(s). This form has been fully explained to me, and I understand its contents. I further understand that no guarantees have been made to me as to the results of treatments or examinations done at the ASMC.

Erica P. Stanley	_April 28, YYYY_
Signature of Patient	Date

  |
--- | ---
Signature of Parent/Legal Guardian for Minor | Date

Relationship to Minor

Andrea Witteman	_April 28, YYYY_
WITNESS: Alfred State Medical Center Staff Member	Date

CONSENT TO RELEASE INFORMATION FOR REIMBURSEMENT PURPOSES

In order to permit reimbursement, upon request, the Alfred State Medical Center (ASMC) may disclose such treatment information pertaining to my hospitalization to any corporation, organization, or agent thereof, which is, or may be liable under contract to the ASMC or to me, or to any of my family members or other person, for payment of all or part of the ASMC's charges for services rendered to me (e.g., the patient's health insurance carrier). I understand that the purpose of any release of information is to facilitate reimbursement for services rendered. In addition, in the event that my health insurance program includes utilization review of services provided during this admission, I authorize ASMC to release information as is necessary to permit the review. This authorization will expire once the reimbursement for services rendered is complete.

Erica P. Stanley	_April 28, YYYY_
Signature of Patient	Date

  |
--- | ---
Signature of Parent/Legal Guardian for Minor | Date

Relationship to Minor

Andrea Witteman	_April 28, YYYY_
WITNESS: Alfred State Medical Center Staff Member	Date

STANLEY, Erica P.   Admission: 04-28-YYYY
Case03   DOB: 04-05-YYYY
Dr. Wylie   ROOM: 0255

ADVANCE DIRECTIVE

Your answers to the following questions will assist your Physician and the Hospital to respect your wishes regarding your medical care. This information will become a part of your medical record.

	YES	NO	PATIENT'S INITIALS
1. Have you been provided with a copy of the information called "Patient Rights Regarding Health Care Decision?"	X		EPS
2. Have you prepared a "Living Will?" If yes, please provide the Hospital with a copy for your medical record.		X	EPS
3. Have you prepared a Durable Power of Attorney for Health Care? If yes, please provide the Hospital with a copy for your medical record.		X	EPS
4. Have you provided this facility with an Advance Directive on a prior admission and is it still in effect? If yes, Admitting Office to contact Medical Records to obtain a copy for the medical record.		X	EPS
5. Do you desire to execute a Living Will/Durable Power of Attorney? If yes, refer to in order: a. Physician b. Social Service c. Volunteer Service		X	EPS

HOSPITAL STAFF DIRECTIONS: Check when each step is completed.

1.   ✓   Verify the above questions where answered and actions taken where required.

2.   ✓   If the "Patient Rights" information was provided to someone other than the patient, state reason:

_____

_____   _____

Name of Individual Receiving Information   Relationship to Patient

3.   ✓   If information was provided in a language other than English, specify language and method.

4.   ✓   Verify patient was advised on how to obtain additional information on Advance Directives.

5.   ✓   Verify the Patient/Family Member/Legal Representative was asked to provide the Hospital with a copy of the Advance Directive which will be retained in the medical record.

File this form in the medical record, and give a copy to the patient.

Name of Patient (Name of Individual giving information if different from Patient)
Erica P. Stanley   *April 28, YYYY*
_____   _____

Signature of Patient   Date

Andrea Witteman   *April 28, YYYY*
_____   _____

Signature of Hospital Representative   Date

ALFRED STATE MEDICAL CENTER ■ 100 MAIN ST, ALFRED, NY 14802 ■ (607) 555-1234

```
STANLEY, Erica P.        Admission: 04-28-YYYY      HISTORY & PHYSICAL EXAM
Case03                   DOB: 04-05-YYYY
Dr. Wylie                ROOM: 0255
```

CHIEF COMPLAINT: Chronic acalculus cholecystitis

HISTORY OF PRESENT ILLNESS: The patient is a 52-year-old white female who, for about 1 year, has been very symptomatic to the point that even water starts to make her have right upper quadrant pain. She had problems with all sorts of foods, fried foods, gravies, and this causes right upper quadrant pains and sometimes nausea radiating around the costal margin straight through to the back underneath the scapula on the right side, very reproducible. Dr. Will ams saw her and obtained an ultra-sound which showed some very subtle thickening of the gallbladder wall but the ultra-sound findings were equivocal. It was suggested that if there were appropriate clinical symptoms that a cholecystokinin HIDA scan might be helpful. Under the circumstances patient is not really anxious to undergo the test in case she gets more pain and with her symptoms being as reproducible as they are, she probably has chronic acalculus gallbladder disease and I think she is getting this every day with every meal it seems a little ridiculous: to try and produce this again so I am going to go ahead and plan for a laparoscopic cholecystectomy with IOC and she understands the procedure as I have explained it to her and agrees to it the way I have explained it to her. I told her that sometimes open procedure is necessary for reasons of safety or bleeding, etc. and I have given her a pamphlet that explains the entire procedure for her to read. She understands and agrees to this the way I have explained it to her.

PAST MEDICAL HISTORY: Reveals that she is allergic to CODEINE AND ASPIRIN. She has been taking Bancap for pain which periodically helps. She has had bilateral implants in her eye and she has had bilateral Stapes operations on her ears and she has had a TAH and BSO. She has had an appendectomy. She has no other known medical illnesses.

SYSTEMIC REVIEW: Consistent with HPI and PMH and otherwise unremarkable.

FAMILY HISTORY: Reveals cancer in the family but nothing hereditary. There is colon cancer, pelvic cancer, etc. She has one daughter who has epilepsy. No bleeding problems or anesthesia problems. No other hereditary problems noted in the family.

SOCIAL HISTORY: She smokes 1/2 pack of cigarettes a day and does not take any alcohol. She is a housewife, married, living at home with her grandchild whom she is taking care of.

At the time of admission, she is a well developed, well nourished, white female in no acute distress. Vital signs are stable. She is afebrile, pleasant, cooperative, and well oriented.

HEENT: Reveals normal cephalic skull. Pupils are round, regular, and reactive to light and accommodation. Extra-ocular movements are intact. Nose and throat - benign.

NECK: Supple. No masses, thyroidomegaly, or adenopathy. She has 2+/4+ bilateral, carotid pulses with good upstrokes. No supraclavicular adenopathy on either side.

CHEST: Clear to auscultation bilaterally.

CARDIAC: Regular sinus rhythm with no murmurs or gallops heard.

BREASTS: Free of any dominant masses or nodules bilaterally.

AXILLA: Free of any adenopathy.

ABDOMEN: Soft. No hernias, masses, or organomegaly. She has some tenderness over the gallbladder in the right upper quadrant area but no rigidity, guarding, or rebound. She has normal bowel sounds.

PELVIC: Deferred today.

PULSES: Equal bilaterally.

NEURO: Within normal limits grossly.

EXTREMITIES: Full range of motion bilaterally with no pain or edema.

IMPRESSION: Chronic acalculus cholecystitis apparently quite symptomatic. The patient will be admitted for a laparoscopic cholecystectomy under antibiotic prophylaxis as noted above as AM admission.

DD: 04-28-YYYY

DT: 04-28-YYYY

E.W. Wylie, M.D.

E.W. Wylie, M.D.

STANLEY, Erica P.	Admission: 04-28-YYYY	PROGRESS NOTES
Case 03	DOB: 04-05-YYYY	
Dr. Wylie	ROOM: 0255	

Date	(Please skip one line between dates.)
4/28/YYYY	cc: chronic acalculus cholecystitis.
0700	Plan of Treatment: Laparosopic cholecystomy.
	Discharge Plan: Home - No services needed. E.W. Wylie, M.D.
04-28-yyyy	Anesthesia Pre Op Note
0715	This 52 y o w female scheduled for Lap Chole. PMHx: ⊕ tobacco hx. ⊕ Past Surgical Hx - appendectomy, total abdominal hysterectomy.
	Cataracts, bilaterally. Bilaterial stapes repair. Meds preop. Alergies: Codeine, ASA, ASA II.
	Plan and GETA, Risks, Benefits, Options Explained. Understood and agreed upon.
	Don Galloway, M.D.
04-28-YYYY	Brief Op. note
1400	Laparoscopic cholecystectomy done under A.E.T. Over
	without pain or complications. E.B.c. min. Pt. tolerated the
	procedure well & left the O.R. in satisfactory condition.
04-28-YYYY	Post Op
1439	Awake, Aert, Vital signs stable. Normal pulse, pressure.
	Abd. soft, w/o distention. Wound is clean and dry. No
	Problems.
	E.W. Wylie, M.D.

STANLEY, Erica P. Case03 Dr. Wylie		Admission: 04-28-YYYY DOB: 04-05-YYYY ROOM: 0255	DOCTORS ORDERS
Date	Time	Physician's signature required for each order. (Please skip one line between dates.)	
04-28-YYYY	0800	**Allergies:** codeine, ASA	E Wylie, M.D.
04-28-YYYY	0805	PATIENT NAME: Stanley, Erica	
		AGE: 52	
		ADMIT TO GEN. SURGERY: a.m. admit	
		CONDITION: satisfactory	
		OUT OF BED, AD LIB.	
		DIET: N.S.D.	
		US – ROUTINE	done in lab 4/23 hj
		CBC, UA, ~~RPR~~, BUN, GLUCOSE, LYTES → pre-op	
		EKG 04-23-YYYY → pre-op	
		CHEST X-RAY done 04-23 → pre-op	
		SHAVE & PREP for laparoscopic cholecystectomy	
		FOR OR ON: 04-28-YYYY	
		NPO	
		M/N OF 04-27-YYYY	
		anes. will pre-op.	
		IN SAME DAY SURGERY: Begin IV of lactate ringers at 125 CC PER Hr.	
		Ancef IV, On al to O.R. placed transderm- scop	
		Patch behind ear A.S.A.P.	
		Measure for thigh-high TED's	
		Bilateral mammogram	
			E Wylie, M.D.

ALFRED STATE MEDICAL CENTER ■ 100 MAIN ST, ALFRED, NY 14802 ■ (607) 555-1234

STANLEY, Erica P.	Admission: 04-28-YYYY	
Case 03	DOB: 04-05-YYYY	DOCTORS ORDERS
Dr. Wylie	ROOM: 0255	

Date	Time	Physician's signature required for each order. (Please skip one line between dates.)
04-28-YYYY	1530	POST OP ORDERS
		1. Routine post-op vital signs
		2. OOB ad lib
		3. Surg. clear liq diet to house diet ad lib
		4. P.O.R.T.
		5. D5 ½ NS w/2 0mEq KCL/L at 100ml/hr
		May d/c when tolerating PO fluids
		6. Cefazolin 1 gm at 1900 hr. and 0300 hr.
		7. May cath., if needed.
		8. Nalbuphine (Nubain) 20 mg IM/IV q3h prn pain, if Toradol is not sufficient
		9. ~~Meperidine 75 mg and Hydroxyzine 25 mg IM q4h prn pain if nalbuphine not sufficient.~~
		10. Percocet 1 P.O. q4h with food prn pain.
		11. Prochlorperasinze (copazine) 10mg IM/IV q6h prn nausea.
		12. Flurazepam (Dalmane) 30mg P.O. qhs prn sleep.
		13. Acetaminophen 650mg. P.O. temp of 101 degrees or above
		14. MOM 30 ml P.O. qhs prn constipation.
		15. Bisacodyl suppository or fleet enema bid prn "gas" or constipation.
		16. Toradol 30 mg IM, q6h, XX doses, then d/c
		E Wylie, M.D.
4-28-YYYY	1430	Discharge from PACU 1430 R.A.V. T.O. Dr. Wylie per H. Figgs RN
4-28-YYYY	0900	Cancel mammogram pre-op (scheduled for 5-18-YYYY at 10:30 am)
		R.A.V. T.O. Dr. Wylie/ Ross, RN
		E Wylie, M.D.

STANLEY, Erica P.		Admission: 04-28-YYYY	DOCTORS ORDERS
Case03		DOB: 04-05-YYYY	
Dr. Wylie		ROOM: 0255	

Date	Time	Physician's signature required for each order. (Please skip one line between dates.)
4-28-YYYY	1530	Pt. See Dr. Wilson in One wk and me in two.
		E Wylie, M.D.
4-29-YYYY		Pt. may d/c today
		S&D done.
		E Wylie, M.D.

STANLEY, Erica P.	Admission: 04-28-YYYY	Consent for Operation(s) and/or
Case 03	DOB: 04-05-YYYY	Procedure(s) and Anesthesia
Dr. Wylie	ROOM: 0255	

PERMISSION. I hereby authorize Dr. _Wylie_ , or associates of his/her choice at the

Alfred State Medical Center (the "Hospital") to perform upon _Erica P. Stanley_

the following operation(s) and/or procedure(s): _Laparoscopic cholecystectomy_

including such photography, videotaping, televising or other observation of the operation(s)/procedure(s) as may be purposeful for the advance of medical knowledge and/or education, with the understanding that the patient's identity will remain anonymous.

EXPLANATION OF PROCEDURE, RISKS, BENEFITS, ALTERNATIVES. Dr. _Wylie_

has fully explained to me the nature and purposes of the operation(s)/procedures named above and has also informed me of expected benefits and complications, attendant discomforts and risks that may arise, as well as possible alternatives to the proposed treatment. I have been given an opportunity to ask questions and all my questions have been answered fully and satisfactorily.

UNFORESEEN CONDITIONS. I understand that during the course of the operation(s) or procedure(s), unforeseen conditions may arise which necessitate procedures in addition to or different from those contemplated. I, therefore, consent to the performance of additional operations and procedures which the above-named physician or his/her associates or assistants may consider necessary.

ANESTHESIA. I further consent to the administration of such anesthesia as may be considered necessary by the above-named physician or his/her associates or assistants. I recognize that there are always risks to life and health associated with anesthesia. Such risks have been fully explained to me and I have been given an opportunity to ask questions and all my questions have been answered fully and satisfactorily.

SPECIMENS. Any organs or tissues surgically removed may be examined and retained by the Hospital for medical, scientific or educational purposes and such tissues or parts may be disposed of in accordance with accustomed practice and applicable State laws and/or regulations.

NO GUARANTEES. I acknowledge that no guarantees or assurances have been made to me concerning the operation(s) or procedure(s) described above.

MEDICAL DEVICE TRACKING. I hereby authorize the release of my Social Security number to the manufacturer of the medical device(s) I receive, if applicable, in accordance with federal law and regulations which may be used to help locate me if a need arises with regard to this medical device. I release the Alfred State Medical Center from any liability that might result from the release of this information.*

UNDERSTANDING OF THIS FORM. I confirm that I have read this form, fully understand its contents, and that all blank spaces above have been completed prior to my signing. I have crossed out any paragraphs above that do not pertain to me.

Patient/Relative/Guardian*

Erica P. Stanley   Erica P. Stanley

Signature   Print Name

Relationship, if other than patient signed:

Witness: _Shirley Thompson_   Shirley Thompson

Signature   Print Name

Date: _April 28, YYYY_

*The signature of the patient must be obtained unless the patient is an unemancipated minor under the age of 18 or is otherwise incompetent to sign.

PHYSICIAN'S CERTIFICATION. I hereby certify that I have explained the nature, purpose, benefits, risks of and alternatives to the operation(s)/procedure(s), have offered to answer any questions and have fully answered all such questions. I believe that the patient (relative/guardian) fully understands what I have explained and answered.

PHYSICIAN: _E Wylie, M.D._   _April 28, YYYY_

Signature   Date

ALFRED STATE MEDICAL CENTER ■ 100 MAIN ST, ALFRED, NY 14802 ■ (607) 555-1234

ANESTHESIA RECORD

STANLEY, Erica P.	Admission: 04-28-YYYY
Case03	DOB: 04-05-YYYY
Dr. Wylie	ROOM: 0255

		START	STOP
PROCEDURE(S): *Laparoscopic cholecystectomy*	ANESTHESIA	1219, 1228	1345
SURGEON(S): *Wylie*	PROCEDURE	1248	1331
DATE OF SURGERY: 04/28/YYYY	ROOM TIME	IN: 1200	OUT: 1345

PRE-PROCEDURE

- ☑ Patient Identified   ☑ ID band verified
- ☑ Patient questioned   ☑ Chart reviewed
- ☑ Consent form signed
- ☑ Patient reassessed prior to anesthesia (ready to proceed)
- ☑ Peri-operative pain management discussed with patient/guardian (plan of care completed)
- Pre-Anesthetic State:
- ☑ Awake   ☑ Anxious   ☐ Calm
- ☐ Lethargic   ☐ Uncooperative
- ☐ Unresponsive
- ☐ Other: _____
- ☑ Anesthesia machine #5626984 checked
- ☑ Secured with safety belt
- ☑ Arm secured on board   ☑ Left   ☐ Right

MONITORS/EQUIPMENT

- ☑ Stethoscope   ☐ Precordial
- ☑ Suprasternal   ☐ Esoph
- ☑ Non-invasive B/P   ☐ V-lead ECG
- ☑ Continuous ECG   ☐ ST Analysis
- ☑ Pulse oximeter   ☐ End tidal CO$_2$
- ☐ Nerve stimulator: ☐ Ulnar ☐ Tibial ☐ Facial
- ☑ Oxygen monitor   ☐ Cell Saver
- ☑ ET agent analyzer ☐ B/S   ☐ TEE
- ☐ Fluid/Blood warmer ☐ Temp:
- ☐ BIS   ☐ ICS
- ☑ NG/OG tube   ☐ FHT monitor
- ☑ Foley catheter   ☐ EEG
- ☐ Airway humidifier
- ☐ Evoked potential: ☐ SSEP ☐ BAEP ☐ MEP
- ☐ Arterial line _____ ☐ CVP _____

ANESTHESTIC TECHNIQUES

- *GA Induction:* ☑ IV ☐ Pre-O$_2$ ☐ RSI ☐ PR
- ☐ Cricoid pressure ☐ Inhalation ☐ IM
- *GA Maintenance:* ☐ TIVA ☐ Inhalation
- ☑ Inhalation/IV ☐ GA/Regional Comb.

Regional:
- Epidural: ☑ Thoracic ☐ Lumbar ☐ Caudal
- ☐ Femoral ☐ Auxiliary ☐ Interscalene
- ☐ CSE ☐ Bier ☐ SAB ☐ Ankle
- ☐ Continuous Spinal ☐ Cervical Plexus

Regional Techniques:
- ☐ Position _____   ☐ See Remarks
- ☐ Site _____   ☐ Prep _____
- ☐ LA _____   ☐ Needle _____
- ☐ Additive _____   ☐ Narcotic _____
-                   ☐ Test dose Rx ___

AIRWAY MANAGEMENT

- ☑ Oral ETT   ☐ LTA   ☐ RAE
- ☐ Nasal ETT   ☐ LMA # ____
- ☐ Stylet   ☐ LMA Fastrach # ____
- ☐ DVL   ☐ LMA ProSeal # ____
- ☐ EMG ETT   ☐ Bougie
- ☐ Armored ETT   ☐ LIS
- ☑ Breath sounds = bilateral
- ☐ Cuffed – min occ pres with ☑ air ☐ NS
- ☐ Uncuffed – leaks at _____ cm H$_2$O
- ☑ Oral airway ☐ Nasal airway ☐ Bite block
- *Circuit:* ☐ Circle system ☐ NRB ☐ Bain
- ☐ Via tracheotomy/stoma ☐ Mask case
- ☐ Nasal cannula   ☑ Simple O$_2$ mask
- Nebulizer: _____
- Nerve Block(s): _____

AGENTS

TIME:

		15	30	45	15	30	45	15	30	45	15	30	45	15	30	45	TOTALS
☐ Des ☐ Iso ☐ Sevo ☐ Halo (%)																	
☑ Air	(L/min)	1	1	1	1	1*											
☑ Oxygen	(L/min)	10 1	1	1	1	1	2/12										
☑ Tracrium	mg			5													
☑ Forane	(%)	.25	25	25	25	25											
☑ Anectine	(mg)	150	120	120	150	150	X										
☑ Pentothal	(mg)	100															226

FLUIDS

Urine	foley																
EBL																	
Gastric																	

SYMBOLS

⌄⌃ BP cuff pressure

⊥ Arterial line pressure

✕ Mean arterial pressure

● Pulse

○ Spontaneous Respirations

∅ Assisted Respirations

T Tourniquet

MONITORS

	15	30	45	15	30	45
☑ ECG						
☑ % Oxygen Inspired (FI0$_2$)		98	98	98	98	
☑ ETCO$_2$			49	49	49	
☑ Temp: ☐ C ☑ F		98			98	
☑ BP Monitor						

PERI-OP MEDS

Atropine .4
Ketorolec 60
Sublimaze 3 cc
Tacrium 5 mg
D-Tubo 2.5 mg

mmHg								
200								
180								
160								
140	⌄	⌄	⌄					
120				⌄	⌄	⌄	⌄	
100				•	•	•	•	•
80	•	•	⌃	⌃	•	⌃		
60	⌃	⌃			⌃		⌃	
40								
20	○	○	○	○	○	○	○	
10								

Time of Delivery: _____

Gender: ☐ M ☐ F

Apgars: ____/____

VENT

		15	30	45	15	30
Tidal Volume (ml)						
Respiratory Rate		SV	SV	SV	SV	SV
Peak Pressure	(cm H$_2$O)					
☐ PEEP ☐ CPAP	(cm H$_2$O)					

Position: *Lithotomy*	
	Surgeon: *Wylie*
Pt ID, chart and machine ☑ed. Pt. brought to OR no. 2 Monitors applied. Pt preoxygenated. IV induction smooth. Laryngoscopy $1GT.CV MAC3.0 intubation $1 7.52 MOP BS = BS. DETC02 cuff palpable. Tube taped 20 cm. Eyes taped. OA. Thermovent OG.	Assistant: *Johnson*
	Scrub Nurse: *Mary Marks, RN*
	Circulating Nurse: *Cynthie Lewis, RN*
	Signature of Anesthesiologist or C.R.N.A.: *Don Galloway, M.D.*

STANLEY, Erica P. Case 03 Dr. Wylie	Admission: 04-28-YYYY DOB: 04-05-YYYY ROOM: 0255	PRE-ANESTHESIA AND POST-ANESTHESIA RECORD

PRE-ANESTHESIA EVALUATION

HISTORY TAKEN FROM: ☑ Patient ☐ Parent/ Guardian ☐ Significant Other ☑ Chart ☐ Poor Historian ☐ Language Barrier

PROPOSED PROCEDURE: | **DATE OF SURGERY:** 04/28/YYYY

AGE	GENDER	HEIGHT	WEIGHT	BLOOD PRESSURE	PULSE	RESPIRATIONS	TEMPERATURE	O2 SAT%
52	☐ Male ☑ Female	5' ½"	112#	98/68	75	18	98.6	96

PREVIOUS ANESTHESIA: ☐ None GETA without complications.

PREVIOUS SURGERY: ☐ None Appendectomy. TAH. Cataract x 2. Both ear stap-y.

CURRENT MEDICATIONS: ☑ None

FAMILY HX – ANES. PROBLEMS: ☑ None

ALLERGIES ☐ None Codeine. ASA.

AIRWAY (Enter X in appropriate boxes.)

☐ MP1 ☐ MP2 ☐ MP3 ☐ MP4 ☐ Unrestricted neck ROM ☐ T-M distance = _____
☐ Obesity ☐ ↓ neck ROM ☐ History of difficult airway ☐ Short muscular neck
☐ Teeth poor repair ☐ Teeth chipped/loose ☑ Edentulous ☐ Facial hair

BODY SYSTEM — COMMENTS

RESPIRATORY ☑ WNL Tobacco Use: ☑ Yes ☐ No ☐ Quit ½ Packs/Day for 32 Years
Adequate oral airway. Negative asthma, bronchitis, URI.

CARDIOVASCULAR ☑ WNL Pre-procedure Cardiac Assessment:
Negative hypertension, MI, CHF, arrhythmia, angina. Good exercise tolerance. Regular rhythm. No carotid bruits.
Positive CTA. Negative SEM.

GASTROINTESTINAL ☑ WNL Ethanol Use: ☐ Yes ☑ No ☐ Quit
Frequency _____ ☐ History of Ethanol abuse

MUSCULOSKELETAL ☑ WNL
Full cervical ROM.

GENITOURINARY ☐ WNL

OTHER ☐ WNL
Negative seizures, stroke. Negative D.M., thyroid, kidney, coag, PUD, hepatitis. ASA risk class. 2

PREGNANCY ☐ WNL ☐ AROM ☐ SROM ☐ Pitocin Drip
☐ Induction ☐ MgDrip EDC: _____
Weeks Gestation: _____ G: _____ P: _____

Plan: GETA, Risks, Benefits, options, explained, understood and agreed upon.

DIAGNOSTIC STUDIES

ECG
CHEST X-RAY WNL
PULMONARY STUDIES

LABORATORY STUDIES
PT/PTT/INR:
T&S / T&C:
HCG: 15.0
UA

OTHER DIAGNOSTIC TESTS
Hct 43.3

PLANNED ANESTHESIA/MONITORS
ECG. ETCO2. O2. Temp.
O2 Sat. BP monitor.

PRE-ANESTHESIA MEDICATION

SIGNATURE OF ANESTHESIOLOGIST OR C.R.N.A.
Don Galloway, M.D.

POST-ANESTHESIA EVALUATION

Location	Time	B/P	O2Sat	Pulse	Respirations	Temperature
Recovery Room	1345	125/50	99	85	18	97.1

☑ Awake ☐ Mask O2 ☐ Somnolent ☐ Unarousable ☐ Oral/nasal airway
☑ Stable ☐ NC O2 ☐ Unstable ☐ T-Piece ☐ Intubated ☐ Ventilator
☐ Regional – dermatome level: ☐ Continuous epidural analgesia
☐ Direct admit to hospital room ☑ No anesthesia related complications noted
☐ See progress notes for anesthesia related concerns ☑ Satisfactory postanesthesia/analgesia recovery

CONTROLLED MEDICATIONS

Medication	Used	Destroyed	Returned

Pt experiencing nausea. Gave pt 10 mg Reglar.

SIGNATURE OF ANESTHESIOLOGIST OR C.R.N.A.
Don Galloway, M.D.

ALFRED STATE MEDICAL CENTER ■ 100 MAIN ST, ALFRED, NY 14802 ■ (607) 555-1234

RECOVERY ROOM RECORD

STANLEY, Erica P. Admission: 04-28-YYYY
Case 03 DOB: 04-05-YYYY
Dr. Wylie ROOM: 0255

DATE: 4/28/YYYY **TIME:** 1345

OPERATION: Laparoscopy cholecyst.

ANESTHESIA: General

AIRWAY: N/A

O₂ USED: ☒ YES ☐ NO

ROUTE: 4 French cath, d/c 1414

TIME	MEDICATIONS	SITE
	Scopolamine patch	behind
	(intact)	left ear

INTAKE	AMOUNT
700 cc LR, L distal forearm	
site w/o edema or redness	
iV intact & infusing at disch.	
TOTAL	200 cc

OUTPUT	AMOUNT
CATHETER N/A	
LEVINE N/A	
HEMOVAC N/A	
TOTAL	

DISCHARGE STATUS

ROOM: 0255 **TIME:** 1450

CONDITION: Satisfactory

TRANSFERRED BY Stretcher

R.R. NURSE: Sally James, RN

PREOP VISIT:

POSTOP VISIT: Report to Dr. Galloway at 1445 by S. James, R.N.

POSTANESTHESIA RECOVERY SCORE

		Adm	30 min	1 hr	2 hr	Disch
Moves 4 extremities voluntarily or on command (2) Moves 2 extremities voluntarily or on command (1) Moves 0 extremities voluntarily or on command (0)	Activity	2	2	2	2	2
Able to deep breathe and cough freely (2) Dyspnea or limited breathing (1) Apneic (0)	Respiration	2	2	2	2	2
BP ± 20% of preanesthetic level BP + 20% of preanesthetic level BP + 50% of preanesthetic level	Circulation	2	2	2	2	2
Fully awake (2) Arouseable on calling (1) Not responding (0)	Consciousness	2	2	2	2	2
Pink (2) Pale, dusky, blotchy, jaundiced, other (1) Cyanotic (0)	Color	2	2	2	2	2

COMMENTS & OBSERVATIONS:

Resp easy, spont at arrival. Four band-aids dry and intact over wounds. c/o nausea at arrival. Dry Emesis. DB encouraged and good compliance 1350. Pt admits to stomach settling a little now. Resting, eyes closed.

Mary Crawford, RN
SIGNATURE OF RECOVERY ROOM NURSE

ALFRED STATE MEDICAL CENTER ■ 100 MAIN ST, ALFRED, NY 14802 ■ (607) 555-1234

STANLEY, Erica P.   Admission: 04-28-YYYY
Case03   DOB: 04-05-YYYY
Dr. Wylie   ROOM: 0255

LABORATORY DATA

SPECIMEN COLLECTED: 04-23-YYYY   SPECIMEN RECEIVED: Blood

TEST	RESULT	FLAG	REFERENCE
Sodium	142		136-147 meq/L
Potassium	3.9		3.6-5.0 mmol/L
Chloride	102		99-110 mmol/L
CO2	29		24-32 mg/dl
Glucose	95		70-110 mg/dl
Urea Nitrogen	6	**L**	7-18 mg/dl

End of Report

STANLEY, Erica P.   Admission: 04-28-YYYY   LABORATORY DATA
Case03   DOB: 04-05-YYYY
Dr. Wylie   ROOM: 0255

SPECIMEN COLLECTED: 04-23-YYYY   SPECIMEN RECEIVED: 04-23-YYYY

TEST	RESULT	FLAG	REFERENCE
URINALYSIS			
DIPSTICK ONLY			
COLOR	CLOUDY YELLOW		
SP GRAVITY	1.025		≤ 1.030
GLUCOSE	110		≤ 125 mg/dl
BILIRUBIN	NEG		≤ 0.8 mg/dl
KETONE	TRACE		≤ 10 mg/dl
BLOOD	0.03		0.06 mg/dl hgb
PH	5.0		5-8.0
PROTEIN	NORMAL		≤ 30 mg/dl
UROBILINOGEN	NORMAL		≤ -1 mg/dl
NITRITES	NEG		NEG
LEUKOCYTE	NEG		≤ 15 WBC/hpf
W.B.C.	5-10		≤ 5/hpf
R.B.C.	RARE		≤ 5/hpf
BACT.	4f		1+(≤ 20/hpf)
URINE PREGNANCY TEST			
	NEG		

End of Report

STANLEY, Erica P.   Admission: 04-28-YYYY   RADIOLOGY REPORT
Case03   DOB: 04-05-YYYY
Dr. Wylie   ROOM: 0255

Initial Diagnosis/History: Preoperative chest X-ray.

Date Requested: 04-23-YYYY

Transport: ☐ Wheelchair   ☐ Stretcher   ☐ O$_2$ ☐ IV
             ☑ IP   ☐ OP   ☐ ER
             ☑ PRE OP   ☐ OR/RR   ☐ Portable

CHEST: PA and lateral views show that the heart, lungs, thorax and
mediastinum are normal.

DD: 04-23-YYYY

DT: 04-24-YYYY   *Philip Rogers, M.D.*
                                       _____
                                       Philip Rogers, M.D., Radiologist

```
STANLEY, Erica P.      Admission: 04-28-YYYY         RADIOLOGY REPORT
Case03                 DOB: 04-05-YYYY
Dr. Wylie              ROOM: 0255
```

Initial Diagnosis/History: Screening mammogram, bilateral.

Date Requested: 04-23-YYYY

Transport: ☐ Wheelchair   ☐ Stretcher   ☐ O$_2$ ☐ IV
             ☑ IP   ☐ OP   ☐ ER
             ☑ PRE OP   ☐ OR/RR   ☐ Portable

BILATERAL MAMMOGRAM: Normal.

DD: 04-23-YYYY

DT: 04-24-YYYY

Philip Rogers, M.D.
_____
Philip Rogers, M.D., Radiologist

STANLEY, Erica P.   Admission: 04-28-YYYY   **EKG REPORT**
Case03   DOB: 04-05-YYYY
Dr. Wylie   ROOM: 0255

           Date of EKG: 04-23-YYYY   Time of EKG: 13:56:20

Rate	66
PR	184
QRSD	60
QT	363
QTC	380
-- Axis --	
P	76
QRS	79
T	71

Normal.

Bella Kaplan
_____
Bella Kaplan, M.D.

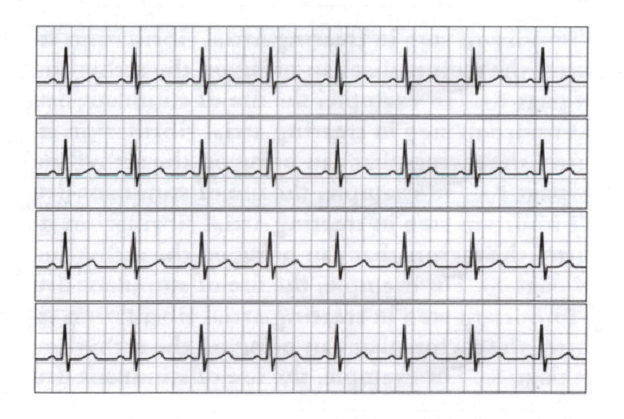

Case 04

ALFRED STATE MEDICAL CENTER 100 MAIN ST, ALFRED, NY 14802 (607) 555-1234 HOSPITAL #: 000999				INPATIENT FACE SHEET			

PATIENT NAME AND ADDRESS				GENDER	RACE	MARITAL STATUS	PATIENT NO.
HOWE, Mary C. 55 Upland Drive Alfred, New York 14802				F	W	S	Case04
				DATE OF BIRTH	MAIDEN NAME		OCCUPATION
				03-31-YYYY	Same		Student

ADMISSION DATE	TIME	DISCHARGE DATE	TIME	LENGTH OF STAY	TELEPHONE NUMBER	
04-29-YYYY	09:00	04-29-YYYY	16:00	01 DAY	(607)555-1511	

GUARANTOR NAME AND ADDRESS	NEXT OF KIN NAME AND ADDRESS
Howe, Shirley 55 Upland Drive Alfred, New York 14802	HOWE, Shirley 55 Upland Drive Alfred, New York 14802

GUARANTOR TELEPHONE NO.	RELATIONSHIP TO PATIENT	NEXT OF KIN TELEPHONE NUMBER	RELATIONSHIP TO PATIENT
(607)555-1511	Mother	(607)555-1511	Mother

ADMITTING PHYSICIAN	SERVICE	ADMIT TYPE	ROOM NUMBER/BED
Donald Thompson, MD	Surgical	3	0254/02

ATTENDING PHYSICIAN	ATTENDING PHYSICIAN UPIN	ADMITTING DIAGNOSIS	
Donald Thompson, MD	100B01	Nasal Fracture	

PRIMARY INSURER	POLICY AND GROUP NUMBER	SECONDARY INSURER	POLICY AND GROUP NUMBER
Empire Plan	857062234		

DIAGNOSES AND PROCEDURES	ICD-9-CM	ICD-10-CM/PCS
PRINCIPAL DIAGNOSIS		
Nasal Fx	802.0	S022XXA
SECONDARY DIAGNOSES		
Nasal Laceration	873.20	S0120XA
	E819.9	V892XXA
PRINCIPAL PROCEDURE		
Nasal Septal Fx Reduction	21.72	0NSB0ZZ
SECONDARY PROCEDURES		
Closure Nasal Laceration	21.81	09QKXZZ
TOTAL CHARGES: $ 1,850.75		

ACTIVITY:	☐ Bedrest	☑ Light	☐ Usual	☐ Unlimited	☐ Other:
DIET:	☑ Regular	☐ Low Cholesterol	☐ Low Salt	☐ ADA	☐ ____ Calorie
FOLLOW-UP:	☑ Call for appointment	☐ Office appointment on ____	☐ Other:		

SPECIAL INSTRUCTIONS: *Do not blow nose*

Signature of Attending Physician: *Donald Thompson, MD*

HOWE, Mary C.　　　　Admission: 04-29-YYYY
Case 04　　　　　　　DOB: 03-31-YYYY
Dr. Thompson　　　　ROOM: 0254

Consent To Admission

I, _Mary C. Howe_ hereby consent to admission to the Alfred State Medical Center (ASMC) , and I further consent to such routine hospital care, diagnostic procedures, and medical treatment that the medical and professional staff of ASMC may deem necessary or advisable. I authorize the use of medical information obtained about me as specified above and the disclosure of such information to my referring physician(s). This form has been fully explained to me, and I understand its contents. I further understand that no guarantees have been made to me as to the results of treatments or examinations done at the ASMC.

Mary C. Howe　　　　　　　　　　_April 29, YYYY_

Signature of Patient | Date

Shirley Howe　　　　　　　　　　_April 29, YYYY_

Signature of Parent/Legal Guardian for Minor | Date

Mother

Relationship to Minor

Andrea Witteman　　　　　　　　　_April 29, YYYY_

WITNESS: Alfred State Medical Center Staff Member | Date

Consent To Release Information For Reimbursement Purposes

In order to permit reimbursement, upon request, the Alfred State Medical Center (ASMC) may disclose such treatment information pertaining to my hospitalization to any corporation, organization, or agent thereof, which is, or may be liable under contract to the ASMC or to me, or to any of my family members or other person, for payment of all or part of the ASMC's charges for services rendered to me (e.g., the patient's health insurance carrier). I understand that the purpose of any release of information is to facilitate reimbursement for services rendered. In addition, in the event that my health insurance program includes utilization review of services provided during this admission, I authorize ASMC to release information as is necessary to permit the review. This authorization will expire once the reimbursement for services rendered is complete.

Mary C. Howe　　　　　　　　　　_April 29, YYYY_

Signature of Patient | Date

Shirley Howe　　　　　　　　　　_April 29, YYYY_

Signature of Parent/Legal Guardian for Minor | Date

Mother

Relationship to Minor

Andrea Witteman　　　　　　　　　_April 29, YYYY_

WITNESS: Alfred State Medical Center Staff Member | Date

ALFRED STATE MEDICAL CENTER ■ 100 MAIN ST, ALFRED, NY 14802 ■ (607) 555-1234

HOWE, Mary C.	Admission: 04-29-YYYY	ADVANCE DIRECTIVE
Case04	DOB: 03-31-YYYY	
Dr. Thompson	ROOM: 0254	

Your answers to the following questions will assist your Physician and the Hospital to respect your wishes regarding your medical care. This information will become a part of your medical record.

	YES	NO	PATIENT'S INITIALS
1. Have you been provided with a copy of the information called "Patient Rights Regarding Health Care Decision?"	X		MCH
2. Have you prepared a "Living Will?" If yes, please provide the Hospital with a copy for your medical record.		X	MCH
3. Have you prepared a Durable Power of Attorney for Health Care? If yes, please provide the Hospital with a copy for your medical record.		X	MCH
4. Have you provided this facility with an Advance Directive on a prior admission and is it still in effect? If yes, Admitting Office to contact Medical Records to obtain a copy for the medical record.		X	MCH
5. Do you desire to execute a Living Will/Durable Power of Attorney? If yes, refer to in order: a. Physician b. Social Service c. Volunteer Service		X	MCH

HOSPITAL STAFF DIRECTIONS: Check when each step is completed.

1. ✓ Verify the above questions where answered and actions taken where required.

2. ✓ If the "Patient Rights" information was provided to someone other than the patient, state reason:

_____

_____   _____
Name of Individual Receiving Information   Relationship to Patient

3. ✓ If information was provided in a language other than English, specify language and method.

4. ✓ Verify patient was advised on how to obtain additional information on Advance Directives.

5. ✓ Verify the Patient/Family Member/Legal Representative was asked to provide the Hospital with a copy of the Advance Directive which will be retained in the medical record.

File this form in the medical record, and give a copy to the patient.

_____
Name of Patient (Name of Individual giving information if different from Patient)
Mary C. Howe   *April 29, YYYY*

_____   _____
Signature of Patient   Date
Andrea Witteman   *April 29, YYYY*

_____   _____
Signature of Hospital Representative   Date

HOWE, Mary C.	Admission: 04-29-YYYY
Case 04	DOB: 03-31-YYYY
Dr. Thompson	ROOM: 0254

SHORT STAY RECORD

CHIEF COMPLAINT AND HISTORY:	**HEART:**
S/P MVA. Hit steering wheel. Nose hurts.	S1, S2 within normal limits.
PERTINENT PAST HISTORY:	**LUNGS:**
Asthma. S/P cleft surgery.	Clear without wheezing.
MEDICATIONS:	**ABDOMEN:**
Ventolin p.r.n.	Within normal limits.
FAMILY HISTORY:	**ENDOCRINE:**
Mother has Parkinson Disease. Asthma.	Neck negative. Groin, and axilla deferred.
REVIEW OF SYSTEMS:	**GENITALIA:**
Nonessential except asthma – last attack.	Deferred.
ALLERGIES:	**EXTREMITIES**
Negative.	Full range of motion.
PHYSICAL EXAMINATION	**NEUROLOGIC:**
GENERAL: 18 yo white female.	Oriented x 3.
EENT:	**DIAGNOSIS:**
PERRLA.	S/P M.V.A. Nasal fx.
	PLAN:
	Reduction of nasal fx.
	Donald Thompson, M.D.

HOWE, Mary C. Case04 Dr. Thompson	Admission: 04-29-YYYY DOB: 03-31-YYYY ROOM: 0254	PROGRESS NOTES

Date	Time	Physician's signature required for each order. (Please skip one line between dates.)
4-29-yyyy	1000	Preanesthesia eval: 18 y/o WF for closed reduction of nasal fracture. Smokes, asthma, ASA II. Explained GA
		and risks. Indicates understanding of risks, answered questions and concerns.
		Don Galloway, M.D.
4-29-yyyy	1415	Postanesthesia eval: Tolerated GA well, no complications, sleeping, stable.
		Don Galloway, M.D.
4/29/YYYY	1400	Short Op Note:
		Preop Dx: Nasal septal fx. Nasal laceration.
		Postop Dx: Same.
		Procedure: Open reduction, nasal septal fx. Closure, nasal lacerations.
		Anesthesia: General, oral.
		Patient tolerated well.
		Donald Thompson, MD

ALFRED STATE MEDICAL CENTER ■ 100 MAIN ST, ALFRED, NY 14802 ■ (607) 555-1234

HOWE, Mary C.		Admission: 04-29-YYYY	DOCTORS ORDERS
Case 04		DOB: 03-31-YYYY	
Dr. Thompson		ROOM: 0254	

Date	Time	Physician's signature required for each order. (Please skip one line between dates.)
04/29/YYYY	0930	PRE-OP ORDERS
		1) ~~Admit to S.D.S.~~ or AM Admit.
		2) Diet: NPO
		3) Allergies: ∅
		4) CBC, UA
		5) I.V. D5 LR at 75 cc/hr *Wait until OR anesthesia to start IV*
		6) Solumedrol 125 mg I.V. PUSH
		7) Antibiotics: *Keflex 500 mg*
		8) PRE-MED: As per anesthesia.
		9) Pre Op Rinse. (Labeled for home use BID)
		10) Old Chart: Yes ~~or No~~.
		Donald Thompson, MD
4/29/YYYY	1155	*Post op*
		Diet – regular
		Toradil 30 mg IM q4h PRN severe pain
		Codeine 1 or 2 q4h PRN moderate pain
		Tylenol 650 mg q4h PRN mild pain
		Donald Thompson, MD
4/29/YYYY	1115	*Discharge from PACU at 1115. R.A.V. T.O. Dr. Thompson/B. Dewshare, RN*
		Donald Thompson, MD
4/29/YY	1150	*Clarify IV – D5LR 25 CC/hr Donald Thompson, MD*
		R.A.V. T.O. Dr. Thompson/C. Smith, RN
4/29/YY	1500	*D/C IV. Discharge home. Donald Thompson, MD*

HOWE, Mary C.	Admission: 04-29-YYYY	
Case04	DOB: 03-31-YYYY	Consent for Operation(s)
Dr. Thompson	ROOM: 0254	and/or Procedure(s) and
		Anesthesia

PERMISSION. I hereby authorize Dr. _Thompson_ , or associates of his/her choice at the

Alfred State Medical Center (the "Hospital") to perform upon _Mary C. Howe_

the following operation(s) and/or procedure(s): _Nasal Septal Fx Reduction /Closure Nasal Laceration_

including such photography, videotaping, televising or other observation of the operation(s)/procedure(s) as may be purposeful for the advance of medical knowledge and/or education, with the understanding that the patient's identity will remain anonymous.

EXPLANATION OF PROCEDURE, RISKS, BENEFITS, ALTERNATIVES. Dr. _Thompson_

has fully explained to me the nature and purposes of the operation(s)/procedures named above and has also informed me of expected benefits and complications, attendant discomforts and risks that may arise, as well as possible alternatives to the proposed treatment. I have been given an opportunity to ask questions and all my questions have been answered fully and satisfactorily.

UNFORESEEN CONDITIONS. I understand that during the course of the operation(s) or procedure(s), unforeseen conditions may arise which necessitate procedures in addition to or different from those contemplated. I, therefore, consent to the performance of additional operations and procedures which the above-named physician or his/her associates or assistants may consider necessary.

ANESTHESIA. I further consent to the administration of such anesthesia as may be considered necessary by the above-named physician or his/her associates or assistants. I recognize that there are always risks to life and health associated with anesthesia. Such risks have been fully explained to me and I have been given an opportunity to ask questions and all my questions have been answered fully and satisfactorily.

SPECIMENS. Any organs or tissues surgically removed may be examined and retained by the Hospital for medical, scientific or educational purposes and such tissues or parts may be disposed of in accordance with accustomed practice and applicable State laws and/or regulations.

NO GUARANTEES. I acknowledge that no guarantees or assurances have been made to me concerning the operation(s) or procedure(s) described above.

MEDICAL DEVICE TRACKING. I hereby authorize the release of my Social Security number to the manufacturer of the medical device(s) I receive, if applicable, in accordance with federal law and regulations which may be used to help locate me if a need arises with regard to this medical device. I release The Alfred State Medical Center from any liability that might result from the release of this information.*

UNDERSTANDING OF THIS FORM. I confirm that I have read this form, fully understand its contents, and that all blank spaces above have been completed prior to my signing. I have crossed out any paragraphs above that do not pertain to me.

Patient/Relative/Guardian*

Mary C. HOWE   Mary C. Howe
Signature   Print Name

Relationship, if other than patient signed:

Witness: _Shirley Thompson_   Shirley Thompson
Signature   Print Name

Date: _April 29, YYYY_

*The signature of the patient must be obtained unless the patient is an unemancipated minor under the age of 18 or is otherwise incompetent to sign.

PHYSICIAN'S CERTIFICATION. I hereby certify that I have explained the nature, purpose, benefits, risks of and alternatives to the operation(s)/ procedure(s), have offered to answer any questions and have fully answered all such questions. I believe that the patient (relative/guardian) fully understands what I have explained and answered.

PHYSICIAN: _Donald Thompson, MD_   April 29, YYYY
Signature   Date

ALFRED STATE MEDICAL CENTER ■ 100 MAIN ST, ALFRED, NY 14802 ■ (607) 555-1234

ANESTHESIA RECORD

HOWE, Mary C.
Case 04
Dr. Thompson

Admission: 04-29-YYYY
DOB: 03-31-YYYY
ROOM: 0254

			START	STOP
PROCEDURE(S):	Nasal Septal Fx Reduction	ANESTHESIA	0945	1015
SURGEON(S):	Donald Thompson	PROCEDURE	0950	1015
DATE OF SURGERY:	4/29/YYYY	ROOM TIME	IN: 0930	OUT: 1030

PRE-PROCEDURE

- ☑ Patient Identified ☑ ID band verified
- ☑ Patient questioned ☑ Chart reviewed
- ☑ Consent form signed
- ☑ Patient reassessed prior to anesthesia (ready to proceed)
- ☑ Peri-operative pain management discussed with patient/guardian (plan of care completed)
- Pre-Anesthetic State:
- ☑ Awake ☑ Anxious ☐ Calm
- ☐ Lethargic ☐ Uncooperative
- ☐ Unresponsive
- ☐ Other: _____
- ☑ Anesthesia machine #5626984 checked
- ☑ Secured with safety belt
- ☑ Arm secured on board ☑ Left ☐ Right

MONITORS/EQUIPMENT

- ☑ Stethoscope ☐ Precordial
- ☐ Suprasternal ☐ Esoph
- ☑ Non-invasive B/P ☐ V-lead ECG
- ☑ Continuous ECG ☐ ST Analysis
- ☑ Pulse oximeter ☐ End tidal CO_2
- ☐ Nerve stimulator: ☐ Ulnar ☐ Tibial ☐ Facial
- ☑ Oxygen monitor ☐ Cell Saver
- ☐ ET agent analyzer ☐ B/S ☐ TEE
- ☐ Fluid/Blood warmer ☐ Temp:
- ☐ BIS ☐ ICS
- ☑ NG/OG tube ☐ FHT monitor
- ☑ Foley catheter ☐ EEG
- ☐ Airway humidifier
- ☐ Evoked potential: ☐ SSEP ☐ BAEP ☐ MEP
- ☐ Arterial line _____ ☐ CVP _____

ANESTHESTIC TECHNIQUES

- GA Induction: ☑ IV ☐ Pre-O₂ ☐ RSI ☐ PR
- ☐ Cricoid pressure ☐ Inhalation ☐ IM
- GA Maintenance: ☐ TIVA ☐ Inhalation
- ☑ Inhalation/IV ☐ GA/Regional Comb.

Regional:
- Epidural : ☑ Thoracic ☐ Lumbar ☐ Caudal
- ☐ Femoral ☐ Auxiliary ☐ Interscalene
- ☐ CSE ☐ Bier ☐ SAB ☐ Ankle
- ☐ Continuous Spinal ☐ Cervical Plexus

Regional Techniques: ☐ See Remarks
- ☐ Position _____ ☐ Prep _____
- ☐ Site _____ ☐ Needle _____
- ☐ LA _____ ☐ Narcotic _____
- ☐ Additive _____ ☐ Test dose Rx ___

AIRWAY MANAGEMENT

- ☑ Oral ETT ☐ LTA ☐ RAE
- ☐ Nasal ETT ☐ LMA #
- ☐ Stylet ☐ LMA Fastrach # ____
- ☐ DVL ☐ LMA ProSeal # ____
- ☐ EMG ETT ☐ Bougie
- ☐ Armored ETT ☐ LIS
- ☑ Breath sounds = bilateral
- ☐ Cuffed – min occ pres with ☑ air ☐ NS
- ☐ Uncuffed – leaks at _____ cm H_2O
- ☑ Oral airway ☐ Nasal airway ☐ Bite block
- Circuit: ☐ Circle system ☐ NRB ☐ Bain
- ☐ Via tracheotomy/stoma ☐ Mask case
- ☐ Nasal cannula ☑ Simple O_2 mask
- Nebulizer: _____
- Nerve Block(s): _____

		TIME:	15	30	45	15	30	45	15	30	45	15	30	45	15	30	45	TOTALS
AGENTS	☐ Des ☐ Iso ☐ Sevo ☐ Halo (%)																	
	☑ N²O ☑ Air (L/min)			2.5	2.5	X												
	☑ Oxygen (L/min)		66	2	2	66												
	☑ N₂O (L/min)																	
	☑ Forane (%)			1/5	2/5	2/0	X											
	☑ Anectine (mg)																	
	☑ Pentothal (mg)			100	100	100	X											226
FLUIDS	Urine																	**SYMBOLS**
	EBL																	
	Gastric																	▾ ▴
MONITORS	☑ ECG																	BP cuff pressure
	☑ % Oxygen Inspired (FI0₂)			98	98	98	98											⊥
	☑ End Tidal CO_2				49	49	49											Arterial line pressure
	☑ Temp: ☐ C ☑ F			98			98											✕
	☑ BP Monitor																	Mean arterial pressure

PERI-OP MEDS	200																	
	180																	
	160																	●
	140		▾	▾	▾													Pulse
	120					▾	▾											○
	100				•	•	•											Spontaneous Respirations
	80		•	•	▴	▴												
	60		▴	▴			▴											∅
	40																	Assisted Respirations
	20		○	○	○	○	○											
	10																	T

VENT	Tidal Volume (ml)																	Time of Delivery:
	Respiratory Rate		SA	SA	SA	SA												
	Peak Pressure (cm H_2O)																	Gender: ☐ M ☐ F
	☐ PEEP ☐ CPAP (cm H_2O)																	Apgars: ___/___

Position:	LIthogomy	Surgeon	Thompson
#20 Oral tubing. Intake DSLR 1000.		Assistant	
Total 650 cc. #18 gu. left.		Scrub Nurse	Mary Marks, RN
		Circulating Nurse	Cynthie Lewis, RcN
		Signature of Anesthesiologist or C.R.N.A.	Don Galloway, M.D.

HOWE, Mary C. Case04 Dr. Thompson	Admission: 04-29-YYYY DOB: 03-31-YYYY ROOM: 0254	PRE-ANESTHESIA AND POST-ANESTHESIA RECORD

PRE-ANESTHESIA EVALUATION

HISTORY TAKEN FROM: ☑ Patient ☐ Parent/ Guardian ☐ Significant Other ☑ Chart ☐ Poor Historian ☐ Language Barrier

| PROPOSED PROCEDURE: | | | | | | DATE OF SURGERY: | 04-29-YYYY |

AGE	GENDER	HEIGHT	WEIGHT	BLOOD PRESSURE	PULSE	RESPIRATIONS	TEMPERATURE	O2 SAT%
18	☐ Male ☑ Female	5 ft 2 in	100	105065	70	18	98.6	98

PREVIOUS ANESTHESIA:	☑ None
PREVIOUS SURGERY:	☑ None
CURRENT MEDICATIONS:	☑ None
FAMILY HX – ANES. PROBLEMS:	☑ None
ALLERGIES:	☑ None

AIRWAY	☐ MP1 ☐ MP2 ☐ MP3 ☐ MP4	☐ Unrestricted neck ROM	☐ T-M distance = _____
(Enter **X** in appropriate boxes.)	☐ Obesity ☐ ↓ neck ROM	☐ History of difficult airway	☐ Short muscular neck
	☐ Teeth poor repair ☐ Teeth chipped/loose	☐ Edentulous	☐ Facial hair

BODY SYSTEM	COMMENTS	DIAGNOSTIC STUDIES
RESPIRATORY	☑ WNL Tobacco Use: ☐ Yes ☑ No ☐ Quit _____ Packs/Day for _____ Years	ECG CHEST X-RAY Negative PULMONARY STUDIES
CARDIOVASCULAR	☑ WNL Pre-procedure Cardiac Assessment:	**LABORATORY STUDIES** PT/PTT/INR: T&S / T&C:
GASTROINTESTINAL	☑ WNL Ethanol Use: ☐ Yes ☑ No ☐ Quit Frequency _____ ☐ History of Ethanol abuse	HCG: 13.2 UA
		OTHER DIAGNOSTIC TESTS Hct 38.4
MUSCULOSKELETAL	☑ WNL	**PLANNED ANESTHESIA/MONITORS** ECG. ETCO2. O2. Temp. O2 Sat. BP monitor.
GENITOURINARY	☐ WNL	
OTHER ASA risk classification I	☐ WNL	**PRE-ANESTHESIA MEDICATION**
PREGNANCY	☐ WNL ☐ AROM ☐ SROM ☐ Pitocin Drip ☐ Induction ☐ MgDrip EDC: _____ Weeks Gestation: _____ G: _____ P: _____	
		SIGNATURE OF ANESTHESIOLOGIST OR C.R.N.A. Don Galloway, M.D.

POST-ANESTHESIA EVALUATION

CONTROLLED MEDICATIONS

Location	Time	B/P	O₂Sat	Pulse	Respirations	Temperature
Room	1430	110/70	96	70	18	98.6

Medication	Used	Destroyed	Returned

☑ Awake ☐ Mask O₂   ☐ Somnolent   ☐ Unarousable ☐ Oral/nasal airway

☑ Stable ☐ NC 0₂   ☐ Unstable   ☐ T-Piece ☐ Intubated ☐ Ventilator

☐ Regional – dermatome level: ☐ Continuous epidural analgesia

☐ Direct admit to hospital room   ☑ No anesthesia related complications noted

☐ See progress notes for anesthesia related concerns   ☑ Satisfactory postanesthesia/analgesia recovery

SIGNATURE OF ANESTHESIOLOGIST OR C.R.N.A.
Don Galloway, M.D.

ALFRED STATE MEDICAL CENTER ■ 100 MAIN ST, ALFRED, NY 14802 ■ (607) 555-1234

RECOVERY ROOM RECORD

HOWE, Mary C.
Case04
Dr. Thompson

Admission: 04-29-YYYY
DOB: 03-31-YYYY
ROOM: 0254

DATE: 4/29/YYYY **TIME:** 1030
OPERATION: Nasal Septal Fx Reduction
ANESTHESIA: General
AIRWAY: N/A
O₂ USED: ☒ YES ☐ NO
ROUTE: Nasal @ 4 l/min. d/c 1100.

TIME	MEDICATIONS	SITE

INTAKE	AMOUNT
350 D5L R antecubital	
IV site w/o redness or edema	
200 D5L R on discharge	
TOTAL	150 cc

OUTPUT	AMOUNT
CATHETER N/A	
LEVINE N/A	
HEMOVAC N/A	
TOTAL	

DISCHARGE STATUS
ROOM: 0254 **TIME:** 1115
CONDITION: Stable
TRANSFERRED BY Stretcher
R.R. NURSE: Sally James, RN
PREOP VISIT:

Dinamap left arm, 15.

POSTANESTHESIA RECOVERY SCORE		Adm	30 min	1 hr	2 hr	Disch
Moves 4 extremities voluntarily or on command (2) / Moves 2 extremities voluntarily or on command (1) / Moves 0 extremities voluntarily or on command (0)	Activity	2	2	2	2	2
Able to deep breathe and cough freely (2) / Dyspnea or limited breathing (1) / Apneic (0)	Respiration	2	2	2	2	2
BP ± 20% of preanesthetic level / BP + 20% of preanesthetic level / BP + 50% of preanesthetic level	Circulation	2	2	2	2	2
Fully awake (2) / Arouseable on calling (1) / Not responding (0)	Consciousness	1	2	2	2	2
Pink (2) / Pale, dusky, blotchy, jaundiced, other (1) / Cyanotic (0)	Color	2	2	2	2	2

POSTOP VISIT: Report given to Dr. Galloway at 1125 by S. James, R.N.

COMMENTS & OBSERVATIONS:

Patient arousable on arrival to PACU with respirations deep, easy and regular.
Denver splint in place. Dry hacking cough noted. HOB elevated 30°.

Mary Crawford, RN
SIGNATURE OF RECOVERY ROOM NURSE

HOWE, Mary C.   Admission: 04-29-YYYY   **LABORATORY DATA**
Case04   DOB: 03-31-YYYY
Dr. Thompson   ROOM: 0254

SPECIMEN COLLECTED: 04-29-YYYY   **SPECIMEN RECEIVED:** 04-29-YYYY

TEST	RESULT	FLAG	REFERENCE
URINALYSIS			
DIPSTICK ONLY			
COLOR	CLOUDY YELLOW		
SP GRAVITY	1.025		≤ 1.030
GLUCOSE	110		≤ 125 mg/dl
BILIRUBIN	NEG		≤ 0.8 mg/dl
KETONE	TRACE		≤ 10 mg/dl
BLOOD	0.03		0.06 mg/dl hgb
PH	5.0		5-8.0
PROTEIN	NORMAL		≤ 30 mg/dl
UROBILINOGEN	NORMAL		≤ -1 mg/dl
NITRITES	NEG		NEG
LEUKOCYTE	NEG		≤ 15 WBC/hpf
W.B.C.	5-10		≤ 5/hpf
R.B.C.	RARE		≤ 5/hpf
BACT.	4f		1+(≤ 20/hpf)
URINE PREGNANCY TEST			
	NEG		

End of Report

ALFRED STATE MEDICAL CENTER ■ 100 MAIN ST, ALFRED, NY 14802 ■ (607) 555-1234

HOWE, Mary C.   Admission: 04-29-YYYY   **LABORATORY DATA**
Case 04   DOB: 03-31-YYYY
Dr. Thompson   ROOM: 0254

SPECIMEN COLLECTED: 04-29-YYYY   SPECIMEN RECEIVED: 04-29-YYYY

CBC c̄ DIFF

TEST	RESULT	FLAG	REFERENCE
WBC	7.4		4.5-11.0 thous/UL
RBC	5.02	**L**	5.2-5.4 mill/UL
HGB	15.0		11.7-16.1 g/dl
HCT	45.8		35.0-47.0 %
MCV	91.2		85-99 fL.
MCHC	32.8	**L**	33-37
RDW	15.2	**H**	11.4-14.5
Platelets	165		130-400 thous/UL
MPV	8.4		7.4-10.4
LYMPH %	21.1		20.5-51.1
MONO %	7.8		1.7-9.3
GRAN %	71.1		42.2-75.2
LYMPH x 10^3	1.6		1.2-3.4
MONO x 10^3	.6	**H**	0.11-0.59
GRAN x 10^3	5.3		1.4-6.5
EOS x 10^3	< .7		0.0-0.7
BASO x 10^3	< .2		0.0-0.2
ANISO	SLIGHT		

End of Report

Case 05

ALFRED STATE MEDICAL CENTER						INPATIENT FACE SHEET	

ALFRED STATE MEDICAL CENTER
100 MAIN ST, ALFRED, NY 14802
(607) 555-1234
HOSPITAL #: 000999

PATIENT NAME AND ADDRESS				GENDER	RACE	MARITAL STATUS	PATIENT NO.
GIBBON, Andrew				M	W	M	Case05
22 Market Street				DATE OF BIRTH		MAIDEN NAME	OCCUPATION
Alfred, NY 14802				08-19-YYYY		N/A	Retired

ADMISSION DATE	TIME	DISCHARGE DATE	TIME	LENGTH OF STAY	TELEPHONE NUMBER		
04-27-YYYY	13:00	04-29-YYYY	00:00	02 DAYS	(607) 555-4500		

GUARANTOR NAME AND ADDRESS	NEXT OF KIN NAME AND ADDRESS
GIBBON, Andrew 22 Market Street Alfred, NY 14802	GIBBON, Cynthia 22 Market Street Alfred, NY 14802

GUARANTOR TELEPHONE NO.	RELATIONSHIP TO PATIENT	NEXT OF KIN TELEPHONE NUMBER	RELATIONSHIP TO PATIENT
(607) 555-4500	Self	(607) 555-4500	Wife

ADMITTING PHYSICIAN	SERVICE	ADMIT TYPE	ROOM NUMBER/BED
Alan Norris, MD	Medical	2	0362/02

ATTENDING PHYSICIAN	ATTENDING PHYSICIAN UPIN	ADMITTING DIAGNOSIS	
Alan Norris, MD	100G02	Chest pain	

PRIMARY INSURER	POLICY AND GROUP NUMBER	SECONDARY INSURER	POLICY AND GROUP NUMBER
Medicare			

DIAGNOSES AND PROCEDURES	ICD-9-CM	ICD-10-CM/PCS
PRINCIPAL DIAGNOSIS		
Unstable Angina	411.1	I20.0
SECONDARY DIAGNOSES		
Hypertension	401.9	I10
Status post myocardial infarction	412	I25.2
PRINCIPAL PROCEDURE		
SECONDARY PROCEDURES		
TOTAL CHARGES: $ 4,855.65		

ACTIVITY:	☐ Bedrest	☑ Light	☐ Usual	☐ Unlimited	☐ Other:
DIET:	☑ Regular	☐ Low Cholesterol	☐ Low Salt	☐ ADA	☐ _____ Calorie

FOLLOW-UP: ☐ Call for appointment ☐ Office appointment on ____ ☐ Medications: Procardia, Isordil, Vasotec, Inderal, Aldoril, Aspirin.

SPECIAL INSTRUCTIONS: See Dr. Derby next week. Do not take Dyazide until you see Dr. Derby.

Signature of Attending Physician: Alan Norris, MD

GIBBON, Andrew
Case 05
Dr. Norris

Admission: 04-27-YYYY
DOB: 08-19-YYYY
ROOM: 0362

CONSENT TO ADMISSION

I, _Andrew Gibbon_ hereby consent to admission to the Alfred State Medical Center (ASMC) , and I further consent to such routine hospital care, diagnostic procedures, and medical treatment that the medical and professional staff of ASMC may deem necessary or advisable. I authorize the use of medical information obtained about me as specified above and the disclosure of such information to my referring physician(s). This form has been fully explained to me, and I understand its contents. I further understand that no guarantees have been made to me as to the results of treatments or examinations done at the ASMC.

Andrew Gibbon

April 27, YYYY

Signature of Patient

Date

Signature of Parent/Legal Guardian for Minor

Date

Relationship to Minor

Andrea Witteman

April 27, yyyy

WITNESS: Alfred State Medical Center Staff Member

Date

CONSENT TO RELEASE INFORMATION FOR REIMBURSEMENT PURPOSES

In order to permit reimbursement, upon request, the Alfred State Medical Center (ASMC) may disclose such treatment information pertaining to my hospitalization to any corporation, organization, or agent thereof, which is, or may be liable under contract to the ASMC or to me, or to any of my family members or other person, for payment of all or part of the ASMC's charges for services rendered to me (e.g., the patient's health insurance carrier). I understand that the purpose of any release of information is to facilitate reimbursement for services rendered. In addition, in the event that my health insurance program includes utilization review of services provided during this admission, I authorize ASMC to release information as is necessary to permit the review. This authorization will expire once the reimbursement for services rendered is complete.

Andrew Gibbon

April 27, YYYY

Signature of Patient

Date

Signature of Parent/Legal Guardian for Minor

Date

Relationship to Minor

Andrea Witteman

April 27, yyyy

WITNESS: Alfred State Medical Center Staff Member

Date

GIBBON, Andrew	Admission: 04-27-YYYY	ADVANCE DIRECTIVE
Case05	DOB: 08-19-YYYY	
Dr. Norris	ROOM: 0362	

Your answers to the following questions will assist your Physician and the Hospital to respect your wishes regarding your medical care. This information will become a part of your medical record.

	YES	NO	PATIENT'S INITIALS
1. Have you been provided with a copy of the information called "Patient Rights Regarding Health Care Decision?"	X		AG
2. Have you prepared a "Living Will?" If yes, please provide the Hospital with a copy for your medical record.		X	AG
3. Have you prepared a Durable Power of Attorney for Health Care? If yes, please provide the Hospital with a copy for your medical record.		X	AG
4. Have you provided this facility with an Advance Directive on a prior admission and is it still in effect? If yes, Admitting Office to contact Medical Records to obtain a copy for the medical record.		X	AG
5. Do you desire to execute a Living Will/Durable Power of Attorney? If yes, refer to in order: a. Physician b. Social Service c. Volunteer Service		X	AG

HOSPITAL STAFF DIRECTIONS: Check when each step is completed.

1. ✓ Verify the above questions where answered and actions taken where required.

2. ✓ If the "Patient Rights" information was provided to someone other than the patient, state reason:

_____

_____   _____
Name of Individual Receiving Information   Relationship to Patient

3. ✓ If information was provided in a language other than English, specify language and method.

4. ✓ Verify patient was advised on how to obtain additional information on Advance Directives.

5. ✓ Verify the Patient/Family Member/Legal Representative was asked to provide the Hospital with a copy of the Advance Directive which will be retained in the medical record.

File this form in the medical record, and give a copy to the patient.

_____
Name of Patient (Name of Individual giving information if different from Patient)

Andrew Gibbon   April 27, YYYY
_____   _____
Signature of Patient   Date

Andrea Witteman   April 27, YYYY
_____   _____
Signature of Hospital Representative   Date

ALFRED STATE MEDICAL CENTER ■ 100 MAIN ST, ALFRED, NY 14802 ■ (607) 555-1234

GIBBON, Andrew	Admission: 04-27-YYYY	HISTORY & PHYSICAL EXAM
Case05	DOB: 08-19-YYYY	
Dr. Norris	ROOM: 0362	

CHIEF COMPLAINT: 72 yr. old gentleman of Dr. K. Derby's who presents with chest pain.

HISTORY OF PRESENT ILLNESS: Mr. Gibbon is a very cheery sort of fellow. He is very pleasant. He looks as though he probably should be running some sort of hardware store commercial. He states that today while he was preparing breakfast, in the restroom he suffered some chest discomfort. He is a little bit vague as to where his chest really is. He felt it in his back, he felt it in his jaw. He took a couple of Nitroglycerin in sequence three minutes apart and felt better. Apparently this has been occurring a little more frequently recently. All these things are nebulous. If it wasn't for his wife I think he would deny everything. According to her he has been having more frequent episodes and has gained a fair amount of weight over the winter. He had been fairly active. His pastor who is with him and often serves as his spokesman, stated that he had hunted this past fall without having to take any Nitroglycerin. However he said the pace was quite controlled and he really didn't do very much in the way of heavy exercise. The patient has a history of an infarction in 1981. Underwent catheterization. Apparently no surgery was necessary. There is also some question about him having a lot of indigestion from time to time and it is not clear whether it is cardiac or GI. Because of his prior cardiac history, the progression of his chest pain, the uncertainty of its origin, he will be admitted for further evaluation and treatment.

PAST MEDICAL HISTORY: Is essentially that listed above.

MEDICATIONS: He is on Dyazide once a day. Isordil 10 mg. q.i.d. Vasotec 2.5 mg. daily. Aspirin one a day. Propranolol 40 mg. q.i.d.

ALLERGIES: Sulfa.

SOCIAL HISTORY & FAMILY HISTORY: The patient is married. Doesn't smoke, although he had in the past. Doesn't drink. There is no disease common in the family.

REVIEW OF SYSTEMS: Negative.

GENERAL: Reveals a very pleasant 72 yr. old gentleman.

VITAL SIGNS: Temperature of 97.6, pulse is 64, respirations 18, blood pressure 178/94.

HEAD: Normocephalic.

ENT: Eyes -sclera and conjunctiva normal. PERRL, EOM's intact. Fundi reveal arteriolar narrowing. ENT are unremarkable.

NECK: Supple. No thyromegaly. Carotids are 2 out of 4. No bruits, no jugular venous distention.

CHEST: Symmetrical. Clear to auscultation and percussion.

HEART: Regular rhythm without any particular murmurs or gallops.

ABDOMEN: Nontender. No organomegaly. Bowel sounds normal activity. No bruits or masses.

BACK: No CVA tenderness nor tenderness to percussion over the spinous processes.

GENITALIA: Normal male.

RECTAL: Good sphincter tones. Stool is hemoccult negative. Prostate is normal in size.

EXTREMITIES: No cyanosis, clubbing or edema. Pulses equal and full.

NEUROLOGIC: Is physiologic.

IMPRESSION: 1) Chest pain, etiology to be determined

2) Hypertension

PLAN: Outlined in the order sheet.

DD:04-28-YYYY

DT: 04-30-YYYY

Alan Norris, MD

Alan Norris, MD

ALFRED STATE MEDICAL CENTER ■ 100 MAIN ST, ALFRED, NY 14802 ■ (607) 555-1234

GIBBON, Andrew Case 05 Dr. Norris	Admission: 04-27-YYYY DOB: 08-19-YYYY ROOM: 0362	PROGRESS NOTES

Date	(Please skip one line between dates.)
4-27-YY	Chief Complaint: Unstable angina.
	Diagnosis: Unstable angina.
	Plan of Treatment: See orders.
	Discharge Plan: Home — No services needed
	Alan Norris, MD
4/28/YY	Pt has had no pain overnight. Plan to get pt up and walking. Treadmill Thursday if no pain BG studies today.
	Alan Norris, MD
4/29/YY	Treadmill — pt not able to achieve goal. Shortness of breath.
	Alan Norris, MD

GIBBON, Andrew	Admission: 04-27-YYYY	DOCTORS ORDERS
Case05	DOB: 08-19-YYYY	
Dr. Norris	ROOM: 0362	

Date	Time	Physician's signature required for each order. (Please skip one line between dates.)
4-27-YY	1330	TELEMETRY PROTOCOL
		1. Saline lock, insert and flush every 24 hours and PRN
		2. EKG with chest pain x 1
		3. Oxygen 3 l/min. via nasal cannula PRN for chest pain.
		4. Chest Pain: NTG 0.4mg SL q 5 min x 3.
		5. Bradycardia: Atropine 0.5mg IV q 5 min to total of 2mg for symptomatic heart rate
		(Pulse less than 50 or 60 with decreased BP and/or PVC's)
		6. PVC's: Lidocaine 50mg IV push
		Start drip 500cc D5W Lidocaine 2 gm @ 2mg/Min (30cc/hr) for greater
		than 6 PVC's per min or 3 PVC's in a row.
		7. V-Tach: (If patient is hemodynamically stable)
		Lidocaine 50mg IV push.
		Start drip 500cc D5W Lidocaine 2 gm @ 2mg/min (30cc/hr)
		(If unstable) Cardiovert at 50 watt seconds
		8. V-fib: Immediately defibrillate at 200 watt seconds, if not converted:
		Immediately defibrillate at 300 watt seconds, if not converted;
		Immediately defibrillate at 360 watt seconds, if not converted: Start CPR
		Give Epinephrine (1:10,000) 1 mg IC push
		Give Lidocaine as per V-Tach protocol
		9. Asystole/EMD: Begin CPR
		Epinephrine (1:10,000) 1mg IV push
		Atropine 1 mg IV push if no response with Epinephrine
		10. Respiratory arrest: Intubation with mechanical ventilation.
		11. Notify Physician for chest pain or arrhythmias requiring treatment.
		R.A.V. T.O. Dr. Norris/M. Higgin, R.N.
		Alan Norris, MD

		DOCTORS ORDERS

GIBBON, Andrew Admission: 04-27-YYYY
Case05 DOB: 08-19-YYYY
Dr. Norris ROOM: 0362

Date	Time	Physician's signature required for each order. (Please skip one line between dates.)
27 Apr YY	1340	Inderal 40 mg qid
		Procardia XL 60 mg q day
		Isordil 10 mg qid
		Vasotec 25 mg q day
		Schedule for stress test 4/28, 1230 if possible
		GB US R/O stones
		Reg diet
		Up in room
		Alan Norris, MD
27 Apr YY	1645	Reschedule for treadmill for 1230, 29 Apr YY.
		Hepatobiliary scan tomorrow.
		Alan Norris, MD
28 Apr YY	0830	Ambulate in hall ad lib.
		Lytes SCGII in am.
		Alan Norris, MD
28 Apr YY	1610	Inderal 20 mg po qid
		Lytes SCGII in am.
		Alan Norris, MD

```
GIBBON, Andrew        Admission: 04-27-YYYY
Case 05               DOB: 08-19-YYYY                    LABORATORY DATA
Dr. Norris            ROOM: 0362
```

SPECIMEN COLLECTED: 04-29-YYYY   **SPECIMEN RECEIVED:** 04-29-YYYY

TEST	RESULT	FLAG	REFERENCE
Glucose	97		70-110 mg/dl
BUN	12		8-25 mg/dl
Creatinine	1.0		0.9-1.4 mg/dl
Sodium	135	**L**	135-145 mmol/L
Potassium	4.2		3.6-5.0 mmol/L
Chloride	97	**L**	99-110 mmol/L
CO2	30		21-31 mmol/L
Calcium	9.3		8.8-10.5 mg/dl
WBC	4.7		4.5-11.0 thous/UL
RBC	5.80		5.2-5.4 mill/UL
HGB	17.0		11.7-16.1 g/dl
HCT	50.1		35.0-47.0 %
Platelets	102	**L**	140-400 thous/UL
Protime	11.4		11.0-13.0
PTT	21		< 32 seconds

End of Report

ALFRED STATE MEDICAL CENTER ■ 100 MAIN ST, ALFRED, NY 14802 ■ (607) 555-1234

```
GIBBON, Andrew       Admission: 04-27-YYYY
Case05               DOB: 08-19-YYYY                    LABORATORY DATA
Dr. Norris           ROOM: 0362
```

SPECIMEN COLLECTED: 04-29-YYYY   **SPECIMEN RECEIVED:** 04-29-YYYY

URINALYSIS

URINE DIPSTICK

COLOR	STRAW	
SP GRAVITY	1.010	1.001-1.030
GLUCOSE	NEGATIVE	< 125 mg/dl
BILIRUBIN	NEGATIVE	NEG
KETONE	NEGATIVE	NEG mg/dl
BLOOD	NEGATIVE	NEG
PH	7.5	4.5-8.0
PROTEIN	NEGATIVE	NEG mg/dl
UROBILINOGEN	NORMAL	NORMAL-1.0 mg/dl
NITRITES	NEGATIVE	NEG
LEUKOCYTES	NEGATIVE	NEG
WBC	RARE	0-5 /HPF
RBC	--	0-5 /HPF
EPI CELLS	RARE	/HPF
BACTERIA	--	/HPF
CASTS.	--	< 1 HYALINE/HPF

End of Report

ALFRED STATE MEDICAL CENTER ■ 100 MAIN ST, ALFRED, NY 14802 ■ (607) 555-1234

```
GIBBON, Andrew          Admission: 04-27-YYYY      NUCLEAR MEDICINE REPORT
Case05                  DOB: 08-19-YYYY
Dr. Norris              ROOM: 0362
```

Reason for Ultrasound (please initial): *r/o stones*

Date Requested:

Transport: ☑ Wheelchair ☐ Stretcher ☐ O₂ ☐ IV
            ☑ IP ☐ OP ☐ ER
            ☐ PRE OP ☐ OR/RR ☐ Portable

HEPATOBILIARY SCAN: Following injection of isotope there is prompt demonstration of the liver, gallbladder, biliary system and small bowel. This would indicate no significant obstruction of either the cystic or the common duct.

CONCLUSION: Normal hepatobiliary scan.

ABDOMINAL ULTRASOUND: Multiple real time images show that the gallbladder is of normal size without evidence of any stones or wall thickening. Portions of the kidneys, spleen, pancreas and upper aorta are demonstrated and are unremarkable.

CONCLUSION: Normal ultrasound

DD: 04-28-YYYY

DT: 04-29-YYYY

D. Lane
_____
D. Lane, M.D.

GIBBON, Andrew   Admission: 04-27-YYYY   EKG REPORT
Case05   DOB: 08-19-YYYY
Dr. Norris   ROOM: 0362

            Date of EKG 04-27-YYYY   Time of EKG 11:42:03

Rate   61
PR   158   Abnormal: Old inferior MI
QRSD   64
QT   383   non specific st-t changes
QTC   386
                     no old tracings for comparison
    -- Axis --
P   1   clinical correlation needed.
QRS   -27
T   28

                                          Bella Kaplan, M.D.
                                          _____
                                               Name of Physician

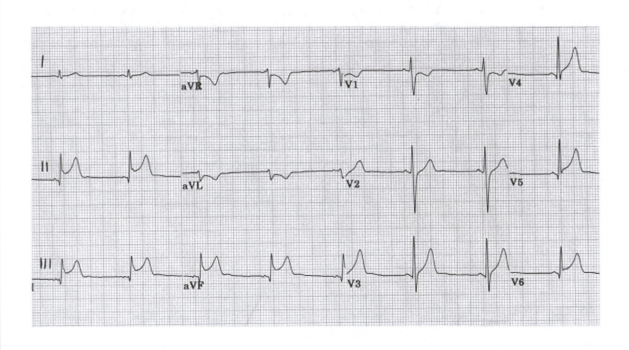

GIBBON, Andrew
Case 05
Dr. Norris

Admission: 04-27-YYYY
DOB: 08-19-YYYY
ROOM: 0362

TREADMILL STRESS TEST

Date of EKG 04-29-YYYY   Time of EKG 13:00

Protocol	Manual	Time	6:41
Age	72	Rate	116, 78% of Expected Max (148)
Race	Caucasian	BP	13/85
Sex	Male	Stage	3
Ht	66 in.	Speed	3.4
Wt	160 lbs.	Grade	14.0
Opt	362	RPP	156
Rate	92	METS	6.4
BP	110/70		

Inconclusive. Pt developed dyspnea, probably due to
Inderal. No change on EKG to suggest ischemic disease.
            Bella Kaplan, M.D.
_____
            Name of Physician

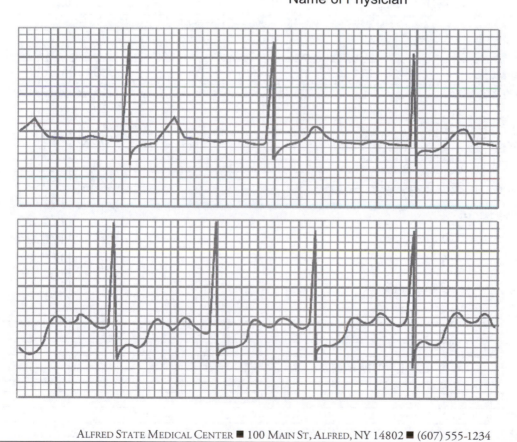

Case 06

ALFRED STATE MEDICAL CENTER 100 MAIN ST, ALFRED, NY 14802 (607) 555-1234 HOSPITAL #: 000999				INPATIENT FACE SHEET			

PATIENT NAME AND ADDRESS				GENDER	RACE	MARITAL STATUS	PATIENT NO.
BENSON, Charles 42 Sherwood Street Alfred, NY 14802				M	W	M	Case06
				DATE OF BIRTH		MAIDEN NAME	OCCUPATION
				12-13-YYYY			Cabinetmaker

ADMISSION DATE	TIME	DISCHARGE DATE	TIME	LENGTH OF STAY	TELEPHONE NUMBER
04-24-YYYY	14:30	04-29-YYYY	10:00	5 DAYS	(607) 555-2032

GUARANTOR NAME AND ADDRESS	NEXT OF KIN NAME AND ADDRESS
BENSON, Charles 42 Sherwood Street Alfred, NY 14802	BENSON, Laura 42 Sherwood Street Alfred, NY 14802

GUARANTOR TELEPHONE NO.	RELATIONSHIP TO PATIENT	NEXT OF KIN TELEPHONE NUMBER	RELATIONSHIP TO PATIENT
(607) 555-2032	Self	(607) 555-2032	Wife

ADMITTING PHYSICIAN	SERVICE	ADMIT TYPE	ROOM NUMBER/BED
Thompson MD, Donald	ICU	2	0204/02

ATTENDING PHYSICIAN	ATTENDING PHYSICIAN UPIN	ADMITTING DIAGNOSIS
Thompson, Donald MD	100B01	Chest Pain

PRIMARY INSURER	POLICY AND GROUP NUMBER	SECONDARY INSURER	POLICY AND GROUP NUMBER
Medicare	18712166A	AARP	50873240 2

DIAGNOSES AND PROCEDURES	ICD-9-CM	ICD-10-CM/PCS
PRINCIPAL DIAGNOSIS		
Costochondritis	733.6	M94.0
SECONDARY DIAGNOSES		
Arteriosclerotic cardiovascular disease	429.9	I51.9
w/ arteriosclerosis	440.9	I52 I70.90
Past myocardial infarction	412	I70.91
Old CVA	V12.59	I25.2 Z86.79
Status post bypass surgery	V45.81	Z95.1
PRINCIPAL PROCEDURE		
SECONDARY PROCEDURES		
TOTAL CHARGES: $ 2,335.50		

ACTIVITY:	☐ Bedrest	☑ Light	☐ Usual	☐ Unlimited	☐ Other:
DIET:	☐ Regular	☐ Low Cholesterol	☐ Low Salt	☐ ADA	☐ _____ Calorie
FOLLOW-UP:	☑ Call for appointment	☑ Office appointment in <u>one week</u>	☐ Other:		

SPECIAL INSTRUCTIONS: : O₂ 4L/min. Albuterol inhaler w/ aerochamber 2 puffs 4 times a day.

Signature of Attending Physician: Donald Thompson, MD

ALFRED STATE MEDICAL CENTER ■ 100 MAIN ST, ALFRED, NY 14802 ■ (607) 555-1234

BENSON, Charles	Admission: 04-24-YYYY	CONSENT TO ADMISSION
Case 06	DOB: 12-13-YYYY	
Dr. Thompson	ROOM: 0204	

I, _Charles Benson_ hereby consent to admission to the Alfred State Medical Center (ASMC) , and I further consent to such routine hospital care, diagnostic procedures, and medical treatment that the medical and professional staff of ASMC may deem necessary or advisable. I authorize the use of medical information obtained about me as specified above and the disclosure of such information to my referring physician(s). This form has been fully explained to me, and I understand its contents. I further understand that no guarantees have been made to me as to the results of treatments or examinations done at the ASMC.

Charles Benson _____ _April 24, YYYY_ _____
Signature of Patient   Date

_____ _____
Signature of Parent/Legal Guardian for Minor   Date

_____
Relationship to Minor

Andrea Witteman _____ _April 24, yyyy_ _____
WITNESS: Alfred State Medical Center Staff Member   Date

CONSENT TO RELEASE INFORMATION FOR REIMBURSEMENT PURPOSES

In order to permit reimbursement, upon request, the Alfred State Medical Center (ASMC) may disclose such treatment information pertaining to my hospitalization to any corporation, organization, or agent thereof, which is, or may be liable under contract to the ASMC or to me, or to any of my family members or other person, for payment of all or part of the ASMC's charges for services rendered to me (e.g., the patient's health insurance carrier). I understand that the purpose of any release of information is to facilitate reimbursement for services rendered. In addition, in the event that my health insurance program includes utilization review of services provided during this admission, I authorize ASMC to release information as is necessary to permit the review. This authorization will expire once the reimbursement for services rendered is complete.

Charles Benson _____ _April 24, YYYY_ _____
Signature of Patient   Date

_____ _____
Signature of Parent/Legal Guardian for Minor   Date

_____
Relationship to Minor

Andrea Witteman _____ _April 24, yyyy_ _____
WITNESS: Alfred State Medical Center Staff Member   Date

ALFRED STATE MEDICAL CENTER ■ 100 MAIN ST, ALFRED, NY 14802 ■ (607) 555-1234

BENSON, Charles	Admission: 04-24-YYYY	**ADVANCE DIRECTIVE**
Case06	DOB: 12-13-YYYY	
Dr. Thompson	ROOM: 0204	

Your answers to the following questions will assist your Physician and the Hospital to respect your wishes regarding your medical care. This information will become a part of your medical record.

	YES	NO	PATIENT'S INITIALS
1. Have you been provided with a copy of the information called "Patient Rights Regarding Health Care Decision?"	X		C B
2. Have you prepared a "Living Will?" If yes, please provide the Hospital with a copy for your medical record.		X	C B
3. Have you prepared a Durable Power of Attorney for Health Care? If yes, please provide the Hospital with a copy for your medical record.		X	C B
4. Have you provided this facility with an Advance Directive on a prior admission and is it still in effect? If yes, Admitting Office to contact Medical Records to obtain a copy for the medical record.		X	C B
5. Do you desire to execute a Living Will/Durable Power of Attorney? If yes, refer to in order: a. Physician b. Social Service c. Volunteer Service		X	C B

HOSPITAL STAFF DIRECTIONS: Check when each step is completed.

1. ✓ Verify the above questions where answered and actions taken where required.

2. ✓ If the "Patient Rights" information was provided to someone other than the patient, state reason:

_____

_____   _____

Name of Individual Receiving Information   Relationship to Patient

3. ✓ If information was provided in a language other than English, specify language and method.

4. ✓ Verify patient was advised on how to obtain additional information on Advance Directives.

5. ✓ Verify the Patient/Family Member/Legal Representative was asked to provide the Hospital with a copy of the Advance Directive which will be retained in the medical record.

File this form in the medical record, and give a copy to the patient.

_____

Name of Patient (Name of Individual giving information if different from Patient)

CHARLES BENSON   *April 24, YYYY*

Signature of Patient   Date

Andrea Witteman   *April 24, YYYY*

Signature of Hospital Representative   Date

ALFRED STATE MEDICAL CENTER ■ 100 MAIN ST, ALFRED, NY 14802 ■ (607) 555-1234

BENSON, Charles	Admission: 04-24-YYYY	CONSULTATION REPORT
Case06	DOB: 12-13-YYYY	
Dr. Thompson	ROOM: 0204	

The patient is a 64 yr. old gentleman of Dr. Thompson's who I was asked to see for chest pain.

HISTORY OF PRESENT ILLNESS: Mr. Benson had about a three day history of somewhat progressive, unprovoked chest pain. It varies in its location and description as the history goes on. I don't think this is intentionally being elusive, I just think he can't well describe it. It is not truly substernal, but more left lateral chest wall. It is exacerbated by movement. It is relieved by Nitroglycerin but a varying dosage. Ultimately he ends up getting Morphine. There is no association with food as far as we can tell. The patient does have a prior cardiac history. He says he has had 2-3 heart attacks and equal number of CVA's, apparently leading to some blindness in one of his eyes. He has had coronary artery bypass, triple vessel I am told. He has a prior history of at least two packs per day smoking for years. He is rather overweight. Interestingly he states that his sternotomy never did heal very well. There is no preceding history of cough, fever, chills, or any kind of muscular activity.

PAST MEDICAL HISTORY: Essentially that mentioned above. He has had back surgery. He has also had hernia repairs.

MEDICATIONS: The patient is on Cardizem 60 mg. q.i.d. Lasix 40 mg. a day. Isordil 40 mg. t.i.d Potassium 10 mEq. Daily. Resteril 30 mg. at bedtime. Theophylline 200 mg. 2 b.i.d. Nitro Patch and Coumadin.

ALLERGIES: None

SOCIAL HISTORY & FAMILY HISTORY: The patient is married. No longer smokes. No strong family history of any particular disease. Interestingly, he served honorably in WWII, was exposed to the radiation blasts where he said he and others were exposed to direct radiation while they were trying to sink the ships with nuclear devices. He also has been exposed to a lot of wood dust in his profession as a cabinetmaker.

REVIEW OF SYSTEMS: Noncontributory.

PHYSICAL EXAMINATION: Reveals a 64 yr. old man in no gross distress at the moment. VITAL SIGNS: Temperature 98, pulse 68 and regular, respirations 16, blood pressure 140/100. HEAD: Normocephalic. Eyes sclera and conjunctiva are normal. PERRLA, EOM's intact. Fundi not visualized. ENT are unremarkable. NECK: Supple, no thyromegaly. Carotids are 2 out of 4. No bruits, no JVD. Chest is symmetrical and clear to A&P. HEART: Reveals a regular rhythm, no particular murmurs or gallops. ABDOMEN: Nontender, no organomegaly. Bowel sounds normal activity. No bruits or masses. BACK: No CVAT, tenderness to percussion over the spinous processes. Anterior chest reveals tenderness to palpation over the left pectoralis muscle and it really makes him whine with light palpation. RECTAL, GENITALIA: Deferred at this time. EXTREMITIES: No cyanosis, clubbing or edema. Pulses are equal and full. NEUROLOGIC: Is physiologic.

IMPRESSION: 1) Chest pain, probably chest wall, although the precipitating event is not clear at this time.

2) ASCVD with history of infarction and CVA's.

RECOMMENDATIONS: I think that if at all possible we ought to put him on NSAIDs, at least temporarily. See if we can't control the discomfort. I am not convinced that there is a cardiac component to this as its presentation is not in pattern. Likewise, there are no changes on the cardiogram and any other objective way of confirming that this is cardiac. Will follow along with you. Thank you for allowing me to participate in his care.

DD: 04-24-YYYY

DT: 04-25-YYYY

Sandra Reese, M.D.
Sandra Reese, M.D.

ALFRED STATE MEDICAL CENTER ■ 100 MAIN ST, ALFRED, NY 14802 ■ (607) 555-1234

BENSON, Charles Admission: 04-24-YYYY	PROGRESS NOTES
Case06 DOB: 12-13-YYYY	
Dr. Thompson ROOM: 0204	

Date	(Please skip one line between dates.)
4/24	Chief Complaint: Chest pain into left lateral chest wall, shortness of breath, and nausea.
	Diagnosis: Chest pain. Unstsable angina. Rule out myocardial infarction.
	Plan of Treatment: ICU observation and work-up. Donald Thompson, MD
04/25	HHN with 0.5 ml proventil/NSS, tolerated well. Breath sounds ↓ clear. Sitting in chair, heart rate 72.
1600	Respirations regular, 18. O2 p+p BLNR. O2 sat. 95%. Rita Childs, R.R.T.
04/25	HHN w/ 0.5 ml proventil and NSS given in mask. Heart rate 84. Respirations regular, 20.
1930	Breath sounds clear, with decreased bases. Patient had good npc, O2 on partial room air. T. Perry, RRT
04-26	Treatment given: HHN with 0.5 ml Proventil/NSS via mask with patient tolerating well.
0715	BS ↓ clear, pulse 64, respirations 16, NPC O2, N/C. L. Seraphin RRT
04-26	Pt. doing better. Still complains of L sided chest pain. Will try to gradually remove O2. D. Thompson, MD
04-26	Treatment given: HHN with 0.5 ml Proventil / NSS via mask. Breath sounds ↓ clear.
1100	Pulse 80, respirations 20, NPC O2 on 6L pre O2 on O2 SL port. L. Seraphin
04-26	Tx given: MDI with Proventil via aerochamber. Pt. instructed on use & using good technique.
1500	BS ↓ w/ rales at bases. P 80. R 20. No cough. O2 on a SL N/C. L. Seraphin
04-26	MDI w/ 2 puffs Proventil treatment given via aerochamber. Patient tolderated treatment well. B.S. clear. ↓'d bases.
1910	No cough. O2 on 5 l n.c. pre and post treatment. C. Steinerly, CPT
04-27	MDI w/ 2 puffs proventil via aerochamber gd. Tx tol well. BS clear ↓, no cough. O2 p+p tx 5L N.C. O2 sat. 97%.
0710	R. Rose CPT
04-27	Pt. has less pain. Continue treatment.

BENSON, Charles	Admission: 04-24-YYYY	PROGRESS NOTES
Case06	DOB: 12-13-YYYY	
Dr. Thompson	ROOM: 0204	

Date	(Please skip one line between dates.)
04-27 0900	Met w/ pt. per multidisciplinary team conference referral by cpt/nursing. Pt. stated to having home O2 but unknown is type of set up he has to meet O_2 demands Presently @ 5 LPM. Interview done w/ pt. this am. He has liquid O_2 @ home (can go ↑ to 10 lpm) and also has access to an O_2 concentrator (usually goes to 4-5 pm). Pt also has E-portable tanks. Pt. utilizes a portable O_2 demand system on a sensor he described as supply/demand by by sensoring constant need w/ rest/activity. Pt. utilizes Hub as O_2 provider + is extremely pleased with company + service. Pt. declines any other needs for discharge planning. No intervention required. Nsg aware. D. Davenport
04-27	MDI w/ 2 puffs proventil gd. tech. Tol well O2 tx. 5L N.C. – N.C. R. Rose, CPT
04-27	MDI w/ 2 puffs proventil / NSS gd. tech. Tol well. No cough. B.S. ↓, clear. Pt. sitting in chair. O2 tx 5L N.C.. R. Rose, CPT
04-27	MDI c̄ 2 puffs Proventil via spacer. BS ↓'d bases. No cough. HR 68. R 16. O2 on 5LN.C. pre & post tx. E. Blossom, RRT
04-28	MDI w/ 2 puffs proventil / Nss gd. tech. tol well no cough BS clear ↓ c̄ Pt. sitting in chair O2 tx 5L N.C. R. Rose, CPT
04-28	Pt says his chest feels better. i feel this is inflammation. Treatment helping. D. Thompson
04-28	mdi w/ 2 puffs proventil gd. tech. tol well feeling better O2 Pre + post tx 5L N.C. – N.C. R. Rose, CPT
04-28	MDI w/ 2 puffs proventil gd. tech. Tol well. O2 sat. 5LNC 95%, ↓ 4LNC O2 sat. No cough. B.S. ↓ appear clear. Pt. shown how to use O2 walker. R. Rose, CPT
04-28	MDI c̄ 2 puffs Proventil via spacer. BS ↓'d bases. HR 68. R 24. O2 4LNC pre-tx. E. Blossom, RRT
04-29	MDI w/ 2 puffs Proventil. tol Rx well. good technique. NPC O2 on pre & post 4 LNC. H. Figgs, CRTT
4/29	Patient feeling much better. No complaints of chest pain. O2 sat 92÷ on 4 L O2. Discharged to home.

BENSON, Charles	Admission: 04-24-YYYY	DOCTORS ORDERS
Case06	DOB: 12-13-YYYY	
Dr. Thompson	ROOM: 0204	

Date	Time	Physician's signature required for each order. (Please skip one line between dates.)
4-24	1501	1) Admit to Dr. Thompson
		2) Admit to ICCU
		3) Daily Protime
		4) Diltiazem 60 mg q.i.d.
		5) Lasix 40 mg in a.m.
		6) Isosorbide 40 mg
		7) KCl 10 mg in a.m.
		8) Theophylline 200 mg bid
		9) Nitro Patch 0.2 mg daily for 12 hours
		10) Coumadin 4 mg
		11) Albuterol MDI with Rigxoir 2 puffs q 4 hours prn for dyspnea and wheezing
		12) Pt. may use own eye drops, right eye
		13) Serum Theophylline level
		14) Mylanta II q 2 hours prn staomch discomfort
		15) Tylenol 4 hrs mild pain
		16) O₂ via N.C. 3L/
		17) Oximetry in 1 hr, q 5 nights
		T.O. Sandra Leary, R.N./D. Thompson, M.D.
		D. Thompson, MD

BENSON, Charles	Admission: 04-24-YYYY	DOCTORS ORDERS
Case06	DOB: 12-13-YYYY	
Dr. Thompson	ROOM: 0204	

Date	Time	Physician's signature required for each order. (Please skip one line between dates.)
04-24		ROUTINE ICU ORDERS
		1. CBC, SR, PT, PTT, SCG II, LYTES, BUN, MAGNESIUM, UA, CPK. Isoenzymes q8h x 24 hrs and
		daily until normal. LDH now and daily x 2 until return to normal range.
		2. EKG STAT and daily x 2 days and with chest pain x one (1).
		3. Oxygen – 3L/min by cannula, PRN. Oximetry PRN.
		4. Chest X-ray.
		5. Diet – Cardiac, clear to regular as tolerated.
		6. MEDICATIONS:
		NTG 0.4mg SL q 5 min x 3 PRN for chest pain.
		Morphine Sulfate 4mg IV q 2 min PRN not to exceed 16mg/hr
		OR Meperidine 50 mg IV q 15 min PRN not to exceed 100mg/4hr for chest pain, dyspnea, extreme restlessness.
		Docusate with Casanthranol BID PRN nausea.
		Acetaminophen 650mg q4h PRN headache.
		7. 500cc D5W at 25CC/HR., if diabetic use Normol R at 25cc/hr.
		8. Bradycardia: Atropine 0.5mg IV q 5 min up to 2mg for symptomatic heart rate. (Pulse less than 50, or less
		than 60 with decreased blood pressure, and/or PVC's).
		9. PVC's: Lidocaine 50mg IV push then start drip of 500ml D5W/Lidocaine 2gm @ 2mg/ml (30cc/hr) for
		greater than six (6) per min or three (3) in a row.
		10. V-Tach: If patient hemodynamically stable Lidocaine 50mg IV push; then start drip of 500 ml
		D5W/Lidocaine 2 gm @ 2 mg/min (30cc/hr.)
		11. V-Tach: If patient becomes unstable, Cardiovert @ 50 watt seconds.
		12. V-Fib: Immediately defibrillate @ 200 watt seconds; if not converted, then
		Immediately defibrillate @ 300 watt seconds; if not converted, then
		Immediately defibrillate @ 360 watt seconds. Give Epinephrine (1:10,000) 1 mg
		IV push, then Lidocaine drip as per V-tach protocol.
		13. Asystole/EMD: Epinephrine (1:10,000) 1mg IV push; if no response, Atropine 1 mg IV push.
		14. Respiratory Arrest: Intubation with Mechanical Ventilation.
		15. Activity: Bedrest with bedside commode if VS stable. Donald Thompson, MD
		16. Notify physician for chest pain or arrhythmias requiring treatment. T.O. Sandra Leary, R.N./D. Thompson, M.D.

BENSON, Charles	Admission: 04-24-YYYY
Case 06	DOB: 12-13-YYYY
Dr. Thompson	ROOM: 0204

DOCTORS ORDERS

Date	Time	Physician's signature required for each order. (Please skip one line between dates.)
04/24	1700	lacrilube eye ung - apply to eyelids @ h.s. daily akwa tears or natural
		tears, drops as needed — may have @ bedside.
		R.A.V. To Dr. Thompson / S. Hollings, RN Donald Thompson, MD
04/24	2220	Increase O$_2$ to 4L min nasal canula
		R.A.V. T.O. Dr. Thompson/S. Hollings, RN Donald Thompson, MD
04-24	0350	ABG in AM
		Increase O$_2$ to 6 LPM - NC
		Consult Dr. Reese to evaluate chest pain in AM
		R.A.V. To Dr. Thompson/R. Underhill Donald Thompson, MD
04-24	0830	Lung Perfusion & Ventilation scan this AM to rule out a PE
		R.A.V. T.O. Dr. Reese/W. Nelson Sandra Reese, M.D.
04-24	0945	Proventil qid Donald Thompson, MD
04-24		Motrin 600 p.o. T.i.D.
		Carafate 1 gm p.o. Q.i.D.
		up in chair
		ABG on RA in AM
		Donald Thompson, MD
4/24	1058	Obtain a.m. blood gas on O2 at 24 min. R.A.V. T.O. Dr. Reese/W. Nelson Sandra Reese, M.D.
04-24		May be out of bed as tolerated Donald Thompson, MD

BENSON, Charles	Admission: 04-24-YYYY	DOCTORS ORDERS
Case06	DOB: 12-13-YYYY	
Dr. Thompson	ROOM: 0204	

Date	Time	Physician's signature required for each order. (Please skip one line between dates.)
4-24	1851	TELEMETRY PROTOCOL
		1. Saline lock, insert and flush every 24 hours and PRN
		2. EKG with chest pain x 1
		3. Oxygen 3 1/min. via nasal cannula PRN for chest pain.
		4. Chest Pain: NTG 0.4mg SL q 5 min x 3.
		5. Bradycardia: Atropine 0.5mg IV q 5 min to total of 2mg for symptomatic heart rate (Pulse less than 50 or 60 with decreased BP and/or PVC's)
		6. PVC's: Lidocaine 50mg IV push
		Start drip 500 cc D5W Lidocaine 2 gm @ 2mg/Min (30 cc/hr) for greater than 6 PVC's per min or 3 PVC's in a row.
		7. V-Tach: (If patient is hemodynamically stable)
		Lidocaine 50mg IV push.
		Start drip 500cc D5W Lidocaine 2 gm @ 2mg/min (30cc/hr)
		(If unstable) Cardiovert @ 50 watt seconds.
		8. V-fib: Immediately defibrillate @ 200 watt seconds, if not converted:
		Immediately defibrillate @ 300 watt seconds, if not converted;
		Immediately defibrillate @ 360 watt seconds, if not converted: Start CPR
		Give Epinephrine (1:10,000) 1 mg IC push
		Give Lidocaine as per V-Tach protocol
		9. Asystole/EMD: Begin CPR
		Epinephrine (1:10,000) 1mg IV push
		Atropine 1 mg IV push if no response with Epinephrine
		10. Respiratory arrest: Intubation with mechanical ventilation.
		11. Notify Physician for chest pain or arrhythmias requiring treatment.
		Donald Thompson, MD

BENSON, Charles	Admission: 04-24-YYYY	DOCTORS ORDERS
Case06	DOB: 12-13-YYYY	
Dr. Thompson	ROOM: 0204	

Date	Time	Physician's signature required for each order. (Please skip one line between dates.)
04-24		1) Transfer to floor on Telemetry. May be up as tolerated.
		2) Heparin IV
		3) O2 via N.C. at 6L/m
		4) Oximetry q shift.
		5) D/C Protimes
		6) Cardizem 60 mg QID
		7) Lasix 40 mg p.o. tib
		8) isosorbium 40 mg p.o. tib
		9) KCi 10 mg in AM
		10) Theophylline 200 mg bid
		11) Nitro patch
		12) Coumadin 5 mg
		13) Motrin 600 mg tid
		14) Lacrilube - apply to eyelids
		15) Tylenol 2 tabs 14h prn for pain
		16) Resteril 30 mg h.s.
		17) Regular diet
		Donald Thompson, MD
4/24	1950	1500 cal ADA diet. May be up ad lib. Donald Thompson, MD
4/25		↓ o2 to 5 L/min and ok oximetry after 1 hr. Donald Thompson, MD
4/26		D/c telemetry. Donald Thompson, MD

ALFRED STATE MEDICAL CENTER ■ 100 MAIN ST, ALFRED, NY 14802 ■ (607) 555-1234

BENSON, Charles	Admission: 04-24-YYYY	DOCTORS ORDERS
Case 06	DOB: 12-13-YYYY	
Dr. Thompson	ROOM: 0204	

Date	Time	Physician's signature required for each order. (Please skip one line between dates.)
04-27	0820	Coumadin 75 mg tid Donald Thompson, MD
04-28	1050	Ambulate ad lib. Donald Thompson, MD
04-29		Discharge Donald Thompson, MD

BENSON, Charles   Admission: 04-24-YYYY   LABORATORY DATA
Case06   DOB: 12-13-YYYY
Dr. Thompson   ROOM: 0204

SPECIMEN COLLECTED: 4-24-YYYY   SPECIMEN RECEIVED: 4-24-YYYY

TEST	RESULT	FLAG	REFERENCE
URINALYSIS			
DIPSTICK ONLY			
COLOR	CLOUDY YELLOW		
SP GRAVITY	1.025		≤ 1.030
GLUCOSE	110		≤ 125 mg/dl
BILIRUBIN	NEG		≤ 0.8 mg/dl
KETONE	TRACE		≤ 10 mg/dl
BLOOD	0.03		0.06 mg/dl hgb
PH	5.0		5-8.0
PROTEIN	NORMAL		≤ 30 mg/dl
UROBILINOGEN	NORMAL		≤ -1 mg/dl
NITRITES	NEG		NEG
LEUKOCYTE	NEG		≤ 15 WBC/hpf
W.B.C.	5-10		≤ 5/hpf
R.B.C.	RARE		≤ 5/hpf
BACT.	4f		1+(≤ 20/hpf)
URINE PREGNANCY TEST			

End of Report

ALFRED STATE MEDICAL CENTER ■ 100 MAIN ST, ALFRED, NY 14802 ■ (607) 555-1234

BENSON, Charles   Admission: 04-24-YYYY   LABORATORY DATA
Case06   DOB: 12-13-YYYY
Dr. Thompson   ROOM: 0204

SPECIMEN COLLECTED: 04-24-YYYY   **SPECIMEN RECEIVED:** Blood

TEST	RESULT	FLAG	REFERENCE
Sodium	142		136-147 meq/L
Potassium	3.9		3.6-5.0 mmol/L
Chloride	102		99-110 mmol/L
CO2	29		24-32 mg/dl
Glucose	95		70-110 mg/dl
Urea Nitrogen	6	**L**	7-18 mg/dl

End of Report

ALFRED STATE MEDICAL CENTER ■ 100 MAIN ST, ALFRED, NY 14802 ■ (607) 555-1234

BENSON, Charles   Admission: 04-24-YYYY   LABORATORY DATA
Case06   DOB: 12-13-YYYY
Dr. Thompson   ROOM: 0204

SPECIMEN COLLECTED: 4-24-YYYY   SPECIMEN RECEIVED: 4-24-YYYY

CBC S DIFF

TEST	RESULT	FLAG	REFERENCE
WBC	7.4		4.5-11.0 thous/UL
RBC	5.02	**L**	5.2-5.4 mill/UL
HGB	15.0		11.7-16.1 g/dl
HCT	45.8		35.0-47.0 %
MCV	91.2		85-99 fL.
MCHC	32.8	**L**	33-37
RDW	15.2	**H**	11.4-14.5
Platelets	165		130-400 thous/UL
MPV	8.4		7.4-10.4
LYMPH %	21.1		20.5-51.1
MONO %	7.8		1.7-9.3
GRAN %	71.1		42.2-75.2
LYMPH x 10^3	1.6		1.2-3.4
MONO x 10^3	.6	**H**	0.11-0.59
GRAN x 10^3	5.3		1.4-6.5
EOS x 10^3	< .7		0.0-0.7
BASO x 10^3	< .2		0.0-0.2
ANISO	SLIGHT		

End of Report

ALFRED STATE MEDICAL CENTER ■ 100 MAIN ST, ALFRED, NY 14802 ■ (607) 555-1234

BENSON, Charles   Admission: 04-24-YYYY
Case06   DOB: 12-13-YYYY   PULSE OXIMETRY
Dr. Thompson   ROOM: 0204

TIME	SPO$_2$	F1O$_2$	TECHNICIAN
04/24/YYYY			
1530	95%	3L	AS
2000	92%	3L	AS
2300	88%	3L NC	RB
04/24/YYYY			
2335	91%	6L	JJ
2340	94%	6L	LL
2345	95%	6L	WW
04/24/YYYY			
2350	93%	6 LPM	PT
2400	94%	6L	RB
04/25/YYYY			
0715	95%	8L	RCH
0945	93%	6L NC	RCH
1600	95%	6L NC	GER
2100	96%	6L NC	RB

End of Report

BENSON, Charles   Admission: 04-24-YYYY

Case 06   DOB: 12-13-YYYY   PULSE OXIMETRY

Dr. Thompson   ROOM: 0204

TIME	SPO$_2$	F1O$_2$	TECHNICIAN
04/26/YYYY			
0730	96%	6L NC	SMC
1520	94%	5L NC	SMC
04/27/YYYY			
1205	93%	5L	SMC
04/28/YYYY			
0715	98%	5L	YE
1530	95%	5L	YE
1615	93%	4L	MM
1630	95%	4L	MM
1640	92%	4L	MM
1650	93%	4L	MM
2310	92%	4L	RB

End of Report

BENSON, Charles   Admission: 04-24-YYYY
Case06   DOB: 12-13-YYYY
Dr. Thompson   ROOM: 0204

RADIOMETRY

SPECIMEN COLLECTED: 04-22-YYYY   SPECIMEN RECEIVED: 04-22-YYYY

TEST	RESULT	REFERENCE
BLOOD GAS VALUES		
pH	7.440	
pCO2	33.4	mmHg
pO2	55.6	mmHg
TEMPERATURE CORRECTED VALUES		
pH	7.440	
pCO2	33.4	mmHg
pO2	55.6	mmHg
ACID BASE STATUS		
HCO3c	22.3	mmol/L
ABEc	-0.4	mmol/L
BLOOD OXIMETRY VALUES		
tHb	17.8	g/dL
O2Hb	89.9	%
COHb	0.6	%
MetHb	0.6	%

End of Report

BENSON, Charles   Admission: 04-24-YYYY

Case06   DOB: 12-13-YYYY

Dr. Thompson   ROOM: 0204

RADIOMETRY

SPECIMEN COLLECTED: 04-23-YYYY   **SPECIMEN RECEIVED:** 04-23-YYYY

TEST	RESULT	REFERENCE
BLOOD GAS VALUES		
pH	7.401	
pCO2	38.5	mmHg
pO2	69.8	mmHg
TEMPERATURE CORRECTED VALUES		
pH	7.401	
pCO2	38.5	mmHg
pO2	69.8	mmHg
ACID BASE STATUS		
HCO3c	23.4	mmol/L
ABEc	-0.6	mmol/L
BLOOD OXIMETRY VALUES		
tHb	17.4	g/dL
O2Hb	92.7	%
COHb	0.3	%
MetHb	0.8	%

End of Report

BENSON, Charles   Admission: 04-24-YYYY
Case 06   DOB: 12-13-YYYY
Dr. Thompson   ROOM: 0204

RADIOMETRY

SPECIMEN COLLECTED: 04-24-YYYY   SPECIMEN RECEIVED: 04-24-YYYY

TEST	RESULT	REFERENCE
BLOOD GAS VALUES		
pH	7.44	
pCO2	36.0	mmHg
pO2	46.3	mmHg
TEMPERATURE CORRECTED VALUES		
pH	7.44	
pCO2	36.0	mmHg
pO2	46.3	mmHg
ACID BASE STATUS		
HCO3c	24.3	mmol/L
ABEc	1.1	mmol/L
BLOOD OXIMETRY VALUES		
tHb	17.0	g/dL
O2Hb	84.6	%
COHb	0.5	%
MetHb	0.7	%

End of Report

BENSON, Charles   Admission: 04-24-YYYY   RADIOLOGY REPORT
Case06   DOB: 12-13-YYYY
Dr. Thompson   ROOM: 0204

Date Requested: 04-22-YYYY

CHEST: PA and lateral views show that the heart, lungs, thorax and mediastinum are normal.

DD: 04-22-YYYY

DT: 04-22-YYYY

Philip Rogers
_____
Philip Rogers, M.D., Radiologist

ALFRED STATE MEDICAL CENTER ■ 100 MAIN ST, ALFRED, NY 14802 ■ (607) 555-1234

BENSON, Charles
Case06
Dr. Thompson

Admission: 04-24-YYYY
DOB: 12-13-YYYY
ROOM: 0204

EKG REPORT

Date of EKG: 04-22-YYYY   Time of EKG: 13:56:20

Rate	66
PR	184
QRSD	60
QT	363
QTC	380
-- Axis --	
P	76
QRS	79
T	71

Normal.

Bella Kaplan
Bella Kaplan, M.D.

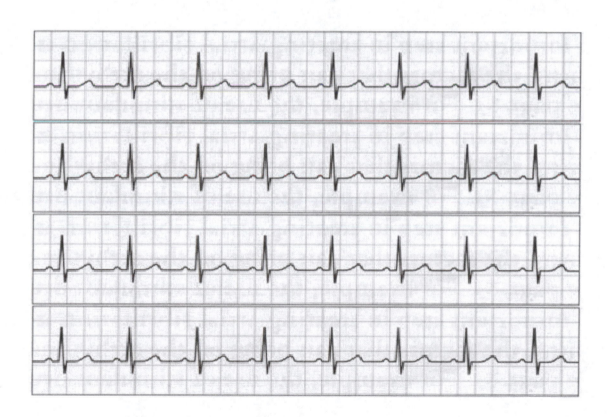

BENSON, Charles   Admission: 04-24-YYYY   EKG REPORT
Case06   DOB: 12-13-YYYY
Dr. Thompson   ROOM: 0204

              Date of EKG: 04-23-YYYY   Time of EKG: 13:56:20

Rate   66
PR   184
QRSD   60
QT   363
QTC   380   Normal.
       -- Axis --
P   76
QRS   79
T   71

                                          Bella Kaplan
                                          Bella Kaplan, M.D.

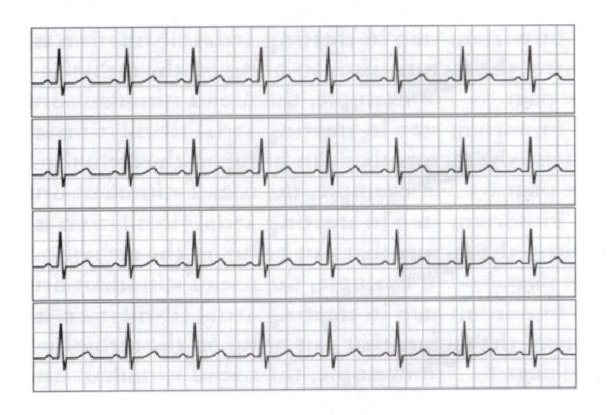

BENSON, Charles   Admission: 04-24-YYYY

Case06   DOB: 12-13-YYYY   **EKG REPORT**

Dr. Thompson   ROOM: 0204

Date of EKG: 04-24-YYYY   Time of EKG: 13:56:20

Rate   66

PR   184

QRSD   60

QT   363   Normal.

QTC   380

-- Axis --

P   76

QRS   79

T   71

Bella Kaplan

Bella Kaplan, M.D.

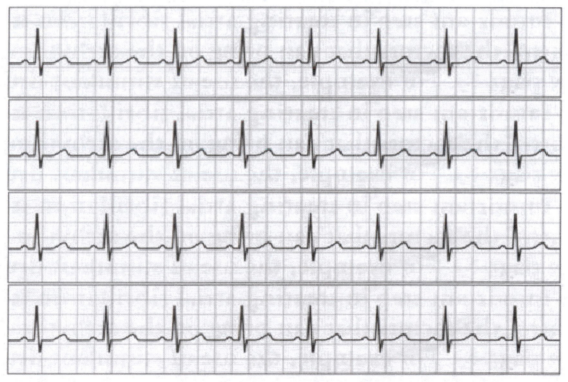

ALFRED STATE MEDICAL CENTER ■ 100 MAIN ST, ALFRED, NY 14802 ■ (607) 555-1234

Case 07

ALFRED STATE MEDICAL CENTER	INPATIENT FACE SHEET

ALFRED STATE MEDICAL CENTER
100 MAIN ST, ALFRED, NY 14802
(607) 555-1234

HOSPITAL #: 000999

PATIENT NAME AND ADDRESS				GENDER	RACE	MARITAL STATUS	PATIENT NO.
HOOVER, Holley E.				F	W	Married	Case07
90 Silver Street				DATE OF BIRTH		MAIDEN NAME	OCCUPATION
Alfred, NY 14802				01-16-YYYY		Berry	Florist

ADMISSION DATE	TIME	DISCHARGE DATE	TIME	LENGTH OF STAY	TELEPHONE NUMBER
04-30-YYYY	15:45	05-02-YYYY	10:10	02 DAYS	(607) 555-6688

GUARANTOR NAME AND ADDRESS	NEXT OF KIN NAME AND ADDRESS
Hoover, Richard	Hoover, Richard
90 Silver Street	90 Silver Street
Alfred, NY 14802	Alfred, NY 14802

GUARANTOR TELEPHONE NO.	RELATIONSHIP TO PATIENT	NEXT OF KIN TELEPHONE NUMBER	RELATIONSHIP TO PATIENT
(607) 555-6688	Husband	(607) 555-6688	Husband

ADMITTING PHYSICIAN	SERVICE	ADMIT TYPE	ROOM NUMBER/BED
Swann MD, Janice	Medical	2	0320/02

ATTENDING PHYSICIAN	ATTENDING PHYSICIAN UPIN	ADMITTING DIAGNOSIS
Swann MD, Janice	100V23	Rule out myocardial infarction

PRIMARY INSURER	POLICY AND GROUP NUMBER	SECONDARY INSURER	POLICY AND GROUP NUMBER
BCBS	332323202 33190	Empire Plan	549087562

DIAGNOSES AND PROCEDURES	ICD-9-CM	ICD-10-CM/PCS
PRINCIPAL DIAGNOSIS		
Reflux esophagitis	530.11	K21.0
SECONDARY DIAGNOSES		
Hiatal hernia	553.3	K44.9
PRINCIPAL PROCEDURE		
SECONDARY PROCEDURES		
TOTAL CHARGES: $ 1,555.95		

ACTIVITY:	☐ Bedrest	☒ Light	☐ Usual	☐ Unlimited	☐ Other:
DIET:	☒ Regular	☐ Low Cholesterol	☐ Low Salt	☐ ADA	☐ _____ Calorie
FOLLOW-UP:	☐ Call for appointment	☒ Office appointment in _one week_	☐ Other:		

SPECIAL INSTRUCTIONS:

Signature of Attending Physician: J Swann, MD

HOOVER, Holley E.   Admission: 04-30-YYYY   CONSENT TO ADMISSION
Case 07   DOB: 01-16-YYYY
Dr. Swann   ROOM: 0320

I, _Holley E. Hoover_ hereby consent to admission to the Alfred State Medical Center (ASMC) , and I further consent to such routine hospital care, diagnostic procedures, and medical treatment that the medical and professional staff of ASMC may deem necessary or advisable. I authorize the use of medical information obtained about me as specified above and the disclosure of such information to my referring physician(s). This form has been fully explained to me, and I understand its contents. I further understand that no guarantees have been made to me as to the results of treatments or examinations done at the ASMC.

Holley E. Hoover
                                  April 30, YYYY

Signature of Patient   Date

Signature of Parent/Legal Guardian for Minor   Date

Relationship to Minor

Andrea Witteman
                                    April 30, yyyy

WITNESS: Alfred State Medical Center Staff Member   Date

CONSENT TO RELEASE INFORMATION FOR REIMBURSEMENT PURPOSES

In order to permit reimbursement, upon request, the Alfred State Medical Center (ASMC) may disclose such treatment information pertaining to my hospitalization to any corporation, organization, or agent thereof, which is, or may be liable under contract to the ASMC or to me, or to any of my family members or other person, for payment of all or part of the ASMC's charges for services rendered to me (e.g., the patient's health insurance carrier). I understand that the purpose of any release of information is to facilitate reimbursement for services rendered. In addition, in the event that my health insurance program includes utilization review of services provided during this admission, I authorize ASMC to release information as is necessary to permit the review. This authorization will expire once the reimbursement for services rendered is complete.

Holley E. Hoover
                                  April 30, YYYY

Signature of Patient   Date

Signature of Parent/Legal Guardian for Minor   Date

Relationship to Minor

Andrea Witteman
                                    April 30, yyyy

WITNESS: Alfred State Medical Center Staff Member   Date

HOOVER, Holley E.	Admission: 04-30-YYYY	ADVANCE DIRECTIVE
Case07	DOB: 01-16-YYYY	
Dr. Swann	ROOM: 0320	

Your answers to the following questions will assist your Physician and the Hospital to respect your wishes regarding your medical care. This information will become a part of your medical record.

	YES	NO	PATIENT'S INITIALS
1. Have you been provided with a copy of the information called "Patient Rights Regarding Health Care Decision?"	X		HEH
2. Have you prepared a "Living Will?" If yes, please provide the Hospital with a copy for your medical record.		X	HEH
3. Have you prepared a Durable Power of Attorney for Health Care? If yes, please provide the Hospital with a copy for your medical record.		X	HEH
4. Have you provided this facility with an Advance Directive on a prior admission and is it still in effect? If yes, Admitting Office to contact Medical Records to obtain a copy for the medical record.		X	HEH
5. Do you desire to execute a Living Will/Durable Power of Attorney? If yes, refer to in order: a. Physician b. Social Service c. Volunteer Service		X	HEH

HOSPITAL STAFF DIRECTIONS: Check when each step is completed.

1. ___✓___ Verify the above questions where answered and actions taken where required.

2. ___✓___ If the "Patient Rights" information was provided to someone other than the patient, state reason:

_____

_____   _____
Name of Individual Receiving Information   Relationship to Patient

3. ___✓___ If information was provided in a language other than English, specify language and method.

4. ___✓___ Verify patient was advised on how to obtain additional information on Advance Directives.

5. ___✓___ Verify the Patient/Family Member/Legal Representative was asked to provide the Hospital with a copy of the Advance Directive which will be retained in the medical record.

File this form in the medical record, and give a copy to the patient.

_____
Name of Patient (Name of Individual giving information if different from Patient)

Holley E. Hoover   April 30, YYYY
_____   _____
Signature of Patient   Date

Andrea Witteman   April 30, YYYY
_____   _____
Signature of Hospital Representative   Date

ALFRED STATE MEDICAL CENTER ■ 100 MAIN ST, ALFRED, NY 14802 ■ (607) 555-1234

HOOVER, Holley E. Admission: 04-30-YYYY	PROGRESS NOTES
Case07 DOB: 01-16-YYYY	
Dr. Swann ROOM: 0320	

Date	(Please skip one line between dates.)
4/30	CC: Chest pain. R/O M.I.
	Plan of Treatment: Rx as needed to R/O M.I.
	Discharge Plan: Home - No services needed J Swann, MD
04/30	MDI 2 puffs each Albuterol/Beclovent. BS harsh. Pulse 68. Resp 20. NPC. Instructed in use of spacer.
	Demonstrated good technique. T. Perry, R.R.T.
05-01 0800	MDI w/ 2 puffs Proventil via spacer – pt. tol well on her own F/B MDI w/ 2 puffs Vanceril – NPC. BS ↓'d clear. L Seraphin C.P.T.
05/01 2035	MDI 2 puffs each Albuterol/Beclovent via spacer w/ excellent technique. BS ↓ clear. T. Perry, R.R.T.
05/01	Pt. has no further pain. She feels well but anxious. Results normal so far. J Swann, MD
05/02	No pain. Results all normal. Will discharge and see in one week. J Swann MD
05-02 0845	MDI w/ 2 puffs Proventil via spacer. F/B MDI w/ 2 puffs Vanceril – pt. tol well on her her own. P 88. RR 20. L Seraphin CPT

HOOVER, Holley E.	Admission: 04-30-YYYY	DOCTORS ORDERS
Case 07	DOB: 01-16-YYYY	
Dr. Swann	ROOM: 0320	

Date	Time	Physician's signature required for each order. (Please skip one line between dates.)
04/30	1815	1. Heparin lock, insert and flush every shift and PRN
		2. EKG with chest pain.
		3. Oxygen – 3 l /min via nasal cannula PRN for chest pain.
		4. Chest pain: NTG 0.4 mg SL q 5 min. x 3. Call physician if not relieved.
		5. Bradycardia: Atropine 0.5 mg IV q 5 min up to 2mg for symptomatic heart
		rate. (Pulse < 50, or > 60 with decreased BP and/or PVC's).
		6. PVC's: Lidocaine 50mg IV push
		Start drip 500 cc D5/W Lidocaine 2gm @ 2 mg/min (30 cc/hr) for
		> six (6) per min or three (3) in a row.
		7.. V-Tach: (If patient hemodynamically stable);
		Lidocaine 50 mg IV push
		Start drip of 500 cc D5/W Lidocaine 2 gm @ 2 mg/min (30cc/hr.)
		(If unstable) Cardiovert @ 50 watt seconds.
		8. V-Fib: Immediately defibrillate @ 200 watt seconds, if not converted;
		Immediately defibrillate @ 300 watt seconds, if not converted;
		Immediately defibrillate @ 360 watt seconds, if not converted;
		Start CPR
		Give Epinephrine (1:10,000) 1 mg IV push
		Give Lidocaine as per V-tach protocol.
		9. Asystole/EMD: Start CPR
		Epinephrine (1:10,000) 1mg IV push
		Atropine 1mg IV push if no response with Epinephrine
		10. Respiratory Arrest: Intubation with mechanical ventilation
		RAV T.O. Dr. Swann/M. Weathers, R.N.
		J Swann, M.D.
4/30		*MDI w/ reservoir b.i.d. and q4 p.r.n. Albuterol 2 puffs. Beclomethasone Dipropionate*
		200 mcg. Goal of Therapy: Bronchodilation. J. Swann, M.D.

HOOVER, Holley E.		Admission: 04-30-YYYY	DOCTORS ORDERS
Case 07		DOB: 01-16-YYYY	
Dr. Swann		ROOM: 0320	

Date	Time	Physician's signature required for each order. (Please skip one line between dates.)
4/30		MDI with reservoir b.i.d. Albuterol Sulfate 1 puff q4h p.r.n.
		Beclomethasone Dipropionate 200 mcg b.i.d.
		Goal of Therapy: Bronchodilation. Bronchial Toilet. Relieve Atelectasis. J. Swann, M.D.
04-30	1537	1) ADMIT TO DR. SWANN
		2) TELEMETRY W/ PROTOCOL
		3) OLD RECORDS
		4) TSH, T4
		5) OXYGEN .625 MG PO / DAILY
		6) TENORETIC - HOLD
		7) DEPAKOTE 500 MG. PO TID
		8) VANCERIL INHALER 2 PUFFS BID
		9) VENTOLIN INHALER 1 PUFF Q4° PRN
		10) ZANTAC 50 MG IV Q8° J. Swann, M.D.
		RAV T.O. DR. SWANN/ C. LOVE RN
04-30		Restoril 30 mg HS. Tylenol tab 2 q 3-4h prn for pain.
		DAT. Telemetr. BRP. J. Swann MD
05/01	1820	Do cardiac profile and EKG now and in AM.
		May take O₂ off and use p.r.n.
		May ambulate as tolerated. RAV T.O. Dr. Swann/ L. Taylor CRN
		J. Swann, M.D.

		HOOVER, Holley E. Case07 Dr. Swann	Admission: 04-30-YYYY DOB: 01-16-YYYY ROOM: 0320	DOCTORS ORDERS

Date	Time	Physician's signature required for each order. (Please skip one line between dates.)
05/01	2100	Continous oximetry during night tonight 05/01/YYYY.　　　J. Swann, M.D.
		RAV　T.O. Dr. Swann/ T. Perry
05/02	0910	D/C IV
		D/C telemetry
		Δ IV Zantac to 150 mg p.o. B.I.D.
		RAV　T.O.Dr. Swann/ L. Taylor CPN
05/02	1010	Discharge
		J. Swann, MD

HOOVER, Holley E.	Admission: 04-30-YYYY	LABORATORY DATA
Case 07	DOB: 01-16-YYYY	
Dr. Swann	ROOM: 0320	

SPECIMEN COLLECTED:	04/30/YYYY	SPECIMEN RECEIVED:	04/30/YYYY

TEST	RESULT	FLAG	REFERENCE
ROUTINE URINALYSIS			
COLOR	STRAW		
SP GRAVITY	1.015		≤ 1.030
GLUCOSE	NEG		≤ 125 mg/dl
BILIRUBIN	NEG		≤ 0.8 mg/dl
KETONE	NEG		≤ 10 mg/dl
BLOOD	NEG		0.06 mg/dl hgb
PH	7.0		5-8
PROTEIN	NEG		≤ 30 mg/dl
UROBILINOGEN	NORMAL		≤ -1 mg/dl
NITRITES	NEG		NEG
LEUKOCYTES	NEG		≤ 15 WBC/hpf
EPITH	4-8		
W.B.C.	RARE		≤ 5/hpf

End of Report

HOOVER, Holley E.   Admission: 04-30-YYYY   LABORATORY DATA
Case07   DOB: 01-16-YYYY
Dr. Swann   ROOM: 0320

SPECIMEN COLLECTED: 4/30/YYYY   **SPECIMEN RECEIVED:**   4/30/YYYY

TEST	RESULT	FLAG	REFERENCE
Glucose	155	**H**	82-115 mg/dl
Creatinine	0.9		0.9-1.4 mg/dl
Sodium	144		136-147 meq/L
Potassium	3.6	**L**	3.7-5.1 meq/L
Chloride	105		98-108 meq/L
Total CO2	29		24-32 meqL
Calcium	9.2		8.8-10.5 mg/dl
WBC	5.0		4.5-10.8 thous/UL
RBC	4.46		4.2-5.4 mill/UL
HGB	13.5		12-16 g/dl
HCT	40.4		37.0-47.0 %
Platelets	288		130-400 thous/UL
PTT	22		< 32 seconds
Protime	12.3		11.0-13.0 seconds

End of Report

HOOVER, Holley E.   Admission: 04-30-YYYY   LABORATORY DATA
Case 07   DOB: 01-16-YYYY
Dr. Swann   ROOM: 0320

SPECIMEN COLLECTED: 4/30/YYYY   **SPECIMEN RECEIVED:**   4/30/YYYY

TEST	RESULT	FLAG	REFERENCE
Urea Nitrogen	17		7-18 mg/dl
Alkaline Phosphatase	90		50-136 U/L
SGOT	27		15-37 U/L
Lactic Dehydrogenase	158		100-190 U/L
Phosphorus	2.8		2.5-4.9 mg/dl
Total Bilirubin	0.3		0.0-1.1 mg/dl
Total Protein	6.7		6.4-8.2 g/dl
Albumin	3.4		3.4-5.0 g/dl
Uric Acid	5.7	**H**	2.6-5.6 mg/dl
Cholesterol	193	***	< 200mg/dl

CARDIAC PROFILE & MG PANEL

Creatine Kinase	177		21-215 U/L
CKMB	5.6		0.0-6.0 ng/ml
Relative Index	3.2	**H**	0.0-2.5 U/L
Magnesium	1.8		1.8-2.4 mg/dl

End of Report

```
HOOVER, Holley E.      Admission: 04-30-YYYY          LABORATORY DATA
Case07                 DOB: 01-16-YYYY
Dr. Swann              ROOM: 0320
```

SPECIMEN COLLECTED: 05/01/YYYY   SPECIMEN RECEIVED: 05/01/YYYY

TEST	RESULT	FLAG	REFERENCE
Creatine Kinase	86		21-215 U/L
CKMB	2.4		0.0-6.0 ng/ml

End of Report

HOOVER, Holley E.   Admission: 04-30-YYYY   LABORATORY DATA
Case 07   DOB: 01-16-YYYY
Dr. Swann   ROOM: 0320

SPECIMEN COLLECTED: 05/02YYYY   SPECIMEN RECEIVED: 05/02YYYY

TEST	RESULT	FLAG	REFERENCE
Creatine Kinase	69		21-215 U/L
CKMB	1.7		0.0-6.0 ng/ml

End of Report

HOOVER, Holley E.   Admission: 04-30-YYYY   LABORATORY DATA
Case 07   DOB: 01-16-YYYY
Dr. Swann   ROOM: 0320

SPECIMEN COLLECTED: 05/03YYYY   **SPECIMEN RECEIVED:**   05/03YYYY

TEST	RESULT	FLAG	REFERENCE
T4	6.3		4.9-10.7 UG/DL
TSH	2.57		0.38-6.15 UIU/ML

End of Report

HOOVER, Holley E.   Admission: 04-30-YYYY   **EKG REPORT**
Case 07   DOB: 01-16-YYYY
Dr. Swann   ROOM: 0320

                           Date of EKG   Time of EKG 14:22:13

Rate   81   04-30-Y Y Y Y
PR   152
QRSD   72
QT   35
QTC   424
          -- Axis --   Sinus Rhythm Normal
P   46
QRS   6
T   -1   Bella Kaplan, MD

                                          Bella Kaplan, M.D.
                                          Name of Physician

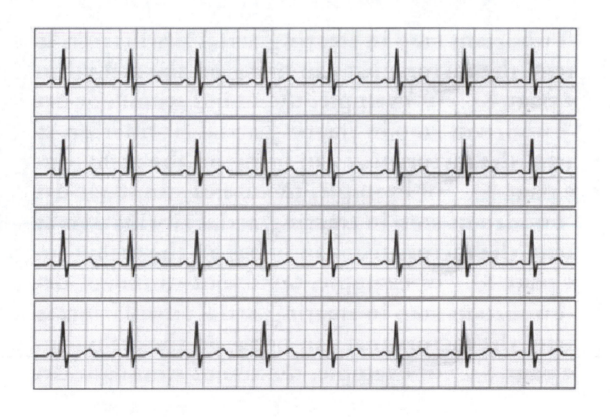

HOOVER, Holley E.
Case 07
Dr. Swann

Admission: 04-30-YYYY
DOB: 01-16-YYYY
ROOM: 0320

Date of EKG   Time of EKG 17:06:34

EKG REPORT

Rate	69
PR	153
QRSD	68
QT	383
QTC	410
-- Axis --	
P	4
QRS	1
T	-14

05-01-YYYY
Tw ↓ sl v3-4
st

Minor nonspecific t-wave lowering.
Stable.

Bella Kaplan, MD

Bella Kaplan, M.D.

Name of Physician

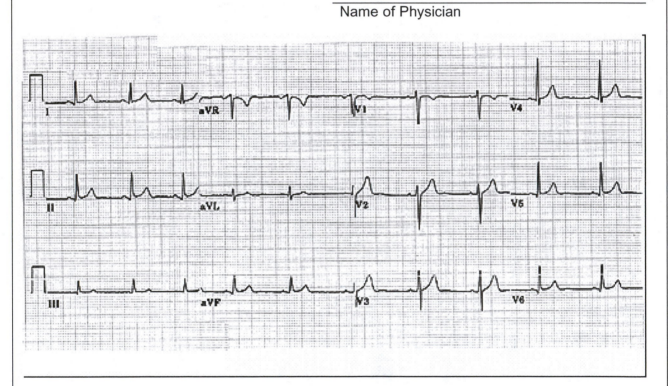

HOOVER, Holley E.
Case 07
Dr. Swann

Admission: 04-30-YYYY
DOB: 01-16-YYYY
ROOM: 0320

EKG REPORT

Date of EKG   Time of EKG 8:20:35

Rate	66
PR	151
QRSD	65
QT	388
QTC	406
-- Axis --	
P	5
QRS	13
T	0

05-02-YYYY

Normal - twaves back to normal today

Bella Kaplan, MD

Bella Kaplan, M.D.
_____
Name of Physician

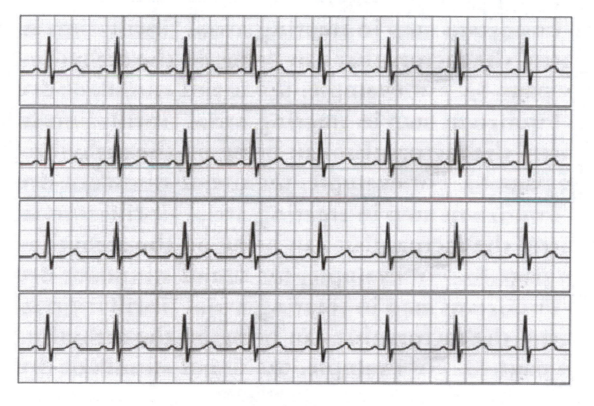

Case 08

ALFRED STATE MEDICAL CENTER 100 MAIN ST, ALFRED, NY 14802 (607) 555-1234 HOSPITAL #: 000999	INPATIENT FACE SHEET

PATIENT NAME AND ADDRESS				GENDER	RACE	MARITAL STATUS	PATIENT NO.
MASON, Molly P. 645 Chicago Lane Alfred, NY 14802				F	W	Single	Case08
				DATE OF BIRTH	MAIDEN NAME		OCCUPATION
				03-01-YYYY			Child

ADMISSION DATE	TIME	DISCHARGE DATE	TIME	LENGTH OF STAY	TELEPHONE NUMBER
04-28-YYYY	23:30	05-02-YYYY	13:00	04 DAYS	(607) 555-8866

GUARANTOR NAME AND ADDRESS	NEXT OF KIN NAME AND ADDRESS
Mason, Irene 645 Chicago Lane Alfred, NY 14802	Mason, Irene 645 Chicago Lane Alfred, NY 14802

GUARANTOR TELEPHONE NO.	RELATIONSHIP TO PATIENT	NEXT OF KIN TELEPHONE NUMBER	RELATIONSHIP TO PATIENT
(607) 555-8866	Mother	(607) 555-8866	Mother

ADMITTING PHYSICIAN	SERVICE	ADMIT TYPE	ROOM NUMBER/BED
Ghann, MD Alan	Ped Med	2	0328/02

ATTENDING PHYSICIAN	ATTENDING PHYSICIAN UPIN	ADMITTING DIAGNOSIS
Ghann, MD Alan	100A90	R/O out respiratory syncytial virus

PRIMARY INSURER	POLICY AND GROUP NUMBER	SECONDARY INSURER	POLICY AND GROUP NUMBER
BC/BS of WNY	262723444 44150	Empire Plan	88765431

DIAGNOSES AND PROCEDURES	ICD-9-CM	ICD-10-CM/PCS
PRINCIPAL DIAGNOSIS		
Bronchiolitis due to RSV ✝	466.11	J21.0
SECONDARY DIAGNOSES		
PRINCIPAL PROCEDURE		
SECONDARY PROCEDURES TOTAL CHARGES: $ 2,605.35		

ACTIVITY:	☐ Bedrest	☑ Light	☐ Usual	☐ Unlimited	☐ Other:
DIET:	☑ Regular	☐ Low Cholesterol	☐ Low Salt	☐ ADA	☐ _____ Calorie
FOLLOW-UP:	☐ Call for appointment	☐ Office appointment on ____	☐ Other:		

SPECIAL INSTRUCTIONS: *Call for appt. w/ Dr. Ghann in 4 days; sooner if any problems (555-3456)*

Signature of Attending Physician: *Alan Ghann, MD*

MASON, Molly P.   Admission: 04-28-YYYY   CONSENT TO ADMISSION
Case 08   DOB: 03-01-YYYY
Dr. Ghann   ROOM: 0328

I, __Molly P. Mason__ hereby consent to admission to the Alfred State Medical Center (ASMC) , and I further consent to such routine hospital care, diagnostic procedures, and medical treatment that the medical and professional staff of ASMC may deem necessary or advisable. I authorize the use of medical information obtained about me as specified above and the disclosure of such information to my referring physician(s). This form has been fully explained to me, and I understand its contents. I further understand that no guarantees have been made to me as to the results of treatments or examinations done at the ASMC.

Molly P. Mason   _April 28, YYYY_
Signature of Patient   Date

Irene Mason   _April 28, YYYY_
Signature of Parent/Legal Guardian for Minor   Date

Mother
Relationship to Minor

Andrea Witteman   _April 28, YYYY_
WITNESS: Alfred State Medical Center Staff Member   Date

CONSENT TO RELEASE INFORMATION FOR REIMBURSEMENT PURPOSES

In order to permit reimbursement, upon request, the Alfred State Medical Center (ASMC) may disclose such treatment information pertaining to my hospitalization to any corporation, organization, or agent thereof, which is, or may be liable under contract to the ASMC or to me, or to any of my family members or other person, for payment of all or part of the ASMC's charges for services rendered to me (e.g. the patient's health insurance carrier). I understand that the purpose of any release of information is to facilitate reimbursement for services rendered. In addition, in the event that my health insurance program includes utilization review of services provided during this admission, I authorize ASMC to release information as is necessary to permit the review. This authorization will expire once the reimbursement for services rendered is complete.

Molly P. Mason   _April 28, YYYY_
Signature of Patient   Date

Irene Mason   _April 28, YYYY_
Signature of Parent/Legal Guardian for Minor   Date

Mother
Relationship to Minor

Andrea Witteman   _April 28, YYYY_
WITNESS: Alfred State Medical Center Staff Member   Date

MASON, Molly P.	Admission: 04-28-YYYY	ADVANCE DIRECTIVE
Case 08	DOB: 03-01-YYYY	
Dr. Ghann	ROOM: 0328	

Your answers to the following questions will assist your Physician and the Hospital to respect your wishes regarding your medical care. This information will become a part of your medical record.

	YES	NO	PATIENT'S INITIALS
1. Have you been provided with a copy of the information called "Patient Rights Regarding Health Care Decision?"	X		IM
2. Have you prepared a "Living Will?" If yes, please provide the Hospital with a copy for your medical record.		X	IM
3. Have you prepared a Durable Power of Attorney for Health Care? If yes, please provide the Hospital with a copy for your medical record.		X	IM
4. Have you provided this facility with an Advance Directive on a prior admission and is it still in effect? If yes, Admitting Office to contact Medical Records to obtain a copy for the medical record.		X	IM
5. Do you desire to execute a Living Will/Durable Power of Attorney? If yes, refer to in order: a. Physician b. Social Service c. Volunteer Service		X	IM

HOSPITAL STAFF DIRECTIONS: Check when each step is completed.

1. ✓ Verify the above questions where answered and actions taken where required.

2. ✓ If the "Patient Rights" information was provided to someone other than the patient, state reason:

IRENE MASON	Mother
Name of Individual Receiving Information	Relationship to Patient

3. ✓ If information was provided in a language other than English, specify language and method.

4. ✓ Verify patient was advised on how to obtain additional information on Advance Directives.

5. ✓ Verify the Patient/Family Member/Legal Representative was asked to provide the Hospital with a copy of the Advance Directive which will be retained in the medical record.

File this form in the medical record, and give a copy to the patient.

Name of Patient (Name of Individual giving information if different from Patient)

Irene Mason (Mother)	April 28, YYYY
Signature of Patient	Date
Andrea Witteman	April 28, YYYY
Signature of Hospital Representative	Date

ALFRED STATE MEDICAL CENTER ■ 100 MAIN ST, ALFRED, NY 14802 ■ (607) 555-1234

```
MASON, Molly P.        Admission: 04-28-YYYY        HISTORY & PHYSICAL EXAM
Case08                 DOB: 03-01-YYYY
Dr. Ghann              ROOM: 0328
```

DATE OF ADMISSION: 04/28/YYYY

CHIEF COMPLAINT, HISTORY OF PRESENT ILLNESS: This six-week-old presented to the office secondary to acute respiratory distress with intercostal retractions, nasal drainage, respiratory distress, difficulty in eating, and rapid respiratory rate. Molly was found to have clinical signs and symptoms of RSV with respiratory decompensation and was recommended admission to the hospital for the same.

PAST MEDICAL HISTORY: Was born of an uncomplicated birth. She had been healthy up until this date. No pre-existing medical problems. No surgeries.

PAST SUGICAL HISTORY: Negative.

HABITS: None.

ALLERGIES: None.

MEDICATIONS: None.

SOCIAL HISTORY: Noncontributory.

FAMILY HISTORY: Noncontributory.

REVIEW OF SYSTEMS: As noted in PMH and CC above.

VITAL SIGNS: TPR's were 98.9, birth weight was 6 lbs. 1 oz., pulse 160, respirations 40, actual weight was 11 lbs. 4 oz. Height was 21 ¼".

HEENT: Head was normocephalic. Ears were clear. She had a serious rhinitis, thick, with posterior pharynx noninjected.

NECK: Noncontributory.

LUNGS: Ausculted with diffuse wheezes and rhonchi with intercostal retraction. Rapid respiratory rate at the time of admission to the office was up to 50-60.

CARDIAC: Noncontributory.

ABDOMEN: Soft without organomegaly or masses.

EXTERNAL GENITALIA: Normal.

RECTAL: Externally was normal.

EXTREMITIES: Revealed good pedal pulses. No ulcerations, cyanosis, clubbing or edema.

NEUROLOGIC: Intact with no neurologic abnormalities.

LABS: RSV testing was positive by EIA testing. She had 9.4 white count on admission with 14.7 hgb, 429 platelets, 18 segs, 70 lymphs, 10 monos, 2 eos. O2 sats on room air were between 96 and 98.

IMPRESSION: 1) RSV with associated bronchiolitis and bronchospasms.

PLAN: Patient is to be admitted to the hospital with croup tent. CPT therapy. See orders.

DD: 04-30-YYYY

DT: 04-30-YYYY

Alan Ghann, MD

Alan Ghann, MD

MASON, Molly P. Admission: 04-28-YYYY	PROGRESS NOTES
Case 08 DOB: 03-01-YYYY	
Dr. Ghann ROOM: 0328	

Date	(Please skip one line between dates.)
04-29	Hhn 0.25 ml Proventil NSS via blow-by w/ pt. held by grandmother; HR 148-150 R 32
0025	O2 Sat R/A 98%. BS ↓'d. Harsh cough w/ /-E squeaks, squaks. Pt out of tent.
	Tent analyzed @ 37 % w/ tent windowed. E. Blossom, CRTT
04-29	HHN w/ 0.25 ml Proventil / N.S.S. tx given blow by while pt.slept in tent. Pt tolerated tx well.
0730	B.S. ↓'d bases – no cough O2 Sat 100% in O2 tent. D. Davenport, CRTT
04-29	Hhn w/ 0.25 ml Proventil + normal saline. Tol. Rx well. BS↓ clear. NPC In tent pre & post.
1130	R. Rose, CPT
04-29	Rx as above. No changes
1530	R. Rose, CPT
04-29	↓ Wheezing and responding to CPT therapy. Lungs difuse ronchi. Wheeze and vitals good. RSV – responding to tx.
1800	Alan Ghann, MD
04-29	Hhn w/ 0.25 ml Proventil / N.S.S. tx given blow by. HR 149, RR 40. Pt cried through entire tx. Pt was in
2005	tent pre- and post. E. Blossom, CRTT
04-30	Hh neb. Rx w/ 025 ml Proventil + NSS given – P 130 – RR 40 BS harsh w/ wheezes in
0750	tent. Sleeping. SPo2 – 99% in tent – tol well. L Seraphin CPT
04-30	~~Slow improvement of croup s&s. Only 3 hrs of cough jag last. Slept 7-7 last evening to a.m.~~
	~~Afebrile. Cough less harsh and throat ↓ soreness. Lungs clear. Cardiac RRR. Ab soft.~~
	~~Imp~~ Error. Note written in wrong patient's chart. M. Harris, M.D.

MASON, Molly P.	Admission: 04-28-YYYY
Case08	DOB: 03-01-YYYY
Dr. Ghann	ROOM: 0328

PROGRESS NOTES

Date	(Please skip one line between dates.)
04-30	No evidence of wheeze today. Green → white nasal drainage. Afebrile.
	Lungs clear. Cardiac RRR. O₂ SAT ↓ last evening.
	Imp: RSV, resolving. Bronchitis.
	Plans as per orders.
	Alan Ghann, MD
04-30 1600	Referral received for hand held nebulizer at home - contact w/ mother - She chooses Hub as DME provider - mother chooses to go to Hub & pick up HHN this noon. Hub's notified. Nursing aware.
	E. Kravitz, RN
04-30 1130	Hh neb. Rx w/ 0.25 ml Proventil + NSS - P 120 - RR 28. BS wheezes - pt. cried for Rx in tent pre + post Rx. L Seraphin CPT
04-30 1520	Hh neb. Rx given by mom w/ 0.25 ml Proventil + NSS - BS harsh - pt. tol. well - Mom understood med + Rx SPO2 - 99% in tent. L Seraphin CPT
04-30 1945	HHN w/ 0.2 ml Albuterol & NSS via blow-by. Slept thru tx. BS harsh. Pulse 150. Resp 30.
	E. Blossom, RRT
04-30	O2 SAT ↓ out of tent. Pt. has loose cough, no active wheezing, and is afebrile. Eats well.
	Imp: RSV resolving. Plan: Home HHN. O2 SAT good
	Alan Ghann, MD
05-01 0745	Hh neb. Rx w/ 0.25 ml Proventil + NSS given - P 164 - RR 44. BS harsh. Pt. in tent, sleeping. For Rx - SPO2 - 96-97% - tent 32% - harsh cough. L Seraphin CPT

MASON, Molly P. Case08 Dr. Ghann	Admission: 04-28-YYYY DOB: 03-01-YYYY ROOM: 0328	PROGRESS NOTES

Date	(Please skip one line between dates.)
05-01 1115	Hh neb. Rx w/ 0.25 ml Proventil + NSS given - P 163 - RR 48. BS harsh. Pt. out of tent for Rx - SPo2 - 98% on RA - pt. cried for Rx - given by dad.
	L. Seraphin CPT
05-01 1520	Hh neb. Rx w/ 0.25 ml Proventil + NSS given - P 162 - RR 28. BS clearing w/ harsh. NPC - out of tent for Rx - SPo2 - 97-98% on RA - Rx given by Grandma. Tol. Well.
	L. Seraphin CPT
05-01 1930	HHN w/ 0.25 ml Albuterol & NSS via blow-by. BS harsh. O2 SAT 93% RA Pulse 160. Resp 40.
	E. Blossom, RRT
05-02	S: Feeding well. Virtually no residual wheeze or cough.
	O: Afebrile. VSS. SATS maintaining outside tent > 92%.
	Chest - good air on vent, no retractions - wheeze or stridor.
	COR: RRR
	ABD: soft
	EXTR: ⊖ cyanosis.
	A/P. RSV +. Bronchiolitis: resolving.
	D/C to home w/ hhn and steroids. See instructions.
	Alan Ghann, MD
05-02 0720	Hh neb. Rx w/ 0.25 ml Proventil + NSS given - P 180 - RR 48 BS harsh w/ wheezes SPo2 - 98% - RA - pt. tol Rx well.
	L. Seraphin CPT
05-02 1100	Rx same as above BS wheezes P 120 RR 40 pt. out of tent. tol. well.
	L. Seraphin CPT

MASON, Molly P.		Admission: 04-28-YYYY	DOCTORS ORDERS
Case08		DOB: 03-01-YYYY	
Dr. Ghann		ROOM: 0328	

Date	Time	Physician's signature required for each order. (Please skip one line between dates.)
04-28		Hand Held Nebulizer (Spontaneous Aerosol) q.i.d. and q4° p.r.n.
		Nebulizer and IPPB Medications: Albuterol Sulfate (Proventil) 0.5% 0.25 ml, Normal Saline 3 ml
		Croupette, low O2 30-50%
		O2 SAT q shift
		Bronchodilation
		Alan Ghann, MD
04-28	2330	Admit to Service Dr. Ghann.
		Dx: RSV - Bronchiolitis
		Chest x-ray - R/O pneumonia
		CBC
		uA
		O2 Croup Tent
		Tylenol 0.4 ml infant dropper q4° prn temp
		RSV - nasal aspirator for titre
		Old chart to floor
		Dict
		Similac formula
		Pedialyte
		Alan Ghann, MD
04-29	0330	Contact isolation.
		R.A.V. T.O. Dr. Ghann/M. Smith, RN
		Alan Ghann, MD

MASON, Molly P.	Admission: 04-28-YYYY	DOCTORS ORDERS
Case08	DOB: 03-01-YYYY	
Dr. Ghann	ROOM: 0328	

Date	Time	Physician's signature required for each order. (Please skip one line between dates.)
04-30	0855	For home HHN
		Begin Decadron 1/2 tsp, t.i.d. x 2 days, then b.i.d.
		Alan Ghann, MD
05-02	1300	D/C to home if home nebulizer & parental instruction in use of HHN is arranged.
		Label Decadron Elixir for home
		1/2 tsp 2x day for 2 days then
		1/2 tsp 1x day for 2 days then stop
		R.A.V. T.O. Dr. Ghann/ G. Goebel, RN
		Alan Ghann, MD

MASON, Molly P.   Admission: 04-28-YYYY
Case08   DOB: 03-01-YYYY
Dr. Ghann   ROOM: 0328

LABORATORY DATA

SPECIMEN COLLECTED: 04/30/YYYY   **SPECIMEN RECEIVED:** 04/30/YYYY

TEST	RESULT	FLAG	REFERENCE
ROUTINE URINALYSIS			
COLOR	STRAW		
SP GRAVITY	1.001		≤ 1.030
GLUCOSE	NEG		NEG
BILIRUBIN	NEG		≤ 0.8 mg/dl
KETONE	NEG		≤ 10 mg/dl
BLOOD	NEG		0.06 mg/dl hgb
PH	8.0		5-8.0
PROTEIN	NEG		≤ 30 mg/dl
UROBILINOGEN	NORMAL		≤ -1 mg/dl
NITRITE	NEG		NEG
LEUKOCYTES	NEG		≤ 15 WBC/hpf
EPITH	5-8		/hpf
W.B.C.	0-3		≤ 5/hpf

End of Report

MASON, Molly P. Admission: 04-28-YYYY
Case08 DOB: 03-01-YYYY LABORATORY DATA
Dr. Ghann ROOM: 0328

SPECIMEN COLLECTED: 04/30/YYYY SPECIMEN RECEIVED: 04/30/YYYY

TEST	RESULT	FLAG	REFERENCE
CBC			
RBC	4.93		4.2-5.4 mill/UL
WBC	9.4		4.5-10.8 thous/UL
HGB	14.7		12-16 g/dl
HCT	43.6		37.0-47.0 %
Platelets	429		130-400 thous/UL
Total CO2	29.8		24-32 meqL
SEGS	18		
LYMPH	70		
MONO	10		
EOS	2		
BASO			

End of Report

MASON, Molly P.   Admission: 04-28-YYYY
Case08   DOB: 03-01-YYYY   LABORATORY DATA
Dr. Ghann   ROOM: 0328

SPECIMEN COLLECTED: 04/29/YYYY   DATE DONE: 04/29/YYYY

TEST   **RESULT**   **FLAG**   **REFERENCE**

RSV - Nasal Aspirate for Titre

POS by EIA Testing

End of Report

MASON, Molly P.   Admission: 04-28-YYYY
Case08   DOB: 03-01-YYYY   PULSE OXIMETRY
Dr. Ghann   ROOM: 0328

TIME	SPO2	F102	TECH
04/28 2235	98%	R/A	RB
2400	Tent analyzed	@	36.7
04/29 0730	100%	O2 tent	GM
2005	84%	R/A	PT
2350	91%	O2 tent	PT
04/30 0750	99%	35.5 tent	DS
1625	99%	tent	DS
1930	98%	R/A out of tent	HK
05/01 0155	96%	O2 tent	GB
0745	96%	32% tent	DS
0830	96%	R/A	DS
1520	97%	R/A	DS
2030	93%	R/A x 1 hr	LT
2245	96%	R/A tent	LT
05/02 0355	98%	R/A	GB
0720	98%	R/A	DS

End of Report

```
MASON, Molly P.          Admission: 04-28-YYYY          RADIOLOGY REPORT
Case08                   DOB: 03-01-YYYY
Dr. Ghann                ROOM: 0328
```

Initial Diagnosis/History:

Date Requested:

Transport: ☑ Wheelchair ☐ Stretcher ☐ O$_2$ ☐ IV
☑ IP ☐ OP ☐ ER ☐ PRE OP ☐ OR/RR ☐ Portable

CHEST: PA and lateral views reveals the heart and mediastinum to be normal. The lung fields are clear and the bony thorax is normal.

CONCLUSION: Normal chest.

DD: 04-29-YYYY

DT: 04-29-YYYY

Philip Rogers
_____
Philip Rogers, M.D., Radiologist

Case 09

ALFRED STATE MEDICAL CENTER 100 MAIN ST, ALFRED, NY 14802 (607) 555-1234 HOSPITAL #: 000999					INPATIENT FACE SHEET		

PATIENT NAME AND ADDRESS				GENDER	RACE	MARITAL STATUS	PATIENT NO.
LUCK, Deborah L. 2399 Route 244 Alfred Station, NY 14802				F	W	M	Case09

				DATE OF BIRTH	MAIDEN NAME		OCCUPATION
				11-21-YYYY	Steinbeck		Teacher

ADMISSION DATE	TIME	DISCHARGE DATE	TIME	LENGTH OF STAY	TELEPHONE NUMBER	
05-01-YYYY	11:30	05-02-YYYY	11:50	01 DAYS	(607) 555-0909	

GUARANTOR NAME AND ADDRESS	NEXT OF KIN NAME AND ADDRESS
LUCK, David 2399 Route 244 Alfred Station, NY 14802	LUCK, David 2399 Route 244 Alfred Station, NY 14802

GUARANTOR TELEPHONE NO.	RELATIONSHIP TO PATIENT	NEXT OF KIN TELEPHONE NUMBER	RELATIONSHIP TO PATIENT
(607) 555-0909	Husband	(607) 555-0909	Husband

ADMITTING PHYSICIAN	SERVICE	ADMIT TYPE	ROOM NUMBER/BED
Ghann, MD Alan	Medical	2	0374/01

ATTENDING PHYSICIAN	ATTENDING PHYSICIAN UPIN	ADMITTING DIAGNOSIS	
Ghann, MD Alan	100A90	Asthma	

PRIMARY INSURER	POLICY AND GROUP NUMBER	SECONDARY INSURER	POLICY AND GROUP NUMBER
Empire Plan	556705250		

DIAGNOSES AND PROCEDURES	ICD-9-CM	ICD-10-CM/PCS
PRINCIPAL DIAGNOSIS		
Severe RAD	493.92	J45.901
SECONDARY DIAGNOSES		
w/ metabolic acidosis	276.2	E87.2
PRINCIPAL PROCEDURE		
SECONDARY PROCEDURES		
TOTAL CHARGES: $ 1,955.95		

ACTIVITY:	❑ Bedrest	❑ Light	❑ Usual	❑ Unlimited	❑ Other:
DIET:	❑ Regular	❑ Low Cholesterol	❑ Low Salt	❑ ADA	❑ _____ Calorie
FOLLOW-UP:	❑ Call for appointment	❑ Office appointment on ____	❑ Other:		

SPECIAL INSTRUCTIONS:

Signature of Attending Physician: *Alan Ghann, MD*

```
LUCK, Deborah L.        Admission: 05-01-YYYY
Case 09                 DOB: 11-21-YYYY
Dr. Ghann               ROOM: 0374
```

CONSENT TO ADMISSION

I, *Deborah L. Luck* hereby consent to admission to the Alfred State Medical Center (ASMC) , and I further consent to such routine hospital care, diagnostic procedures, and medical treatment that the medical and professional staff of ASMC may deem necessary or advisable. I authorize the use of medical information obtained about me as specified above and the disclosure of such information to my referring physician(s). This form has been fully explained to me, and I understand its contents. I further understand that no guarantees have been made to me as to the results of treatments or examinations done at the ASMC.

Deborah L. Luck   *May 1, YYYY*
_____   _____
Signature of Patient   Date

_____   _____
Signature of Parent/Legal Guardian for Minor   Date

_____
Relationship to Minor

Andrea Witteman   *May 1, YYYY*
_____   _____
WITNESS: Alfred State Medical Center Staff Member   Date

CONSENT TO RELEASE INFORMATION FOR REIMBURSEMENT PURPOSES

In order to permit reimbursement, upon request, the Alfred State Medical Center (ASMC) may disclose such treatment information pertaining to my hospitalization to any corporation, organization, or agent thereof, which is, or may be liable under contract to the ASMC or to me, or to any of my family members or other person, for payment of all or part of the ASMC's charges for services rendered to me (e.g. the patient's health insurance carrier). I understand that the purpose of any release of information is to facilitate reimbursement for services rendered. In addition, in the event that my health insurance program includes utilization review of services provided during this admission, I authorize ASMC to release information as is necessary to permit the review. This authorization will expire once the reimbursement for services rendered is complete.

Deborah L. Luck   *May 1, YYYY*
_____   _____
Signature of Patient   Date

_____   _____
Signature of Parent/Legal Guardian for Minor   Date

_____
Relationship to Minor

Andrea Witteman   *May 1, YYYY*
_____   _____
WITNESS: Alfred State Medical Center Staff Member   Date

```
LUCK, Deborah L.        Admission: 05-01-YYYY
Case 09                 DOB: 11-21-YYYY
Dr. Ghann               ROOM: 0374
```

ADVANCE DIRECTIVE

Your answers to the following questions will assist your Physician and the Hospital to respect your wishes regarding your medical care. This information will become a part of your medical record.

		YES	NO	PATIENT'S INITIALS
1.	Have you been provided with a copy of the information called "Patient Rights Regarding Health Care Decision?"	X		DLL
2.	Have you prepared a "Living Will?" If yes, please provide the Hospital with a copy for your medical record.		X	DLL
3.	Have you prepared a Durable Power of Attorney for Health Care? If yes, please provide the Hospital with a copy for your medical record.		X	DLL
4.	Have you provided this facility with an Advance Directive on a prior admission and is it still in effect? If yes, Admitting Office to contact Medical Records to obtain a copy for the medical record.		X	DLL
5.	Do you desire to execute a Living Will/Durable Power of Attorney? If yes, refer to in order: a. Physician b. Social Service c. Volunteer Service		X	DLL

HOSPITAL STAFF DIRECTIONS: Check when each step is completed.

1. ___✓___ Verify the above questions where answered and actions taken where required.

2. ___✓___ If the "Patient Rights" information was provided to someone other than the patient, state reason:

_____

_____   _____
Name of Individual Receiving Information   Relationship to Patient

3. ___✓___ If information was provided in a language other than English, specify language and method.

4. ___✓___ Verify patient was advised on how to obtain additional information on Advance Directives.

5. ___✓___ Verify the Patient/Family Member/Legal Representative was asked to provide the Hospital with a copy of the Advance Directive which will be retained in the medical record.

File this form in the medical record, and give a copy to the patient.

_____
Name of Patient (Name of Individual giving information if different from Patient)

Deborah L. Luck   *May 1, YYYY*
_____   _____
Signature of Patient   Date

Andrea Witteman   *May 1, YYYY*
_____   _____
Signature of Hospital Representative   Date

ALFRED STATE MEDICAL CENTER ■ 100 MAIN ST, ALFRED, NY 14802 ■ (607) 555-1234

LUCK, Deborah L.	Admission: 05-01-YYYY	HISTORY & PHYSICAL EXAM
Case09	DOB: 11-21-YYYY	
Dr. Ghann	ROOM: 0374	PAGE 1 OF 2

Mrs. Luck is a 37-year-old white female with past medical history significant for severe reactive airways disease who presents to the Emergency Room in respiratory distress. CHIEF COMPLAINT: Difficulty breathing progressive over the past two days.

HPI: Patient was in her usual state of health until approximately two days ago when she developed worsening of her asthma. She did not seek medical attention at that time and her symptoms progressed over the point where last night she was having difficulty sleeping. She was sitting on the edge of her bed most of the night in moderate respiratory distress. She presented to the ER this morning for evaluation and was found to be in moderately severe respiratory distress with impaired oxygenation. She is unable to give a meaningful history at this point because she is so dyspneic she cannot talk. However, she states she has not had fevers or chest pain. She has had a slight cough and she is not sure if this is due to bronchitis, infectious process or if this was due to her dyspnea. She has had a scant amount of sputum production over the past 12 hrs.

PAST HISTORY: Reactive airways disease as mentioned in the HPI. She has had one previous hospital admission. Status post C-section times two. Tonsillectomy, adenoidectany. Cholecystectany. Appendectomy. Right shoulder surgery. Bilateral tubal ligation.

MEDICATIONS: Proventil MDI p.rn. Azrnacort 2 puffs bi.d. Prednisone courses are required from time to time. She is currently taking Advil for a toothache. ALLERGIES: Codeine, Penicillin

FAMILY HISTORY: Her father is alive with coronary artery disease post MI. Her mother is alive with diabetes mellitus, CAD, cerebrovascular disease. She has two female siblings who are alive and well with no identified health problems. There is no identified history of reactive airways disease or extrinsic asthma.

SOCIAL HISTORY: She lives with her husband and two children in Alfred Station, NY. Her children are ages 13 and 15. Habits include nonsmoking, minimal alcohol use. No excessive caffeine use. She denies excessive over the counter drug use.

ROS: LMP three weeks ago. She denies swallowing difficulties, chest pain, change in bowel habits. She has had no urinary symptoms of dysuria, frequency or urgency. She has had no joint pain, weight loss, weight gain, temperature intolerance. She performs breast self exam and has noted no new breast lesions. The remainder of the ROS is noncontributory except as mentioned in the HPI.

VITAL SIGNS: Upon presentation to the Emergency Room blood pressure was 180/120. Later repeated was 160/100. Temperature was 97.8 orally, pulse 140, respirations 40 initially. Slowed to 24 after a nebulizer treatment.

GENERAL: The patient is in moderate respiratory distress sitting on the hospital cart, alert and oriented and answers questions although she is severely dyspneic.

HEENT: Head atraumatic, normocephalic. TM's are grey bilaterally. PERRL at 2 mm. diameter. Sclera anicteric. Pharynx is moist with no lesions noted. NECK: Supple. There is no adenopathy.

CHEST: Reveals very poor air movement and marked expiratory wheezing throughout her entire lung field. There are no areas of decreased breath sounds. There are no crackles or rhonchi. HEART: Tachycardic, regular with no murmurs.

ABDOMEN: Soft, obese, nontender. No organomegaly.

BREASTS: Without masses, retractions, dimpling. There is no adenopathy.

PELVIC/RECTAL: Deferred due to patient discomfort. Will be performed during her hospital course.

Continued on next page.

EXTREMITIES: Without edema, cyanosis. They are warm to touch and well perfused. Good distal pulses are appreciated.

NEUROLOGIC: Is nonfocal. She is alert and oriented. Has no motor or sensory deficits. Cranial nerves 2-12 are grossly intact.

LAB DATA: White count 21,300, hgb. 14.8, platelets 369, segs 87, bands 4, lymphs 7. SCG II is pending. Initial blood gas on 15 liters nonrebreather face mask revealed pH of 7.286, PCO2 of 43.8, PO2 90.4, 94.6 saturated. Chest X-ray is pending at the time of this dictation.

IMPRESSION/PLAN: 37-year-old white female with known reactive airways disease with an acute exacerbation probably due to an infectious process. Her white count is markedly elevated with a left shift, however she was given Epinephrine subcutaneously by Dr. Smith in the Emergency Room and this could have conceivably caused demargination of her white blood cells. She is however, breathing more comfortably on a 50% face mask at this time with oxygen saturations in the mid 90's. She is less tachypneic and she is breathing more comfortably. She is mentating well. We will load with IV Aminophyllin at 6 per kilo, ideal body weight, and follow with an infusion. Will check Theophylline level later tonight to be certain that we are avoiding toxicity. Frequent hand held nebulizer treatments, IV steroids. The rest of the regimen can be discerned from the admission orders.

DD: 05-01-YYYY
DT: 05-03-YYYY

_____

Alan Ghann, MD

LUCK, Deborah L.	Admission: 05-01-YYYY	PROGRESS NOTES
Case09	DOB: 11-21-YYYY	
Dr. Ghann	ROOM: 0374	

Date	(Please skip one line between dates.)
05-01	Chief Complaint: Respiratory distress.
	Diagnosis: Severe RAD w/ metabolic acidosis.
	Plan of Treatment: IV steroids, HHN txs, IV Aminophylline, O2 sats.
05-01	3 pm Pt. seen improved. No distress. Alan Ghann, MD
05-01	Late entry
1400	Tx given Hhn w/ 0.5 ml Proventil /nss via mask w/ pt.. tolerating well. BS↓ w/ I + exp. Wheeze.
	P 130. R 28. No cough. O2 on a 50% Venti. R. Rose, CPT
05-01	Tx given as above. BS↓ w/ harsh exp. Wheeze. P 130. R 32. NPC. O2 on a 50% Venti.
1530	R. Rose, CPT
05-01	Tx given as above. BS↓ w/ faint I + exp. Wheeze. P 120. R 32. Harsh NPC. O2 on a 50% Venti mask.
1610	R. Rose, CPT
05-01	HHN 0.5 ml Albuterol/nss. HR 121. RR 20. BS diminished w/ occasional exp. Wheeze. Sa O_2 _ 98% on 3L.
1900	E. Blossom, RRT
05-01	HHN 0.5 ml Albuterol/nss. HR 120. RR 24. BS - occasional rhonchi. No wheezes. Sa O_2 _ 95% on 35% – ↓ to 30% VM,
2230	E. Blossom, RRT
05-02	HHN as above. HR 96. RR 20. BS - occasional exp. Wheeze. Tight NPC O_2 on 28%. Sa O_2 on 30% VM. 95.
0150	E. Blossom, RRT
05-02	HHN tx given w/ .5 ml Albuterol /nss via mask. BS scattered exp. wheeze loose nec HR 112, RR 20.
0450	P 130. R 28. No cough. SA O2 94% on 28%. O2 on @ 28% venti mask. Δ to 2L nasal cannula. R. Rose, CPT

LUCK, Deborah L.	Admission: 05-01-YYYY	PROGRESS NOTES
Case09	DOB: 11-21-YYYY	
Dr. Ghann	ROOM: 0374	

Date	(Please skip one line between dates.)
05-02	Rx given HHN w/ 0.5 ml Proventil / nss via mask w/ pt. tol. well. . BS↓ w/ exp. wheeze. P 110. R 20.
0800	Harsh NPC O2 on a 2L N/C. R. Rose, CPT
05-02	S: Breathing much better. Adament about discharge today.
	O: Afebrile. VSS. O2 sats on 2L = 95%.
	CHEST- good air intake. No wheeze.
	COR - RRR. No murmur.
	ABD - soft.
	A: Severe RAD, prompt resolution. Patient insists on discharge today.
	P. Taper IV meds to p.o. Check sats. Possible disch. later.
	Alan Ghann. MD
05-02	Tx given as above. BS↓ clear. NPC.
1110	P 120. R 20. O2 was ↓ to 1L N/C.
	R. Rose, CPT

		DOCTORS ORDERS

LUCK, Deborah L.
Case09
Dr. Ghann

Admission: 05-01-YYYY
DOB: 11-21-YYYY
ROOM: 0374

Date	Time	Physician's signature required for each order. (Please skip one line between dates.)
05-01		Admit: Ghann MD
		Dx: Severe Asthma w/ resp distress
		Vs Q2 x 24° then Q4°
		Allerg. PCN ⊚ Codeine
		Diet - regular
		IVF- D5 NS @ 125 cc/hr.
		O2 /5 L NRBFM - wean to face mask if SATS > 92%.
		STUDIES: sputum C ⊚ S if not obtained in ED
		Lytes in AM UA w/ c ⊚ s
		MEDS: Albuterol HHN 0.5 cc am 2cc NS Q3° ⊚ Q/° PRN
		Solumedrol 125 mg IV Q6° ATC
		Ancef 1 gm IV Q8 pending sputum results
		Aminophylin 40 mg/hr IV Pharmacist to determine solu ⊚ rate
		Tylenol 650 mg po Q4° PRN
		Theophyline level @ 27:00 - call if < 10 or > 20.
		O2 SATS - continuous x 8 hrs - alarms @ 92%, then Q treatment
		Thank you
		Alan Ghann. MD
5/1	1515	↓ IVF to 75 cc/hr while Aminophylline is infusing. SCG II results to chart please.
		Alan Ghann. MD

LUCK, Deborah L.	Admission: 05-01-YYYY	DOCTORS ORDERS
Case09	DOB: 11-21-YYYY	
Dr. Ghann	ROOM: 0374	

Date	Time	Physician's signature required for each order. (Please skip one line between dates.)
05-02		D/C Aminophyline
		D/C IV Solumedrol
		Start Prednisone 20mg po tid
		D/C Ancef
		Start Ceclor 250mg po tid
		Δ HHN to QID and Q 4° PRN
		D/C IV
		Possible D/C later today
		Alan Ghann, MD
05-02		Wean O2 to off if SATS > 92%.
		Please have pt ambulate off O2. Check O2 sats with ambulatory at 2:00 p.m.
		If sats > 92% please discharge to home.
		Thanks
		Alan Ghann, MD

LUCK, Deborah L.   Admission: 05-01-YYYY
Case09   DOB: 11-21-YYYY   LABORATORY DATA
Dr. Ghann   ROOM: 0374

SPECIMEN COLLECTED: 05-01-YYYY   SPECIMEN RECEIVED: 05-01-YYYY

TEST	RESULT	FLAG	REFERENCE
SCG2, LYTES, BUN PANEL			
Glucose	162		70-110 mg/dl
Creatinine	0.8		0.6-1.0 mg/dl
Sodium	143		136-147 MEQ/L
Potassium	4.9		3.7-5.1 MEQ/L
Chloride	104		98-108 MEQ/L
TOTAL CO2	24		24-32 MEQ/L
Calcium	9.9		8.8-10.5 mg/dl
WBC	21.3	**H**	4.5-11.0 thous/UL
RBC	5.21		5.2-5.4 mill/UL
HGB	14.8		11.7-16.1 g/dl
HCT	45.2		35.0-47.0 %
MCV	86.8		85-99 fL.
MCH	32.7		32-37
Platelets	369		140-400 thous/UL

End of Report

LUCK, Deborah L.   Admission: 05-01-YYYY
Case09   DOB: 11-21-YYYY   LABORATORY DATA
Dr. Ghann   ROOM: 0374

SPECIMEN COLLECTED: 05-01-YYYY   SPECIMEN RECEIVED: 05-01-YYYY

TEST	RESULT	FLAG	REFERENCE
URINALYSIS			
DIPSTICK ONLY			
COLOR	CLOUDY YELLOW		
SP GRAVITY	1.025		≤ 1.030
GLUCOSE	110		≤ 125 mg/dl
BILIRUBIN	NEG		≤ 0.8 mg/dl
KETONE	TRACE		≤ 10 mg/dl
BLOOD	11	**H**	0.06 mg/dl hgb
PH	5.0		5-8.0
PROTEIN	TRACE		≤ 30 mg/dl
UROBILINOGEN	NORMAL		≤ -1 mg/dl
NITRITES	POS		NEG
LEUKOCYTE	NEG		≤ 15 WBC/hpf
EPITH	5-10		
W.B.C.	5-10		≤ 5/hpf
R.B.C.	RARE		≤ 5/hpf
BACT.	4f		1+(≤ 20/hpf)

End of Report

LUCK, Deborah L.   Admission: 05-01-YYYY
Case09   DOB: 11-21-YYYY
Dr. Ghann   ROOM: 0374

LABORATORY DATA

SPECIMEN COLLECTED: 05-01-YYYY   **SPECIMEN RECEIVED:** 05-01-YYYY

TEST	RESULT	FLAG	REFERENCE
Urea Nitrogen	8		7-18 mg/dl
Alkaline Phosphatase	176	**H**	50-136 U/L
GLUCOSE	162	**H**	70-110 mg/dl
SGOT	19		15-37 U/L
Lactic Dehydrogenase	182		100-190 U/L
Phosphorus	2.7		2.5-4.9 mg/dl
Total Bilirubin	0.3		0.0-1.1 mg/dl
Total Protein	7.5		6.4-8.2 g/dl
Albumin	4.2		3.4-5.0 g/dl
Uric Acid	3.0		2.6-5.6 mg/dl
Cholesterol	186		≤ 200mg/dl

End of Report

LUCK, Deborah L.   Admission: 05-01-YYYY
Case09   DOB: 11-21-YYYY   LABORATORY DATA
Dr. Ghann   ROOM: 0374

SPECIMEN COLLECTED: 05-02-YYYY   SPECIMEN RECEIVED: 05-02-YYYY

TEST	RESULT	FLAG	REFERENCE
ELECTROLYTES PANEL			
Sodium	139		136-147 MEQ/L
Potassium	3.9		3.7-5.1 MEQ/L
Chloride	106		98-108 MEQ/L
TOTAL CO2	20		24-32 MEQ/L

End of Report

```
LUCK, Deborah L.      Admission: 05-01-YYYY
Case09                DOB: 11-21-YYYY                LABORATORY DATA
Dr. Ghann             ROOM: 0374
```

SPECIMEN COLLECTED: 05-01-YYYY   SPECIMEN RECEIVED: 05-01-YYYY

Theophylline Level

TEST	RESULT	FLAG	REFERENCE
Theophylline	9.3	**L**	10.0-20.0 UG/ML

End of Report

LUCK, Deborah L.   Admission: 05-01-YYYY
Case09   DOB: 11-21-YYYY   LABORATORY DATA
Dr. Ghann   ROOM: 0374

SPECIMEN COLLECTED: 05-01-YYYY   **SPECIMEN RECEIVED:** 05-01-YYYY

TEST: Urine Culture

2+ gram negative rod

1. cc ≥ 100,000

E. coli

End of Report

LUCK, Deborah L.   Admission: 05-01-YYYY
Case09   DOB: 11-21-YYYY   RADIOMETRY
Dr. Ghann   ROOM: 0374

SPECIMEN COLLECTED: 05-01-YYYY   SPECIMEN RECEIVED: 05-01-YYYY

TEST   RESULT

BLOOD GAS VALUES

pH	7.286
pCO2	43.8 mmHg
pO2	90.4 mmHG

TEMPERATURE CORRECTED VALUES

pH(98.6°)	7.286
pCO2(98.6°)	43.8 mmHg
pO2(98.6°)	90.4 mmHg

ACID BASE STATUS

HCO3c	20.2 mmol/L
ABEc	-5.9 mmol/L

BLOOD OXIMETRY VALUES

tHb	14.4 g/dL
O2Hb	94.6%
COHb	0.2%
MetHb	0.8%

End of Report

Case 10

| ALFRED STATE MEDICAL CENTER
100 MAIN ST, ALFRED, NY 14802
(607) 555-1234
HOSPITAL #: 000999 | | | | INPATIENT FACE SHEET | | | |

PATIENT NAME AND ADDRESS				GENDER	RACE	MARITAL STATUS	PATIENT NO.
PAULSON, Paula P. 49 Hillbottom Way Alfred, NY 14802				F	W	M	Case10
				DATE OF BIRTH	MAIDEN NAME	OCCUPATION	
				01-20-YYYY	King	Waitress	

ADMISSION DATE	TIME	DISCHARGE DATE	TIME	LENGTH OF STAY		TELEPHONE NUMBER	
04-26-YYYY	16:00	05-01-YYYY	09:30	05 DAYS		(607) 555-2836	

GUARANTOR NAME AND ADDRESS		NEXT OF KIN NAME AND ADDRESS	
PAULSON, Patrick 49 Hillbottom Way Alfred, NY 14802		PAULSON, Patrick 49 Hillbottom Way Alfred, NY 14802	

GUARANTOR TELEPHONE NO.	RELATIONSHIP TO PATIENT	NEXT OF KIN TELEPHONE NUMBER	RELATIONSHIP TO PATIENT
(607) 555-2836	Husband	(607) 555-2836	Husband

ADMITTING PHYSICIAN	SERVICE	ADMIT TYPE	ROOM NUMBER/BED
Thompson MD, Donald	Medical	2	0367/01

ATTENDING PHYSICIAN	ATTENDING PHYSICIAN UPIN	ADMITTING DIAGNOSIS	
Thompson MD, Donald	100B01	Congestive Heart Failure	

PRIMARY INSURER	POLICY AND GROUP NUMBER	SECONDARY INSURER	POLICY AND GROUP NUMBER
BCBS	432763201 77690	Empire Plan	5739057512

DIAGNOSES AND PROCEDURES	ICD-9-CM	ICD-10-CM/PCS
PRINCIPAL DIAGNOSIS		
Acute Bronchitis	491.22	J20.8
SECONDARY DIAGNOSES		
Chronic obstructive pulmonary disease	496	J44.9
Restrictive Lung Disease	518.89	J98.4
Congestive heart failure	428.0	I50.9
PRINCIPAL PROCEDURE		
SECONDARY PROCEDURES		
TOTAL CHARGES: $ 7,236.95		

ACTIVITY:	☐ Bedrest	☑ Light	☐ Usual	☐ Unlimited	☐ Other:
DIET:	☐ Regular	☐ Low Cholesterol	☐ Low Salt	☐ ADA	☐ _____ Calorie
FOLLOW-UP:	☑ Call for appointment	☑ Office appointment in 2 wks	Other:		

SPECIAL INSTRUCTIONS: Go to Pulmonary lab for blood test 1 hr before appt.

Signature of Attending Physician: Donald Thompson, MD

PAULSON, Paula P. Admission: 04-26-YYYY CONSENT TO ADMISSION
Case 10 DOB: 01-20-YYYY
Dr. Thompson ROOM: 0367

I, _Paula P. Paulson_ hereby consent to admission to the Alfred State Medical Center (ASMC) , and I further consent to such routine hospital care, diagnostic procedures, and medical treatment that the medical and professional staff of ASMC may deem necessary or advisable. I authorize the use of medical information obtained about me as specified above and the disclosure of such information to my referring physician(s). This form has been fully explained to me, and I understand its contents. I further understand that no guarantees have been made to me as to the results of treatments or examinations done at the ASMC.

Paula P. Paulson _____ _April 26, yyyy_ _____
Signature of Patient Date

_____ _____
Signature of Parent/Legal Guardian for Minor Date

_____
Relationship to Minor

Andrea Witteman _____ _April 26, yyyy_ _____
WITNESS: Alfred State Medical Center Staff Member Date

CONSENT TO RELEASE INFORMATION FOR REIMBURSEMENT PURPOSES

In order to permit reimbursement, upon request, the Alfred State Medical Center (ASMC) may disclose such treatment information pertaining to my hospitalization to any corporation, organization, or agent thereof, which is, or may be liable under contract to the ASMC or to me, or to any of my family members or other person, for payment of all or part of the ASMC's charges for services rendered to me (e.g., the patient's health insurance carrier). I understand that the purpose of any release of information is to facilitate reimbursement for services rendered. In addition, in the event that my health insurance program includes utilization review of services provided during this admission, I authorize ASMC to release information as is necessary to permit the review. This authorization will expire once the reimbursement for services rendered is complete.

Paula P. Paulson _____ _April 26, yyyy_ _____
Signature of Patient Date

_____ _____
Signature of Parent/Legal Guardian for Minor Date

_____
Relationship to Minor

Andrea Witteman _____ _April 26, yyyy_ _____
WITNESS: Alfred State Medical Center Staff Member Date

ALFRED STATE MEDICAL CENTER ■ 100 MAIN ST, ALFRED, NY 14802 ■ (607) 555-1234

		ADVANCE DIRECTIVE
PAULSON, Paula P. Case 10 Dr. Thompson	Admission: 04-26-YYYY DOB: 01-20-YYYY ROOM: 0367	

Your answers to the following questions will assist your Physician and the Hospital to respect your wishes regarding your medical care. This information will become a part of your medical record.

	YES	NO	PATIENT'S INITIALS
1. Have you been provided with a copy of the information called "Patient Rights Regarding Health Care Decision?"	X		PP
2. Have you prepared a "Living Will?" If yes, please provide the Hospital with a copy for your medical record.		X	PP
3. Have you prepared a Durable Power of Attorney for Health Care? If yes, please provide the Hospital with a copy for your medical record.		X	PP
4. Have you provided this facility with an Advance Directive on a prior admission and is it still in effect? If yes, Admitting Office to contact Medical Records to obtain a copy for the medical record.		X	PP
5. Do you desire to execute a Living Will/Durable Power of Attorney? If yes, refer to in order: a. Physician b. Social Service c. Volunteer Service		X	PP

HOSPITAL STAFF DIRECTIONS: Check when each step is completed.

1. ___✓___ Verify the above questions where answered and actions taken where required.

2. ___✓___ If the "Patient Rights" information was provided to someone other than the patient, state reason:

_____

_____   _____
Name of Individual Receiving Information   Relationship to Patient

3. ___✓___ If information was provided in a language other than English, specify language and method.

4. ___✓___ Verify patient was advised on how to obtain additional information on Advance Directives.

5. ___✓___ Verify the Patient/Family Member/Legal Representative was asked to provide the Hospital with a copy of the Advance Directive which will be retained in the medical record.

File this form in the medical record, and give a copy to the patient.

_____
Name of Patient (Name of Individual giving information if different from Patient)

Paula P. Paulson   April 26, yyyy
_____   _____
Signature of Patient   Date

Andrea Witteman   April 26, yyyy
_____   _____
Signature of Hospital Representative   Date

ALFRED STATE MEDICAL CENTER ■ 100 MAIN ST, ALFRED, NY 14802 ■ (607) 555-1234

PAULSON, Paula P. Admission: 04-26-YYYY	PROGRESS NOTES
Case10 DOB: 01-20-YYYY	
Dr. Thompson ROOM: 0367	

Date	(Please skip one line between dates.)
4-26	Chief Complaint: Shortness of breath.
	Diagnosis: CHF
	Plan of Treatment: See orders.
04-26	Hhn w/ 0.25 ml Proventil / N.S.S. tx given. Pt. tol. tx well. P 92 + R 16
1820	B.S. clear RC w/ green sputum. O₂ off pt. pre tx on pot at 3 l n.c.
	D. Davenport, CPT
04-26	Tx given as above. B.S. rhonchi + wheezes — pt. tol. tx well dry N.P.C.
2200	O₂ on 3 l n.c. pre + post tx.
	D. Davenport, CPT
04-27	Pt. is less short of breath today. Weight ↓ 6 lbs. But still has a lot of rales
	at bases Continue same treatment.
	Donald Thompson, MD
04-27	Hh neb. Rx w/ 25 ml Proventil + NSS P 72 — RR 24 BS rales + exp wheezes LNPC
0715	SAT 90% on 3l — pt. tol rx well L. Seraphin CPT
04-27	Hh neb. Rx w/ 25 ml Proventil + NSS P 72 — RR 24 BS rales + wheezes NPC
1140	O2 3l n/c pre + post Respirdyne done.
	L. Seraphin CPT
04-27	Hh neb. Rx w/ 25 ml Proventil + NSS P 72 — RR 20 BS ↓ d NPC O2 on 3l pt. tol rx
1520	Well w/ fine rales bases.
	L. Seraphin CPT

PAULSON, Paula P. Case10 Dr. Thompson	Admission: 04-26-YYYY DOB: 01-20-YYYY ROOM: 0367	PROGRESS NOTES
Date	(Please skip one line between dates.)	
04-27	HHN 25mg Proventil & NSS **BS** ↓ ↓'d **L** ↓'d **R** rales ½ up bilat. LNPC; HR 80; R 20 O2 el NC	
1940	E. Blossom, CPT	
04-28	Hhn rx w/ 05 ml Albuterol/nss **BS** ↓ w/ rales bilaterally in bases. **NPC** at this time.	
0710	P 88 RR 20 stable O2 on 3l nc pre + post rx	
	L. Seraphin CPT	
04-28	Pt. sleeping well with no orthopnea or PND. Rales diminished in bases.	
	Donald Thompson, MD	
04-28	Hhn rx w/ 05 ml Albuterol/nss **BS** rales in bases bilaterally. **NPC**	
1100	O2 on 3l nc	
	L. Seraphin CPT	
04-28	Rx as above. **BS** rales bilaterally in bases. **NPC** O2 on 3l nc	
1500	L. Seraphin CPT	
04-28	HHN 25mg Proventil & NSS **BS** ↓'d **L** ↓'d **R** rales ½ up bilat. LNPC; HR 78; R 20 O2 3l nc pre & post	
1900	E. Blossom, CPT	
04-29	Hhn w/ 025 ml Proventil / N.S.S. tx given Pt. tol. tx well P 86 + R 16	
0710	B.S. clear w/ few scattered rales P.C. w/ clear sputum O2 3l nc pre + post tx	
	D. Davenport, CPT	
04-29	Pt. is steadily improving with breather; few rales at bases yet, will ↑ Act.	
	Home tomorrow if stable. Donald Thompson, MD	

PAULSON, Paula P.	Admission: 04-26-YYYY	DOCTORS ORDERS
Case10	DOB: 01-20-YYYY	
Dr. Thompson	ROOM: 0367	

Date	Time	Physician's signature required for each order. (Please skip one line between dates.)
04-26	1630	ABG and CXR done as OP copy for chart
		O2 3L via NC
		Saline lock
		Lasix 40 mgm IV now then bid
		CBC, BUN, lytes, seg #11. Check iso today and a.m.
		Urinalysis, HIV
		Sputum C & S
		HHN w/ Proventil 2.5 mgm qid
		NAS diet
		Lanoxin 0.25 gm po now and BT then daily
		Capaten 12.5 mgm now and BT then q 12 hrs 8 am – 8 pm
		R.A.V. To Dr. Thompson/T. Perry
04-26		T4 & TSH D Thompson, MD
04-27	1025	BUN & lytes in A.M. D Thompson, MD
04-28		O2 SAT in AM. on Room air
		Ceftin 250 p.o. D Thompson, MD
04-29	0150	Tylenol 650 mg PO Q4° prn pain or fever
		R...A.V. To Dr. Thompson/F. Hill D Thompson, MD
04-30	1100	Cancel O2 sat for today. Chest X-ray in a.m.. Weigh daily.
		ABG room air. Lanoxin level, BUN, Digoxin level. Lasix 40 po bid.
		D Thompson MD

PAULSON, Paula P.	Admission: 04-26-YYYY	DOCTORS ORDERS
Case10	DOB: 01-20-YYYY	
Dr. Thompson	ROOM: 0367	

Date	Time	Physician's signature required for each order. (Please skip one line between dates.)
04-29	1620	Oximetry on RA; if above 90% leave O2 off.
		R.A.V. To Dr. Thompson/T. Perry D Thompson, MD
04-29	1620	Please do a VQ scan & PFT (before & after) today
		R.A.V. To Dr. Thompson/C. Moore D Thompson, MD
04-30	0955	Do diffusion capacity with PFT
		R.A.V. T.O. Dr. Thompson D Thompson, MD
04-30	1410	Instruct pt. on NAS diet
		R.A.V. T.O. Dr. Thompson/T. Perry D Thompson, MD
05-01		Discharge.
		D Thompson MD

PAULSON, Paula P.   Admission: 04-26-YYYY
Case10   DOB: 01-20-YYYY
Dr. Thompson   ROOM: 0367

LABORATORY DATA

SPECIMEN COLLECTED: 04-27-YYYY   **SPECIMEN RECEIVED:** 04-27-YYYY

BLOOD PROFILE

TEST	RESULT	FLAG	REFERENCE
HIV	**Neg**		

End of Report

PAULSON, Paula P.   Admission: 04-26-YYYY
Case10   DOB: 01-20-YYYY
Dr. Thompson   ROOM: 0367

LABORATORY DATA

SPECIMEN COLLECTED: 04-26-YYYY   **SPECIMEN RECEIVED:** 04-26-YYYY

CBC c̄ DIFF

TEST	RESULT	FLAG	REFERENCE
WBC	7.4		4.5-11.0 thous/UL
RBC	5.02	**L**	5.2-5.4 mill/UL
HGB	15.0		11.7-16.1 g/dl
HCT	45.8		35.0-47.0 %
MCV	91.2		85-99 fL.
MCHC	32.8	**L**	33-37
RDW	15.2	**H**	11.4-14.5
Platelets	165		130-400 thous/UL
MPV	8.4		7.4-10.4
LYMPH %	21.1		20.5-51.1
MONO %	7.8		1.7-9.3
GRAN %	71.1		42.2-75.2
LYMPH x 10^3	1.6		1.2-3.4
MONO x 10^3	.6	**H**	0.11-0.59
GRAN x 10^3	5.3		1.4-6.5
EOS x 10^3	< .7		0.0-0.7
BASO x 10^3	< .2		0.0-0.2
ANISO	SLIGHT		

End of Report

ALFRED STATE MEDICAL CENTER ■ 100 MAIN ST, ALFRED, NY 14802 ■ (607) 555-1234

PAULSON, Paula P.   Admission: 04-26-YYYY
Case10   DOB: 01-20-YYYY
Dr. Thompson   ROOM: 0367

LABORATORY DATA

SPECIMEN COLLECTED: 04-26-YYYY   SPECIMEN RECEIVED: 04-26-YYYY

URINALYSIS – DIPSTICK ONLY

TEST	RESULT	FLAG	REFERENCE
COLOR	YELLOW		
SP GRAVITY	1.020		$\leq$ 1.030
GLUCOSE	NEG		$\leq$ 125 mg/dl
BILIRUBIN	NEG		$\leq$ 0.8 mg/dl
KETONE	NEG		$\leq$ 10 mg/dl
BLOOD	NEG		0.06 mg/dl hgb
PH	5.5		5-8.0
PROTEIN	NEGATIVE		$\leq$ 30 mg/dl
UROBILINOGEN	NORMAL		$\leq$ -1 mg/dl
NITRITES	NEG		NEG
LEUKOCYTE	NEG		$\leq$ 15 WBC/hpf
EPITH	10-15		/lpf
W.B.C.	1-2		$\leq$ 5/hpf
R.B.C.	1-2		$\leq$ 5/hpf
BACT.	RARE		1+($\leq$ 20/hpf)

End of Report

PAULSON, Paula P.   Admission: 04-26-YYYY
Case10   DOB: 01-20-YYYY
Dr. Thompson   ROOM: 0367

LABORATORY DATA

SPECIMEN COLLECTED: 04-26-YYYY   SPECIMEN RECEIVED: 04-26-YYYY

UNIT WORKUP PANEL

TEST	RESULT	FLAG	REFERENCE
Sodium	145		136-147 MEQ/L
Potassium	5.1		3.7-5.1 MEQ/L
Chloride	103		98-108 MEQ/L
TOTAL CO2	38	**H**	24-32 MEQ/L
Urea Nitrogen	14		7-18 mg/dl
Creatine Kinase	43		21-215 U/L
Lactic Dehydrogenase	150		100-190 U/L
Alkaline Phosphatase	120		50-136 U/L
GLUCOSE	86		70-110 mg/dl
SGOT	24		15-37 U/L
Creatinine	0.9		0.6-1.0 mg/dl
Calcium	9.3		8.8-10.5 mg/dl
Phosphorus	4.3		2.5-4.9 mg/dl
Total Bilirubin	0.5		0.0-1.1 mg/dl
Total Protein	7.0		6.4-8.2 g/dl
Albumin	3.2	**L**	3.4-5.0 g/dl
Uric Acid	9.3	**H**	2.6-5.6 mg/dl
Cholesterol	157		≤ 200mg/dl
CKMD	1.5		0.0-6.0 ng/ml

End of Report

ALFRED STATE MEDICAL CENTER ■ 100 MAIN ST, ALFRED, NY 14802 ■ (607) 555-1234

PAULSON, Paula P.   Admission: 04-26-YYYY
Case10   DOB: 01-20-YYYY
Dr. Thompson   ROOM: 0367

LABORATORY DATA

SPECIMEN COLLECTED: 04-27-YYYY   SPECIMEN RECEIVED: 04-27-YYYY

CARDIAC PROFILE

TEST	RESULT	FLAG	REFERENCE
Creatine Kinase	35		21-215 U/L
CKMD	0.7		0.0-6.0 ng/ml

End of Report

PAULSON, Paula P.   Admission: 04-26-YYYY
Case10   DOB: 01-20-YYYY
Dr. Thompson   ROOM: 0367

LABORATORY DATA

SPECIMEN COLLECTED: 04-28-YYYY   SPECIMEN RECEIVED: 04-28-YYYY

TEST	RESULT	FLAG	REFERENCE
ELECTROLYTES PANEL			
Sodium	141		136-147 MEQ/L
Potassium	4.5		3.7-5.1 MEQ/L
Chloride	94	**L**	98-108 MEQ/L
Total CO_2	35	**H**	24-32 MEQ/L
UREA NITROGEN	16		7-18 MG/DL
THYROID PANEL			
T4	5.2		4.9-10.7 UG/DL
TSH	1.28		0.38-6.15 UIU/ML

End of Report

PAULSON, Paula P.   Admission: 04-26-YYYY
Case10   DOB: 01-20-YYYY
Dr. Thompson   ROOM: 0367

LABORATORY DATA

SPECIMEN COLLECTED: 04-30-YYYY   **SPECIMEN RECEIVED:** 04-30-YYYY

TEST	RESULT	FLAG	REFERENCE
ELECTROLYTES	PANEL		
Sodium	140		136-147 MEQ/L
Potassium	5.2	**H**	3.7-5.1 MEQ/L
Chloride	92	**L**	98-108 MEQ/L
Total CO_2	34	**H**	24-32 MEQ/L
UREA NITROGEN	25	**H**	7-18 MG/DL
DIGOXIN	1.6		0.5-2.0 NG/ML
DIGOXIN NOTE	REF.INT=RX LEVEL AT PEAK TISSUE LEVEL > 8 HRS POST ORAL DOSE. OTHER FACTORS MAY AFFECT LEVEL AND ACTIVITY.		

End of Report

PAULSON, Paula P.   Admission: 04-26-YYYY
Case10   DOB: 01-20-YYYY
Dr. Thompson   ROOM: 0367

RADIOMETRY

SPECIMEN COLLECTED: 04-26-YYYY   **SPECIMEN RECEIVED:**   04-26-YYYY

TEST	RESULT	REFERENCE
BLOOD GAS VALUES		
pH	7.340	
pCO2	62.1	mmHg
pO2	44.5	mmHg
TEMPERATURE CORRECTED VALUES		
pH(98.6°)	7.340	
pCO2(98.6°)	62.1	mmHg
pO2(98.6°)	44.5	mmHg
ACID BASE STATUS		
HCO3c	32.6	mmol/L
ABEc	5.3	mmol/L
BLOOD OXIMETRY VALUES		
tHb	14.5	g/dL
O2Hb	78.3	%
COHb	1.0	%
MetHb	0.7	%

End of Report

ALFRED STATE MEDICAL CENTER ■ 100 MAIN ST, ALFRED, NY 14802 ■ (607) 555-1234

PAULSON, Paula P.   Admission: 04-26-YYYY
Case10   DOB: 01-20-YYYY   RADIOMETRY
Dr. Thompson   ROOM: 0367

SPECIMEN COLLECTED: 04-30-YYYY   SPECIMEN RECEIVED: 04-30-YYYY

TEST	RESULT	REFERENCE
BLOOD GAS VALUES		
pH	7.385	
pCO2	67.7	mmHg
pO2	40.3	mmHg
TEMPERATURE CORRECTED VALUES		
pH(98.6°)	7.385	
pCO2(98.6°)	67.7	mmHg
pO2(98.6°)	40.3	mmHg
ACID BASE STATUS		
HCO3c	39.6	mmol/L
ABEc	11.2	mmol/L
BLOOD OXIMETRY VALUES		
tHb	16.3	g/dL
O2Hb	74.8	%
COHb	0.7	%
MetHb	0.7	%

End of Report

ALFRED STATE MEDICAL CENTER ■ 100 MAIN ST, ALFRED, NY 14802 ■ (607) 555-1234

```
PAULSON, Paula P.        Admission: 04-26-YYYY
Case10                   DOB: 01-20-YYYY                RADIOLOGY REPORT
Dr. Thompson             ROOM: 0367
```

Initial Diagnosis/History: CHF

Date Requested: 04-26-YYYY

Transport: ☑ Wheelchair ☐ Stretcher ☑ O$_2$ ☐ IV

☐ IP ☑ OP ☐ ER ☐ PRE OP ☐ OR/RR ☐ Portable

Technical Data: PA and left Lat CXR T2 ↑. TBA. Shortness of breath.

CHEST: PA and lateral view show that the heart appears slightly enlarged compared to our study of 06-09-YYYY. The central pulmonary arteries are prominent and there is a tiny right pleural effusion. The left diaphragm is elevated with some overlying fibrosis but this is unchanged from previously.

CONCLUSION: Findings compatible with mild congestive heart failure.

DD: 04-26-YYYY

DT: 04-26-YYYY

Philip Rogers

Philip Rogers, M.D., Radiologist

PAULSON, Paula P.   Admission: 04-26-YYYY   NUCLEAR MEDICINE
Case10   DOB: 01-20-YYYY
Dr. Thompson   ROOM: 0367

Reason for Nuclear Scan: Ventilation Perfusion Scan. Determine the reason for poor oxygenation.

Date Requested: 04-30-YYYY

Transport: ☑ Wheelchair   ☐ Stretcher   ☑ O$_2$ ☐ IV

☑ IP ☐ OP   ☐ ER   ☐ PRE OP   ☐ OR/RR   ☐ Portable

VENTILATION PERFUSION LUNG SCAN: Following inhalation of technetium aerosol and intravenous injection as the MAA films were made of AP, PA and both lateral projections. The activity throughout both lungs is quite patchy which appears to be due to chronic lung disease or residual change from the patient's heart failure. I do not see any segmental perfusion defects or areas of mismatch to suggest an embolus.

CONCLUSION: No evidence of a pulmonary embolus.

DD: 04-30-YYYY

DT: 04-30-YYYY

Philip Rogers

Philip Rogers, M.D., Radiologist

```
PAULSON, Paula P.          Admission: 04-26-YYYY
Case10                     DOB: 01-20-YYYY                    RADIOLOGY REPORT
Dr. Thompson               ROOM: 0367
```

Initial Diagnosis/History: CHF.

Date Requested: 04-30-YYYY

Transport: ☑ Wheelchair ☐ Stretcher ☑ O$_2$ ☐ IV

☑ IP ☐ OP ☐ ER ☐ PRE OP ☐ OR/RR ☐ Portable

CHEST: PA and lateral views show that the interstitial markings are less prominent on today's film than they were in the previous study of 04-26. Other than this, there hasn't really been a significant change. There is no evidence of pneumonia and I certainly would not say that the patient has any congestive heart failure on the current study. There is abnormal elevation of the left diaphragm which is probably due to paralysis or eventration. The overall cardiac size has not increased.

CONCLUSION: Probable resolution of the mild CHF since 04-26.

DD: 04-30-YYYY

DT: : 04-30-YYYY

Philip Rogers
_____
Philip Rogers, M.D., Radiologist

Appendix II

Electronic Health Record Activities

The following is a series of lab activities that allows the student to explore the use of an electronic health record (EHR). These labs are designed to be used with the Neehr Perfect® system. Neehr Perfect® is an educational EHR developed to be utilized to educate students and give them practical experience in using an electronic record system. A subscription is required for using Neehr Perfect®. Please contact your instructor for more information.

LAB 1: Level I Scavenger Hunt: EHR Orientation

This lab needs to be completed as a pre-requisite for the remaining labs.

LAB 2: Level II Scavenger Hunt: Essential Skills and Usability

This lab needs to be completed following Lab 1.

LAB 3: Neehr Perfect Activity: Health Information Terminology

This lab introduces terms used in health care, the medical office, and in the Neehr Perfect system. It is suggested that this lab be used with Chapter 1 of *Essentials of Health Information Management*, third edition.

LAB 4: Neehr Perfect Activity: Approved Abbreviations

This activity involves auditing documents in a patient record found in the Neehr Perfect Electronic Record system and identifying the incorrect use of abbreviations found within patient medical documentation. It is suggested that this lab be used with Chapter 4 of *Essentials of Health Information Management*, third edition.

LAB 5: Neehr Perfect Activity: Retrieval of Data

This activity involves data retrieval within the EHR focusing on finding key information from a patient's chart. It is suggested that this lab be used with Chapter 6 of *Essentials of Health Information Management*, third edition.

LAB 6: Neehr Perfect Activity: Verification of Documentation Requirements

This lab involves abstracting and summarizing patient information abstracted from patients' medical documentation. It is suggested that this lab be used with Chapter 8 of *Essentials of Health Information Management*, third edition.

LAB 7: Neehr Perfect Activity: Introduction to Privacy, Security, and Confidentiality

This lab introduces the basic meaning and application of privacy, security, and confidentiality in the EHR as related to patient's health information. It is suggested that this lab be used with Chapter 9 of *Essentials of Health Information Management*, third edition.

LAB 8: Neehr Perfect Activity: Release of Information

This lab introduces concepts and activities that relate to the release of information function. It is suggested that this lab be used with Chapter 9 of *Essentials of Health Information Management*, third edition.

LAB 1: Level I Scavenger Hunt: EHR Orientation

REQUIRED PRE-REQUISITES

- Review the **Student Guide to Neehr Perfect**.
- Go to www.neehrperfect.com and go to the **Student Resource Network**. Review all of the FAQs located in the **Help** section.

OBJECTIVES

At the end of this assignment, the student should be able to:

- Demonstrate the technical skills necessary to access an EHR system and trouble-shoot and resolve access difficulties.
- Locate patient name and open correct record using patient lookup.
- Navigate essential information viewing areas of a patient electronic medical chart.
- Understand where to go to set personal preferences.
- Demonstrate how to access and use reference tools and materials associated with an education EHR.
- Complete documentation and submission of a progress note.

ASSIGNMENT

- Complete the required pre-requisites.
- Go to www.neehrperfect.com and sign in to the Neehr Perfect EHR by entering your Username and Password in the login section.
- Select the '**Click Here to Start the Neehr Perfect EHR**' link.
- Select your school's EHR and enter your username and password. (You may be prompted to download the Citrix plug-in if you haven't done so already. Refer to the Student Guide for more information.) Note: Your EHR icon may be named differently than in the image below (i.e., EST01 or CST01).

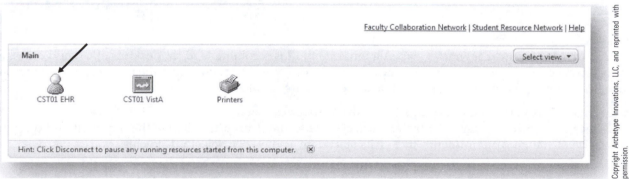

- Once the EHR launches, the patient selection window will appear. Search for patient **ORIENTATION, MYLES**. Note: It will likely have your school's initials incorporated into the name followed by numbers. Double click on the patient name OR once highlighted/selected, select **OK** to open the record.

You will be answering questions related to this patient's information. Near the end of this activity, you will enter your answers as a note in the patient's chart for submission to your instructor. Write down your answers in this document or a separate sheet of paper so they are readily available when you get to that part of the activity.

Navigational tools and user preferences

To resize windows:
Place cursor on lines between sections on cover sheet. When the cursor changes to a double arrow, click and drag to make sections bigger or smaller. Your window should appear as follows (chart information may vary, image shown to demonstrate layout of Cover Sheet):

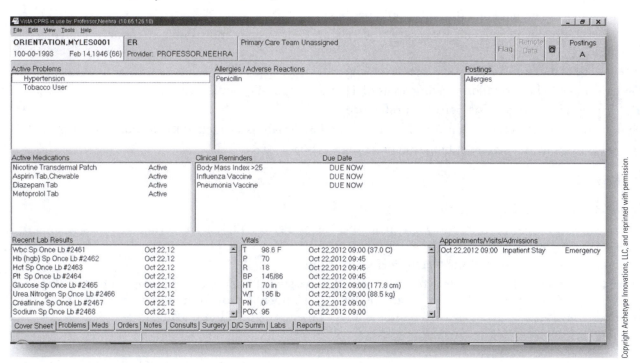

Font size:
Edit menu > Preferences > Fonts: Changing font size to 12 is recommended for desktops, PCs, and Macs. Font size of 8 is recommended for handheld devices and tablets. Note: After changing the font size, you may need to adjust the layout of your Cover Sheet so that all sections are visible.

Date range: This may need to be adjusted to show historical data.
Tools menu > Options > General tab and select **Date Range Defaults**: Change the inpatient and outpatient days to **999**. Change Appointments and Visits start date **Today-999**. Select **OK** to close both windows.

External resources available through the EHR:
Tools menu > select Drug Information Portal – which will take you out of the EHR into another window (the Internet). To get back into the EHR, select the CPRS icon at the bottom of your screen (🔲 or 🔳). Select the **Tools** menu again, this time click on **Health Information**. Again, you will be taken to another Internet window. Return to EHR window and repeat the previous steps and go to **Lab Tests Online**. You will use these resources later in this activity.

Help menu:

Help menu > Contents – You are now in the CPRS Help File. Using the 'Find' or 'Index' allows you to search for a variety of help topics.

Note: There are additional resources and help options available in the Student Resource Network portion of Neehr Perfect.

Cover sheet activities

The cover sheet is time sensitive, showing the most current information that has been entered into the patient chart. **Click on the upper left box with the patient's name, SSN, and date of birth – this will open the Patient Inquiry window.**

1. What ward was the patient admitted to?
2. What is patient's address?
3. Who is the emergency contact and number?

Close the Patient Inquiry window.

Back on the cover sheet, click on the first problem listed.

4. What is the status?
5. Who is the provider?

Close the Problem window.

Click on the patient's allergy listing.

6. What is the patient's allergy and reaction?

Close the Allergy window.

Click on the temperature entry in the Vitals box. You are brought to the Vitals history of the patient. On the left side panel you can choose how much of the vital signs you want to view in a graph. Scroll down and choose **All Results.**

7. What was the most recent set of vitals recorded? List the types and values.

Note that Vital Signs can be entered by clicking on the upper right icon **Enter Vitals**. Click on the icon now. **DO NOT ENTER VITAL SIGNS AT THIS TIME.**
Close the Vitals window.

Back on the Cover Sheet, refer to the vitals section.

8. What is this patient's BMI? (Hint: You may need to scroll down.)
9. Does the patient have a Clinical Reminder related to his BMI?

Clinical Reminders are populated based on the information that has been entered into the patient chart: the age, sex, problems, and vital signs. A single click on a Clinical Reminder will get you information on the clinical maintenance. Right-clicking on the Clinical Reminder will give you the option of looking at the reference information provided for this clinical reminder. Do this now for BMI: Right click – go to **Reference Information,** then click on the top reference listed (Calculate your own BMI).

10. What website are you taken to when you clicked on the first reference?

Return to the EHR by clicking on the CPRS icon at the bottom of your screen (or).

Click on the Problems tab

Notice that you can click on any of the **View Options** and see what problems are active, inactive, and removed. New problems can also be added by clicking on **New Problem.**

Click on the Meds tab

If you have medications showing on this tab that means there are active and current medications. By default, if a medication is more than 100 days old, it is expired and will not show on this tab. To view the patient's medications, both current and expired, go to the Orders tab.

Click on the Orders tab

Double click on one of the medication orders and read the details.

11. What is the medication and its order? The answer should include the name, dose, route, and frequency. Close the order details window.

Click on the Tools menu and select the Drug Information Portal. Search for the medication you chose in question 11. Type in the medication name and click **Go**. The search will provide you with Drug Name, Description, and Category.

12. What is the description of the medication you chose?

Return to the EHR by clicking on the CPRS icon at the bottom of your screen (▣ or ▨).

Click on the Notes tab

Review the Admission Note.

13. What does it say is the patient's admitting diagnosis?

Click on the Tools menu and select Health Information. Search Medline Plus for the admitting diagnosis. Type the diagnosis name and select **Go**. Scroll down and in the **Results** click on the first result.

14. What does it list as alternative names for the diagnosis?

Return to the EHR by clicking on the CPRS icon at the bottom of your screen (▣ or ▨).

Click on the Labs tab

Under Lab Results click on **Cumulative** – under **Date Range** click on **All Results.**

Locate the lab **Creat** (short for Creatinine). What is the result and the normal ranges for creatinine?

Go back to the Notes tab. Now you will submit your answers to this exercise as a documentation note.

- Click on **New Note** on the bar to the left. Type in **"NURS"** in the **Progress Note Title field.**
- Scroll through the results and choose the note template called **NURS: PROGRESS NOTE (UNTEMPLATED).**
- Select your instructor as the co-signer.
- In the note, document the answers for questions 1-15. Enter your text on the right side of the screen. Leave the Subject field blank.

- When you are finished with the note, right-click on the body of your note and select **Sign Note Now.** You will need to sign the note using your Username. Note: You may also click on the Action menu and choose **Sign Note Now.**

Consults tab

If a consult was ordered and completed, the consult note would show on this tab.

D/C Summary tab

If a Discharge Summary had been completed it would show on this tab.

Reports tab

From this tab you can view or print any report in this chart.

To view another chart, it is not necessary to log out of the EHR or to go back to www.neehrperfect.com. Simply click on **File > Select New Patient** – you will be brought back to the Patient Selection Screen. Now, click **Cancel.** You are still in the Orientation chart.

Select File > Refresh Patient Information. This will refresh the patient chart with any newly entered information. Under the Notes tab, you may now see that more notes have been entered by your classmates since you entered your note.

Exit the chart

Go to the File menu in the upper left hand corner of the screen. Select **Exit.**

Congratulations! You have completed the Neehr Perfect EHR Orientation Scavenger Hunt!

LAB 2: Level II Scavenger Hunt: Essential Skills and Usability

OVERVIEW

This second Scavenger Hunt is to follow the Level I Scavenger Hunt: EHR Orientation. It reviews some essential skills introduced in Level I and adds to the skill of using an electronic health record and its usability.

PRE-REQUISITES

1. Review the Neehr Perfect Student Guide you received.
2. Complete the Level I Scavenger Hunt: EHR Orientation.

STUDENT INSTRUCTIONS

1. If you have questions about this activity, contact your instructor for assistance.
2. Sign in with your username and password on www.neehrperfect.com. Select **Click Here to Start the Neehr Perfect EHR** and double click on the icon labeled **EHR**. Use your username and password to sign in and access the Patient Selection screen.

OBJECTIVES

At the end of this assignment, the student should be able to:

1. Demonstrate the technical skills necessary to access an EHR system and troubleshoot and resolve access difficulties.
2. Use various filter options to select a patient chart.
3. Understand various options to select a patient chart.
4. Demonstrate how to create personal patient selection list.
5. Identify how to change presentation preferences.
6. Demonstrate how to create preferred notes list.
7. Evaluate examples of usability in the EHR system.

GLOSSARY

A **skill** is something that you learn and can do competently. It is often a physical task and is the ability to use what you have learned, your own knowledge, to effectively execute or complete a task.

Usability is defined by ISO as "the extent to which a product can be used by specified users to achieve specified goals with effectiveness, efficiency, and satisfaction in a specified context of use." The EHR is used by many different health care professionals, from physicians and nurses to clinical managers and administrators. To effectively accommodate different agendas, modifications can be made in the EHR. This activity will explore some of those modifications.

THE ACTIVITY

Patient selection practice

The Patient Selection screen contains many options for filtering patient charts in the EHR to make it easier for you to locate and open the correct chart. Practice using some of these filter options below.

Skill: Selecting a patient chart with a unique last name

1. Look at the list labeled **All Patients**. Find a patient with a unique name (i.e., a name that only one patient in the list has). Try Brady, Leanne, Olson, Warren, or Armand, Vivian.
2. Click once with your mouse on the patient's name to select the patient.
3. Record the name, date of birth, and SSN number of the patient you have selected here.
4. Now press **OK**. What happened when you pressed **OK**?

Skill: Selecting a new patient

5. You should now have a patient chart open. To return to the Patient Selection screen to open a different chart, open the File menu located in the upper left-hand corner of the screen. Which option do you think will allow you to select and open a different chart? *TIP: Do not click on the "X" in the upper right corner. It will close you out of the EHR.*
6. When you selected that option from the File menu, what happened?

Skill: Selecting a patient chart with a non-unique last name (the same last name)

7. On the Patient Selection screen, look at the list labeled **All Patients**. Scroll down the patient list until you find two or more charts with the same last name (i.e., Smith).
8. List the patient names here:
9. Click once with your mouse one of the patient names to select that patient. What happened?
10. Now scroll down this abbreviated list and click once more on the listing of the patient name you chose the first time (in question 9) and describe what changes occur.
11. Record the name, date of birth, and full SSN number of the patient you have selected here.

Skill: Exploring patient chart filters by location

12. Open the File menu again and select a new patient. Find the filter options in the upper left-hand corner of the Patient Selection screen. Which filtering options are available?
13. Select the option to filter patient charts by **Ward**. Click on the various Ward names. Which Ward has the most patients?
14. List the name of a Ward and the Name and SSN number of one of the patients in that unit.

Skill: Selecting a patient using the SSN number

15. Click on filtering option **All**. In the patient search box, type the full SSN number of the patient with the non-unique name from question 9 above. What happened?

16. Many health professionals prefer looking up patient charts by SSN or medical record number rather than patient name. Why do you think this is?

Skill: Searching for and opening a patient chart by name

17. In the patient search box, type the first 3 letters of your last name. Double check that you have selected the correct patient chart by confirming the last name and first name are yours, with the middle name of **Portfolio**. Agree to access this restricted record and click **OK** to open this patient chart, which is your personal portfolio.

18. How is this chart different from the other charts in the list?

OPTIMIZING THE VIEWS IN THE EHR

Skill: Noticing data fields displayed on the Cover Sheet

19. Go to the Patient Selection screen again by clicking on the File Menu and Select New Patient. Type in the last name or the SSN of the chart you listed in question 11. Go into the patients chart.

20. The default display is the **Cover Sheet**. Notice the tabbed organization along the bottom. What are the data fields displayed on the Cover Sheet? *Hint: Active Problems is one of the data fields displayed.*

Skill: Optimizing the data displayed on the Cover Sheet

21. In the patient chart, notice the data displayed in the windows of the Cover Sheet. Are there any Lab Results displayed on the Cover Sheet?

22. Click on the Labs tab. Are there any lab results listed on the Labs tab?

23. Now, go back to the Cover Sheet and open the top menu (i.e., located at the top of the screen) called **Tools**. Select the very last tool in the list called **Options**. The options interface allows users to customize their own preferences in the EHR.

24. On the first tab of the Options window, called **General**, press the **Date Range Defaults** button. Change the EHR Lab Results Inpatient and Outpatient days to 999 days by typing "999" in the boxes. *(Note: This may have already been completed in the Level I Scavenger Hunt. If so, leave it at 999.)* Your new default should read "Lab results will be displayed on the cover sheet back 999 days for inpatients and 999 days for outpatients." Press **OK** to save your new default lab range and close the Options window.

Skill: Changing font size in the EHR

25. In the patient chart, open the upper menu marked **Edit** (found on the top left-hand side of the screen to the right of **File**). What options do you find in the **Edit** menu?

26. Open Preferences and select **Font Size**. What is the currently selected font size in the chart?

27. Change the font size to 18 point. What are the data fields displayed on the Cover Sheet now? Which fields are missing from view?

CURSOR ACTIONS USED IN THE EHR

There are four main cursor (i.e., mouse, actions used in the EHR):
1) The **single left click** to open menus or select data
2) The **hover**, click, hold, and drag to resize

3) The **double left click** to open reports
4) The **right-click** to access actions

Skill: Resizing and moving borders in the EHR

28. Without changing the font size (currently at size 18), resize the displayed chart windows to uncover all data on the Cover Sheet. On the Cover Sheet, hover your cursor over the window border that you believe is covering the hidden windows. When you see a double-sided arrow appear on the border, click and hold your mouse to drag the border down the screen. Which data display windows did you uncover?

29. Now, change your font size to your preferred size and resize the data display window borders as needed. What is your preferred font size and why? *TIP: 8 point font is the best size for using the EHR on handheld mobile devices.*

Skill: The double click in the EHR

30. To open a report about content on the Cover Sheet, hover your cursor over one of the active problems, allergies, or clinical reminders. Double click on any one of these data elements. Describe what appeared when you double clicked.

31. Open the Orders tab by clicking on the tab labeled **Orders** at the bottom of the chart screen. Double click on one of the orders listed in the Orders tab. What details are you looking at? *Hint: The type of details is identified at the top of the screen.*

Skill: Resizing and moving windows in the EHR

32. Continuing with the same window open (from question 31), place your cursor on the blue bar along the top of the window. Left-click on the blue bar and hold your left button on your mouse. While holding your left mouse button, move the window to the far left side of the chart screen. Close the window by pressing the 'X' in the upper right corner or pressing **Close** along the bottom of the window. Double click on the order to re-open the window. Does the order window re-open on the far left-hand side of the chart screen? If not, where does it re-open?

33. With the same window open, place your cursor along the lower right-hand corner of the window border. Left-click on the window border and hold your left button on your mouse. While holding your left mouse button drag the window border to the far lower right side of the chart screen to make the window larger or drag the window border up to the left to make the widow smaller. Close the report window by pressing the 'X' in the upper right corner or pressing **Close** along the bottom of the window. Double click on the order to re-open the window. Does the order window re-open the same size it was when you closed it?

Skill: Resizing note template windows in the EHR

34. Click on the Notes tab. Click on **New Note** to open the Progress note template search screen and search for "Health" and open the template called **Health History**. The template will load in a separate, pop-up window (called the **Boilerplate text**). Expand the template window to full screen. Use the **Maximize** button located in the upper right-hand corner of the template window. Once the template is maximized, press **Cancel** to exit out of the template window. When you press cancel, you will receive a Cancel Dialogue Processing message asking if you are sure you want to cancel without saving. Press **Yes**. Open a new template window by pressing the **Change** button on the upper-right side of your Notes tab screen. Search for "Care" and open the template called **Clinical Assessment & Care Plan**. Did the Clinical Assessment & Care Plan template window open maximized?

Skill: The right-click in the EHR

35. On the Orders tab, place your cursor on an order and perform a right-click with your mouse. What actions appear? *Note: These Order actions will be different for providers and non-providers or students and faculty.*

36. While on the Orders tab, select the **Action** menu found at the top of the screen. What additional Order actions are listed here?

37. Navigate from the Orders tab to the Notes tab in the chart. To open the Note action menu, right-click in the body of a note (anywhere on the right-hand side of the screen). What menu options are available for Notes?

38. Compare the Action menu at the top of the Notes tab screen with the action menu available via right-click. Are there any differences in the actions? If so, what are they?

APPLYING USABILITY

You have already applied some usability by changing default date ranges and font size. Let's do one more.

Create a favorite note list

39. Go to the **Tools** menu and select **Options**.

40. On the next pop up screen, select the Notes tab and select **Document Titles**.

41. In the Document Titles search box on the left, type in "**Assessment**" and select **NURS: CLINICAL ASSESSMENT & CARE PLAN** to add to your preferred list, or "favorites." Highlight the note(s) and click **Add**. This will move the selected document title to the box on the right. Repeat this again with the note **CODE STATUS.** List all of the notes you added to your favorites.

42. When you have completed adding the note(s) titles, click **Save Changes** then **OK**. Then **OK** again to leave the Options box. Now when you go to the **Notes** tab and click on **New Note** the note(s) you selected as favorites will appear at the top of the other notes in the EHR, above the dividing line. Review the notes above the line. Do they match the notes you listed in question 41? If not, repeat the steps to correct your listing.

43. Now go back and remove one of the titles you just added. **Tools > Options > Notes > Document Titles**. Highlight one of the notes from the list on the right and click on **Remove**. Which note did you remove? Click on **Save Changes** and **OK**. Exit from the Options box.

EXIT THE CHART

Open the top **File** menu in the upper left hand corner of the screen. Select **Exit**.

> **Congratulations! You have completed the Level II Scavenger Hunt: Essential Skills and Usability!**

References

International Organization for Standardization. Retrieved July 31, 2013 from http://www.iso.org/iso/home.html

LAB 3: Neehr Perfect Activity: Health Information Terminology

OVERVIEW

This activity is designed for the beginning EHR student user. This activity introduces terms used in health care, the medical office, and in Neehr Perfect.

PRE-REQUISITES

1. Completion of Level I and Level II Scavenger Hunts

STUDENT INSTRUCTIONS

1. If you have questions about this activity, please contact your instructor for assistance.
2. Access the EHR and select your **personal ePortfolio**.
3. Using your ePortfolio, enter a NEW NOTE titled: **HEALTH INFORMATION TERMINOLOGY ACTIVITY**. Select your instructor as your expected cosigner.
4. Document your answers to the 25 questions in the HEALTH INFORMATION TERMINOLOGY ACTIVITY note.

OBJECTIVES

At the end of this assignment, the student should be able to:
1. Demonstrate the technical skills necessary to access an EHR system.
2. Demonstrate the ability to filter and locate the correct chart.
3. Document in a templated note.

THE ACTIVITY

Once you have opened your ePortfolio, click on the **Notes** tab and then click on **New Note**. Begin typing in "Health" and the HEALTH INFORMATION TERMINOLOGY ACTIVITY note will pull to the top. Select your instructor as your expected cosigner and click **OK** to open the note. Use the terms below to answer the 25 questions in the note. When you are finished, sign your note to submit your answers it to your instructor.

Terms

Abstracting: The process of extracting information from a document to create a brief summary of a patient's illness, treatment and outcome.

Addendum: Note that is added (and attached to) to a completed note after it has been finalized (signed by the author).

Authentication: Identifying the source of health record entries by attaching a handwritten signature, the author's initials, or an electronic signature.

Authorization: The granting of permission to disclose confidential information. As defined in terms of the HIPAA privacy rule, an individual's written permission to use or disclose his or her personally identifiable health information for purposes other than treatment, payment, or health care operations.

Bioethics: The study and formulation of health care ethics. Bioethics takes on relevant ethical problems experienced by health care providers in the provision of care to individuals and groups.

Care plan: A written plan for your care. It provides information on which services you will receive to reach and keep your best physical, mental, and social well-being.

Centers For Medicare & Medicaid Services (CMS): The federal agency that runs the Medicare program. In addition, CMS works with the states to run the Medicaid program. CMS works to make sure that the beneficiaries in these programs are able to receive high quality health care.

Certificate of destruction: A document that constitutes proof that a health record was destroyed and that includes the method of destruction, the signature of the person responsible for destruction, and the date(s) for destruction.

Clinical coding: The process of assigning numeric or alphanumeric classifications to diagnostic and procedural statements in a patient record.

Clinical data: Captured during the process of diagnosis and treatment, supports direct patient care and is used for health care reimbursement, planning, and research purposes.

Clinical Information System (CIS): Collection of applications and functionality; consolidation of systems, medical equipment, and technologies working together to collect, store, and manipulate health care data and information and provide secure access to interdisciplinary clinicians navigating the continuum of patient care.

Coded data: Controlled data entered into specific fields in the EHR which enable the retrieval, or data mining, of the entered information. Examples of coded data include ICD diagnostic codes, CPT procedural codes, and health factors.

Code of Ethics: Guides the practice of people who choose a given profession and sets forth the values and principles defined by the profession as acceptable behavior within a practice setting.

Cohort: A population group that shares a common property, characteristic, or event, such as a year of birth or year of marriage.

Commission of Accreditation for Health Informatics and Information Management (CAHIIM): The accrediting body established by AHIMA in 2004 that accredits undergraduate HIM programs that were previously accredited by CAAHEP (Council on Accreditation of Allied Health Educational Programs). The CAHIIM also offers an approval process for master's degree programs in HIM that will convert to an accreditation process in the future.

Computer-assisted Coding (CAC): Utilizes natural language processing (NLP) and algorithmic software to electronically analyze entire medical charts to pre-code with both CPT procedure and ICD9 diagnostic nomenclatures

Computerized Patient Record System (CPRS): A Veterans Health Information Systems and Technology Architecture (VISTA) product that integrates Adverse Reaction Tracking, Bed Control, Consults, Dietetics, Encounter Forms, Order Check Expert System, Inpatient Pharmacy, Laboratory, Order Entry, Outpatient Pharmacy, Problem List, Radiology/Nuclear Medicine, Registration, Scheduling, Text Integration Utilities, and Vitals. This is what makes up the Neehr Perfect EHR.

Conditions of Participation (COP): (by CMS) These regulations require that providers develop, implement, and maintain an effective organization-wide, data-driven quality assessment and performance improvement program. The regulation specifics vary according to the provider setting.

Credentials: Similar to a Username and Password, this is used to access Neehr Perfect or other electronic health records.

Current Procedural Terminology (CPT): A coding system used to provide uniform language that accurately describes medical, surgical, and diagnostic services.

Data: The raw facts and figures expressed in text, number, symbols, and images.

Data mining: Compiling and reporting of data from coded fields within the EHR for accurate bio-surveillance, public health reporting, and performance measurement.

Deficiency slip: A written document for tracking information missing from a medical health record.

Delinquent record: An incomplete record not finished or made complete within the time frame determined by the facility.

Digital dictation: A process in which vocal sounds are converted to bits and stored on a computer for random access.

Diagnosis: The name for the health problem that you have.

Diagnosis code: A code describing the principal diagnosis, additional conditions that coexisted at the time of admission, or developed subsequently, and which had an effect on the treatment received or the length of stay.

Diagnosis Related Groups (DRG): A classification system that groups patients according to diagnosis, type of treatment, age, and other relevant criteria. Under the prospective payment system, hospitals are paid a set fee for treating patients in a single DRG category, regardless of the actual cost of care for the individual.

E-health: The use of emerging information and communication technology, especially the Internet, to improve or enable health and health care. Health services and information delivered or enhanced through the internet or other technologies.

Electronic Health Information Management: The use of emerging information and communications technology to manage health information systems.

Electronic Health Record (EHR): Patient records that are maintained electronically in a manner that is accessible to the caregiver, the patient, and others who need access to specific information or to aggregate information to prevent illness and improve future treatment.

Electronic Medical Record (EMR): Electronic patient records that are developed by individual health care providers/organizations. EMRs are composed of whole files as opposed to individual data elements. The data from the EMR are the source of data for the electronic health record.

Encoder: Specialty software used to facilitate the assignment of diagnostic and procedural codes according to the rules of the coding system.

Encounter data: Detailed data about individual services provided by a capitated managed care entity. Encounter data are also sometimes referred to as "shadow claims".

Health care provider: A person who is trained and licensed to give health care. Also, a place that is licensed to give health care. Doctors, nurses, and hospitals are examples of health care providers.

Health factor: A type of coded data that captures patient health information for which no standard diagnostic code exists, such as Family History of Alcohol Abuse, Lifetime Non-smoker, No Risk Factors for Hepatitis C, etc.

Health Informatics (aka: Healthcare Informatics): The intersection of information science, medicine, and health care. It deals with the resources, devices, and methods required to optimize the acquisition, storage, retrieval, and use of information in health and biomedicine. Health informatics tools include not only

computers, but also clinical guidelines, formal medical terminologies, and information and communication systems.

Health Information Exchange (HIE): Allows doctors, nurses, pharmacists, other health care providers, and patients to appropriately access and securely share a patient's vital medical information electronically—improving the speed, quality, safety, and cost of patient care.

Health Information Technology: Broadly defined as the use of information and communication technology in health care.

Health Information Technology for Economic and Clinical Health (HITECH) Act: Provides the Department of Health & Human Services (HHS) with the authority to establish programs to improve health care quality, safety, and efficiency through the promotion of health IT, including electronic health records and private and secure electronic health information exchange.

Health Insurance Portability and Accountability Act (HIPAA): (1) This law expands your health care coverage if you have lost your job, or if you move from one job to another, HIPAA protects you and your family if you have: pre-existing medical conditions, and/or problems getting health coverage, and you think it is based on past or present health. (2) Sets national standards for the security of electronic protected health information.

Health record number: A unique numeric or alphanumeric identifier assigned to each patient's record upon admission to a health care facility. Often called Medical Record Number.

Hybrid record: A combination of paper-based and electronic patient record.

ICD & ICD-N-CM & ICD-N-PCS: International Classification of Diseases, with "n" = "9" for Revision 9 or "10" for Revision 10, with "CM" = "Clinical Modification", and with "PCS" = "Procedure Coding System".

Index: An organized (usually alphabetical) list of specific data that serves to guide, indicate, or otherwise facilitate reference to the data.

Information: Data that has been organized and processed into meaningful form to make it valuable to the user.

Inpatient: Health care you receive when you are admitted to a hospital.

Institute of Medicine (IOM): Branch of the National Academy of Sciences whose goal is to advance and distribute scientific knowledge with the mission or improving human health

International Classification of Diseases, Ninth Revision, Clinical Modification (ICD-9-CM): The official system used in the United States to classify and assign codes to health conditions and related information. The use of standardized codes improves consistency among physicians in recording patient symptoms and diagnoses.

International Classification of Diseases, Tenth Revision (ICD-10): Created in 1992 as the successor to the previous ICD-9 system. In the United States, an official use of the ICD-10 system began in 2014. It is split into two systems: ICD-10-CM (clinical modification) for diagnostic coding and ICD-10-PCS (procedure coding system) for inpatient hospital procedure coding.

J-Codes: A subset of the HCPCS Level II code set with a high-order value of "J" that has been used to identify certain drugs and other items.

Joint Commission: An organization that accredits health organizations. Formerly known as the Joint Commission on Accreditation of Healthcare Organizations (JCAHO).

Knowledge: Derived from information once information is organized, analyzed, and synthesized by the user.

Longitudinal record: A comprehensive record that provides the complete history of a patient, from birth to death.

Managed care plans: A generic term for a health care reimbursement system that is designed to minimize utilization of services and contain costs while ensuring the quality of care.

Master Patient Index (MPI): A list or database created to record the name and identification number of every patient who has ever been admitted or treated in the facility.

Meaningful use: Meaningful use describes the use of health information technology (HIT) that leads to improvements in health care and furthers the goals of information exchange among health care professionals. To become Meaningful Users, health professionals need to demonstrate they are using certified EHR technology in ways that can be measured in quantity and in quality, such as the recording and tracking of key patient health factors to enable the planning and delivery of timely and effective care.

Medicaid: A joint federal and state program that helps with medical costs for some people with low incomes and limited resources. Medicaid programs vary from state to state, but most health care costs are covered if you qualify for both Medicare and Medicaid.

Medical transcription: The conversion of verbal medical reports dictated by health care providers into written form for inclusion in patients' health records.

Medicare: The federal health insurance program for people 65 years of age or older, certain younger people with disabilities, and people with End-Stage Renal Disease (permanent kidney failure with dialysis or a transplant, sometimes called ESRD).

National patient safety goals: Set of goals published each year by the Joint Commission and designed to improve patient safety in specific health care areas identified as problematic by the Sentinel Event Advisory Group

Natural Language Processing (NLP): A field of computer science and linguistics concerned with the interactions between computers and human (natural) languages that converts information from computer databases into readable human language.

Outcome: The result of performance (or nonperformance) of a function or process.

Outpatient: Medical or surgical care that does not include an overnight hospital stay.

Overlap: Situation in which a patient is issued more than one medical record number from an organization with multiple facilities

Overlay: Situation in which a patient is issued a medical record number that has been previously issued to a different patient

Patient account number: A number used assigned by a health care facility for billing purposes that is unique to a particular episode of care; a new account number is assigned each time the patient receives care or services at the facility

Patient record: Primary source of health data and information for the health care industry. The record can be paper-based, electronic, or a combination of both referred to as a hybrid record. It is the legal documentation of care provided to an individual by the medical or health care professionals who practice in the setting.

Plan of care: A doctor or practitioner's written plan saying what kind of services and care needed for a health problem.

Policies: Governing principles that describe how a department or an organization is supposed to handle a specific situation.

Purged records: Patient health records that have been removed from the active file area.

Quality improvement: Formal approach to the analysis of performance and systematic efforts to improve it.

Quantitative analysis: A review of the health record to determine its completeness and accuracy.

Record completion: The process where health care professionals are able to access, complete, and/or authenticate a specific patient's medical information.

Record processing: The processes that encompass the creation, maintenance, and updating of each patient's medical record.

Record reconciliation: The process of assuring that all the records of discharged patients have been received by the HIM department for processing.

Reference data: Refers to literature, research outcomes, protocol, formulary, care plan, clinical alert or reminder, and so on, which enhance clinical knowledge or operation decision making.

Registry: A collection of care information related to a specific disease, condition, or procedure that makes health record information available for analysis and comparison.

Release of Information (ROI): The process of disclosing patient-identifiable information from the health record to another party. Requires a signed form by the patient allowing the release of their information.

Research data: Collected as part of care or gathered for specific research purposes or clinical trials.

Retraction: Removal of a document from standard view within an electronic document management system (EDMS)

Retrospective review: The part of the utilization review process that concentrates on a review of clinical information following patient discharge.

Secondary patient data: Data from the record that are shared in government and private.

Security keys (or privileges): Controls what a user can and cannot do in any area of the EHR. *See User Class.*

Sentinel event: An unexpected occurrence involving death or serious physical or psychological injury, or the risk thereof.

Standard: A model or an example established by authority or general consent, or by a rule established by an authority, as a measure of quantity, quality, or value.

Telemedicine: Professional services given to a patient through an interactive telecommunications system by a practitioner at a distant site.

Template: In the EHR it is a document with instructions, pre-defined documentation choices, and/or narrative documentation in a format that has not been produced as a note yet.

Unsigned: Note has not been signed by the author, on paper or electronically.

User class: Classifying an individual user by professional scope of practice; i.e., Nurse, Doctor, Medical Assistant, etc.

Virtual HIM: Health information management function that takes place outside of a traditional office setting.

LAB 4: Neehr Perfect Activity: Approved Abbreviations

OVERVIEW

This activity involves auditing documents in a patient record found in the Neehr Perfect educational Electronic Health Record system and identifying the incorrect use of abbreviations found within patient medical documentation.

PRE-REQUISITES

1. Completion of the Neehr Perfect Scavenger Hunts I and II

OBJECTIVES

At the end of this assignment, the student should be able to:

- Identify approved medical abbreviations.
- Review health data from an electronic health record to compare with approved medical abbreviations.
- Analyze documentation contained within an electronic health record based on an approved abbreviation list.
- Compile a summary of the findings.

You are the Health Information Manager in a hospital. You have been asked by the quality control director to audit several records because a monthly QA audit has identified that the staff are using unapproved abbreviations when documenting in the electronic record. You are currently auditing Ethel Mertz's August 26 hospital admission. There are several abbreviations in the following notes that are not on the approved abbreviation list. (See approved abbreviation list below.) Also, some medical conditions are abbreviated within a note, and should be written out completely to avoid any misinterpretation of information.

INSTRUCTIONS:

1. Using the Neehr Perfect system locate the record for Mertz, Ethel.

   NOTE: Your version of the chart will also include your school's initials and some numbers in the patient name.

2. After opening the chart, go to the 'Notes' tab and locate the following notes for review:
   - Medic Admit note, August 26, 2014 @ 10:00, Dr. Eight
   - Surgery Note, August 26, 2014 @ 1300, Dr. Eight

   NOTE: There are several other notes in the chart, make sure you have selected the correct notes.

3. Copy each of the notes listed above into separate word documents.

4. Read the notes and identify the abbreviations in each of the documented notes that are not found in the following List of Approved Abbreviations, and highlight them in yellow in the word document that you have created.

5. Following the word document list the unapproved abbreviations that you have identified and then list the word/words that should have been used in place of the abbreviation that was listed in the note.

Example: If a note contained the abbreviation RX you would identify this as an abbreviation that is not on the list of approved abbreviations. You would then record this at the end of the note in the Word document that you have created as a list as follows:

Unapproved Abbreviation	Correction
Rx	Prescription

6. Submit the completed Word documents to your instructor following the instructions given by your instructor.

List of Approved Abbreviations for Neehr Perfect Lab Activity

ACL	Anterior cruciate ligament
BID	Twice (in) a day
Cardio	Cardiology
DJD	Degenerative joint disease
D/T	Due/To
ER	Emergency room
GI	Gastrointestinal
gm	gram
GP	General practitioner
GU	Genitourinary
GYN	Gynecology
ICU	Intensive Care Unit
mg	milligram
mL	milliliter
mm	millimeter
mmHg	Milliliters of mercury
NPO	Nothing by mouth (non per os)
NSG	Nursing
OB	Obstetrics
OR	Operating room
OT	Occupational therapy
O2	Oxygen
Peds	Pediatrics
PT	Physical therapy
PRN	When necessary
Resp.	Respirations
SOB	Short of breath
S/P	Status/Post
ST	Speech therapy
SW	Social work
TID	Three times (in) a day (ter in die)
V/S	Vital/Signs

LAB 5: Neehr Perfect Activity: Retrieval of Data

OVERVIEW

This activity involves data retrieval within the electronic health record focusing on finding key information from a patient's chart. This is best suited for the Intermediate Student.

PRE-REQUISITES

1. Completion of Scavenger Hunts I and II

STUDENT INSTRUCTIONS

1. If you have questions about this activity, please contact your instructor for assistance.
2. Select the patient **Susan Bowers** from the patient list.
   a. Use this patient to answer all questions listed in the below activity.

OBJECTIVES

At the end of this assignment, the student should be able to:

1. Select the correct patient chart.
2. Demonstrate the ability to navigate the patient chart.
3. Demonstrate the ability to retrieve and interpret data from the patient chart.
4. Explain the importance to patient care and safety in relation to nationally approved protocols and guidelines.

GLOSSARY

ICD - International Classification of Diseases (ICD) is the standard diagnostic tool for epidemiology, health management and clinical purposes. This includes the analysis of the general health situation of population groups. It is used to monitor the incidence and prevalence of diseases and other health problems. Example: ICD-9 789.7.

IRB – Institutional Review Board is a committee that has been formally designated to approve, monitor, and review biomedical and behavioral research involving humans. They often conduct some form of risk-benefit analysis in an attempt to determine whether or not research should be done.

Protocol - a system of rules that explain the correct conduct and procedures to be followed in formal situations; a plan for a scientific experiment or for medical treatment.

Guideline - a general rule, principle, or piece of advice.

ACTIVITY

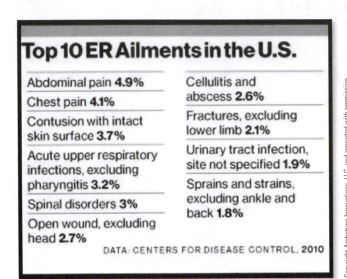

Top 10 ER Ailments in the U.S.

Abdominal pain **4.9%**

Chest pain **4.1%**

Contusion with intact skin surface **3.7%**

Acute upper respiratory infections, excluding pharyngitis **3.2%**

Spinal disorders **3%**

Open wound, excluding head **2.7%**

Cellulitis and abscess **2.6%**

Fractures, excluding lower limb **2.1%**

Urinary tract infection, site not specified **1.9%**

Sprains and strains, excluding ankle and back **1.8%**

DATA: CENTERS FOR DISEASE CONTROL, 2010

Copyright Archetype Innovations, LLC, and reprinted with permission.

You are a Health Information Technician at a large academic hospital. One of your attending physicians, Dr. Jenson, has asked for you to begin to compile data from the EHR. He is conducting a study on angina and has given you specific data to retrieve for it. The study has already been approved by the hospital's IRB (Institutional Review Board) and the start of the study is pending the compilation of this data. Included in the information Dr. Jenson gave you, is a list of 20 patient names with dates of birth. These are the patients that have been preliminarily enrolled in his study. The first patient on the list is Susan Bowers.

Using your knowledge of the Neehr Perfect EHR, locate the following data from Ms. Bowers' chart.

1. Ms. Bowers was diagnosed with Angina, Unstable.
   a. Click on this problem in her chart. What is the ICD-9 code for this diagnosis?
   b. What is the ICD-10 code for this diagnosis?

      To find the ICD-10 code, click on the Problems tab. Then click on **New Problem** on the left side of the screen. You may be prompted to choose an Encounter Provider. Choose your instructor and click **OK** (if prompted to enter a Location, leave it blank).

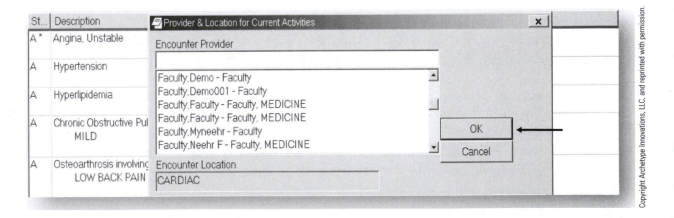

Type "**Angina**" in the Search box that pops up and click **Search**. Search for the ICD-10 code for Angina, Unstable. The ICD-9 codes are at the top of the list; you will need to scroll down to find the ICD-10 code.

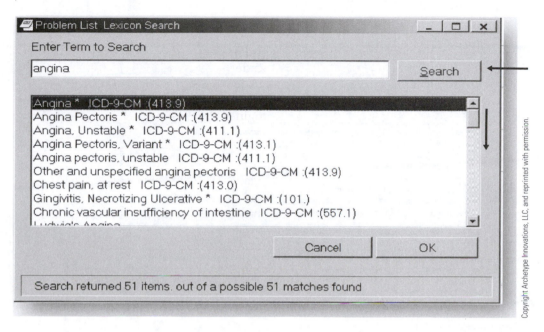

c. Return to the Cover Sheet and click on the problem for Angina, Unstable. What was the date of onset?

2. Was Ms. Bowers admitted to the hospital?
   a. How do you know this?

3. Did Ms. Bowers receive oxygen while at the hospital?
   a. Where did you find this information?

4. What was Ms. Bowers' initial blood pressure?

5. What was Ms. Bowers' glucose level at 1000?
   a. Was this high or low?
   b. What is the reference range for this lab result?

6. Was Ms. Bowers given any medication while in the ER?
   a. If so, what medication was given?

7. Which of the following protocols was followed by the emergency department staff? Hint: Read the NURS: ER NOTE and the MED: HISTORY AND PHYSICAL note.
   a. Acute Coronary Syndrome Protocol
   b. Standard Precautions Protocol
   c. Heparin Administration Protocol

CRITICAL THINKING QUESTIONS

1. Located in the chart documentation immediately after arrival to the ER are a dozen tests or assessment that were completed on Ms. Bowers. Summarize for Dr. Jenson at least eight that would assist him in determining if Ms. Bowers received appropriate evaluation and care per national protocols and guidelines. Hint: Below is an excerpt from the protocol that should be followed for each patient that is suspected of having an acute coronary "event." Refer to Box 3 in the screenshot below to assist in locating what was documented in the patient chart.

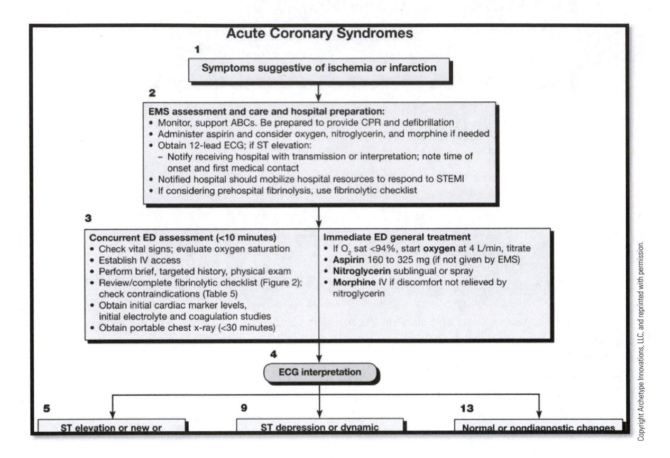

2. In your own words, explain the importance to patient care and safety of following nationally approved protocols and guidelines.

3. Dr. Jenson wants you to present the data to him in a clear and concise manner. If you have 20 patients with multiple data elements for each, what software program would you use to compile the data in an acceptable manner?

4. As an HIM or HIT professional, and from the management perspective, explain the impact of following such protocols as these?

References

Fibrinolytic Checklist for STEMI. ACLS Training Center. Retrieved October 28, 2014 from https://www.acls.net/images/algo-fibrinolytic.pdf

Part 10: Acute Coronary Syndromes. (2010) American Heart Association Guidelines for Cardiopulmonary Resuscitation and Emergency Cardiovascular Care Science. Retrieved October 28, 2014 from http://circ.ahajournals.org/content/122/18_suppl_3/S787.full#cited-by

LAB 6: Neehr Perfect Activity: Verification of Documentation Requirements

OVERVIEW

Health information professionals must be able to navigate through electronic health records to abstract information. This lab involves abstracting and summarizing the information abstracted from patient medical documentation.

PRE-REQUISITES

1. Completion of the Neehr Perfect Scavenger Hunts I and II

OBJECTIVES

At the end of this assignment, the student should be able to:

- Identify organizational documentation requirements.
- Abstract health data from an electronic health record.
- Analyze documentation contained within an electronic health record based on organizational documentation requirements.
- Compile a summary of the abstract findings.

INSTRUCTIONS

You have been asked by Dr. Belle, the medical director of Sunny Valley Hospital, to review the electronic health records of patients. It is the policy of Sunny Valley Hospital that on every discharge summary the provider must record an admitting diagnosis and a final diagnosis at the start of the discharge summary. The discharge summary should have the headings of admitting or admission diagnosis(es) and discharge or final diagnosis(es) clearly recorded followed by the diagnosis(es). Dr. Belle wants to ensure that these documentation requirements are being met. He also wants to determine if there is a correlation between the admitting and discharge diagnoses, so he needs you to abstract the admitting and discharge diagnoses. He will review the data that you abstract to determine if there is a correlation in the diagnoses from a medical perspective. He needs you to complete the following:

(Following the instructions given to you by your instructor, submit in a Word document the data collection tool that summarizes the data that you abstracted from the Neehr Perfect Electronic Health Record and the answers to the critical thinking questions listed below.)

1. Create a data collection tool that gathers the following data:
   - Patient's last and first name
   - Patient's social security number
   - Patient's date of birth
   - Admitting diagnosis—Select the first listed admitting diagnosis from the patient's discharge summary
   - Discharge diagnosis—Select the first listed discharge diagnosis from the patient's discharge summary

2. Using the data collection tool that you developed, collect the data from the following patients' records found in the Neehr Perfect Electronic Health Record.

   Log in to the EHR and select the following patient charts. Note: The chart names in your EHR will also include your school's initials followed by numbers. Once in the patient chart, go to the 'D/C Summary' tab at the bottom to view the patient's Discharge Summary and gather the data.

   Amand, Vivian

   Becker, Regina

Bowers, Susan

Carey, Emily

Dickinson, Garrett

Ehlers, Jackson

Hobbie, Hollie

Knealy, Karen

Olson, Stuart

Wang, Dahuili

3. Critical thinking question

After reviewing the data collection tool Dr. Belle feels that he wants to discuss the findings with the medical staff and with the specific providers that did not document the admitting and discharge diagnoses according to hospital policy.

What additional information would he need to accomplish this?

Do you feel that he should state the names of the specific providers in his report to the entire medical staff?

LAB 7: Neehr Perfect Activity: Introduction to Privacy, Security, and Confidentiality

OVERVIEW

This activity is intended for the beginning EHR user. It will introduce the student to the basic meaning and application of privacy, security, and confidentiality in the EHR and as they are related to patient's health information.

PRE-REQUISITES

1. Completion of Scavenger Hunts Levels I and II.
2. Completion of the Neehr Perfect Activity: Health Information Terminology

STUDENT INSTRUCTIONS

1. If you have questions about this activity, please contact your instructor for assistance.
2. Read through the activity and the cases provided.
3. Access the EHR and follow the steps outlined in the activity below.

OBJECTIVES

At the end of this assignment, the student should be able to:
1. Define privacy, confidentiality, and security.
2. Understand the details of the HIPAA security rule.
3. Compare the different types of HIPAA safeguards.
4. Differentiate role-based security and role-based security elements.
5. Identify the role social security numbers play in patient identification in the EHR and patient privacy.
6. Develop a policy or procedure that protects patient's privacy.

GLOSSARY

Privacy: The right patients have to control who can store, retrieve, and share their health information.

Confidentiality: The practices a provider employs to protect the patient's privacy rights, such as permitting only certain authorized individuals to access a patient's record.

Security: Specific safeguards or controls that are put in place to ensure the confidentiality of patient data. For example, security would include a technical safeguard that requires all individuals in the health care setting to log into a system using a unique account using credentials that are not shared with others, thus providing a mechanism to enforce confidentiality of the information.

Details of the HIPAA Security Rule with implementing HIT systems

The **HIPAA Security Rule** groups its security standards into three categories—administrative safeguards, physical safeguards, and technical safeguards.

Administrative safeguards: The administrative functions that should be implemented to ensure that security standards are met. These standards include designating responsibility for security management, adoption of policies and procedures, and privacy and security training for an organization's staff.

Physical safeguards: The controls put in place to protect electronic systems and hardware and the data stored there, from threats such as natural disasters and unauthorized intrusion. These safeguards may include locks on doors, special rooms, and back-ups to ensure that the data can be retrieved.

Technical safeguards: The automated controls used to protect electronic data and to control access. Examples include using authentication controls to ensure the identity of a person accessing a Health IT system containing electronic PHI, as well as encryption standards for data stored in HIT systems and transferred between them.

Some safety measures that may be built in to EHR systems include:

- "Access controls" like passwords and PIN numbers, to help limit access to your information.
- "Encrypting" your stored information. This means your health information cannot be read or understood except by someone who can "decrypt" it, using a special "key" made available only to authorized individuals.
- An "audit trail," which records who accessed your information, what changes were made and when.

Role-based security and confidentiality

In most computer systems, credentials (username and password) are used as part of an access control system in which users are assigned certain rights to access the data within. This access control system might be part of an operating system (e.g., Windows) or built into a particular application (e.g., an e-prescribing module), often both are true. In any case, an EHR implementation needs to be configured to grant access to personal health information only to people who need to know it. The "need to know" is narrowly defined, so EHR systems should be configured carefully to allow limitation of access in all but the smallest practices.

For many situations in small practices, setting file access permissions may be done manually using an access control list. This can only be done by someone with administrative rights to the system, which means that this individual must be fully trusted. Prior to setting these permissions, it is important to identify which files should be accessible to which staff members.

Additional access controls that may be configured include role-based access control, in which a staff member's role within the practice (e.g., physician, nurse, billing) determines what information may be accessed. In this case, care must be taken to assign staff to the correct roles and then to set the access permissions for each role correctly with respect to the need to know.

Role-based security elements

User class:
Classifying an individual user by professional scope of practice; i.e., Nurse, Doctor, Medical Assistant, etc. Based on the user class determines the user's privileges, or want they can access in the EHR. When using Neehr Perfect, students are given "student access" and faculty are given "provider access."

Menu options:
Controls where you go and what you have access to. In Neehr Perfect, CPRS is actually a menu option. The eMAR is also a menu option. Users can be granted menu options to increase access.

Security keys:
Controls what a user can and cannot do in any area of the EHR. In Neehr Perfect, the CPRS Med Button to order crash cart meds in the BCMA. In order to have the CPRS Med Button, a user must first be in the Nurse User Class AND have the BCMA Menu Option, only then can they be granted the CPRS Med Button Security Key.

WHAT IS HAPPENING IN REAL LIFE?

Case 1

The five-hospital Riverside Health System in southeast Virginia announced earlier this week that close to 1,000 of its patients are being notified of a privacy breach that continued for four years.

From September 2009 through October 2013, a former Riverside employee inappropriately accessed the Social Security numbers and electronic medical records of 919 patients. Reportedly, the employee was a licensed practical nurse, according to a Daily Press account. The breach wasn't discovered until November 1 following a random company audit.

"Riverside would like to apologize for this incident," said Riverside Spokesperson Peter Glagola, in a December 29 notice. "We are truly sorry this happened. We have a robust compliance program and ongoing monitoring in place, and that is how we were able to identify this breach. We are looking at ways to improve our monitoring program with more automatic flags to protect our patients."

The practical nurse who inappropriately accessed the records has had their employment terminated, according to Riverside officials.

Case 2

When you are sick enough to be in the hospital, what is written on your wristband is probably the last thing on your mind.

"I've never paid any attention," said Charles Boyd, a Phoenix Veterans Affairs Health Care Systems patient. Rosemary Anzalone's husband is a World War II veteran. He's been coming to the VA for more than four decades. She, too, had no idea that her husband's Social Security number was printed on the inside of his wristband. "I've just taken them off and thrown them in the trash. And who knows who picks these things up on a daily basis," Anzalone said.

CBS 5 News asked VA officials why the patient's private number was put on the band. Scott McRoberts said the practice is consistent with National Patient Safety Goals.

Patients said the policy puts folks at risk for identity theft. "I think they should change it immediately," Boyd said. "They print them out. So print them out without the numbers," Anzalone said.

Officials from the VA declined to go on camera but sent us this statement that read:

"To protect patient confidentiality and maintain patient safety, Phoenix VA Health Care Systems prints the name on the front of the wrist band and a second unique patient identifier, the patient's SSN, on the inside of the wrist band out of view."

Case 3

Dr. G, 58, was a urologist with a solo practice. His business was thriving, and he employed both a nurse and an office manager to help him.

One morning, the office manager got a call from one of the practice's patients, Mr. M, a 52-year-old, HIV-positive man who had been seeing Dr. G for a decade. Although he was happy with the treatment he had been receiving, Mr. M's company was promoting him and he was relocating to another town. He called to ask Dr. G to fax his medical records to his new urologist.

The office manager was juggling numerous tasks, but managed to send the fax out later that day. The office did not have personalized fax cover sheets, just sheets that the office manager printed off once a week which had spaces to fill in the "to" and "from" sections. She hurriedly filled them in and shot off the fax, one of several she had to do before checking in the next patient.

At the end of the day she told Dr. G that it had been done. He thought nothing of it until the following Monday when the office manager came into the back office to speak to him. She was pale and looked shaken, and the physician immediately asked if she was okay.

"It's Mr. M," the office manager said. "He just called – absolutely furious. He says that we faxed his medical records to his employer rather than his new doctor, and that now his company is aware of his HIV status. He is extremely upset."

THE ACTIVITY

SSN as a Patient Identifier

Social security numbers (SSNs) were first issued in the 1930s as a means to track and calculate retirement benefits. Today, however, the SSN has become a national identifier. The SSN's success as a stable and unique means of identification has led to its use as an identifier in many unanticipated areas such as employee and customer tracking, patient identifier for health care providers, and health insurance records, banking, and utility service records.

Over the years, the health care industry has recognized the inherent risks of using the SSN as a patient identifier and has taken some security measures against identify theft. The most common security measure in use for the health care industry has been to allow only those who have a job-related need full access to SSNs (e.g., registration and patient accounting). Some organizations may restrict access to the SSN further, such as limiting use, access, or display to the last four digits.

In an effort to minimize public concerns regarding privacy and identity theft, the federal government and states have enacted laws to restrict the use and disclosure of the SSN. However, despite the federal government's activities to curtail the use of the SSN, Medicare continues to use the SSN as a patient identifier.

The health care industry and organizations such as the Joint Commission have long recognized the effect a unique patient ID number would have on continuity of care, patient safety, information integrity, and accuracy. However, there continues to be a struggle between correctly identifying a patient's clinical and financial information and the risks to patient privacy that coincides with easy identification.

1. Log into the EHR and at the patient selection screen, locate and open the chart for **Susan Bowers**.
2. Once inside the chart, go to the **Reports** tab. In **Available Reports** click on and expand **Health Summary**, then click on **Patient Personal Hx**.
3. You will copy Susan Bowers' personal history into a Word Document. Place your mouse in the information to the right, where it lists the **Health Summary Patient Personal Hx**. Right-click and **Select All**. Then right-click again and **Copy**. Paste the information you just copied into the Word document.
4. In the document highlight three personal identifiers of this patient.
5. You will submit this Word document to your instructor through your Learning Management System (LMS) as instructed. In addition to the information on Susan Bowers, include your answers to the Critical Thinking exercise below in your Word document.

References

AHIMA. "Limiting the Use of the Social Security Number in Healthcare." *Journal of AHIMA* 82, no.6 (June 2011): 52-56. Retrieved October 29, 2014 from http://library.ahima.org/xpedio/groups/public/documents/ahima/bok1_049016.hcsp?dDocName=bok1_049016

Blair, A. (2014). Social Security numbers on wristbands worry VA patients. Retrieved October 29, 2014 from http://www.kpho.com/story/24659178/va-patients-concerned-about-id-theft-ssn-number-printed-on-wristbands#ixzz3HYvzrI00

neehr
▪▪▪▪▪▪▪▪ ▪▪▪ perfect.®

Latner, A. W. (2013). Fax Sent to Wrong Number Results in HIPAA Violation. Rena & Urology News. Retrieved October 29, 2014 from http://www.renalandurologynews.com/fax-sent-to-wrong-number-results-in-hipaa -violation/article/305022/

McCann, E. (2014). 4-year long HIPAA breach uncovered. *Healthcare IT News*. Retrieved October 28, 2014 from http://www.healthcareitnews.com/news/four-year-long-hipaa-data-breach-discovered

The Nationwide Privacy and Security Framework for Electronic Exchange of Individually Identifiable Health Information.c2008.Availablefrom:http://healthit.hhs.gov/portal/server.pt/gateway/PTARGS_0_10731_848088_0_0_18 /NationwidePS_Framework-5.pdf

LAB 8: Neehr Perfect Activity: Release of Information

OVERVIEW

The release of information sections of Health Information Departments are responsible for responding to requests for patient information. This lab introduces the concepts and activities that relate to the release of information function.

PRE-REQUISITES

1. Completion of the Neehr Perfect Scavenger Hunts I and II

OBJECTIVES

At the end of this assignment, the student should be able to:

1. Identify patient-specific data found within an electronic health record.
2. Release patient-specific data as requested by authorized users.

INSTRUCTIONS

Assume that you are a release of information staff member that has received the following requests for patient information. For this activity assume that you have a valid release for each request.

Following the instructions given to you by your instructor, submit a Word document that answers the questions that relate to the information requested to be released. You need to complete in letter format a response to each request. The name and address of the facility you work at is:

Sunny Valley Health Care Systems
390 Hill Street
Anytown, NC 12345

Within the Neehr Perfect Electronic Health Record, access the following patients' records and answer the questions that relate to each patient. You are to assume for each case that you only need to release the information that will answer the specific questions for each case. Note: The patient names in your EHR will also include your school's initials and numbers.

Case 1—Patient Trulow, Trudie
The ROI staff has received a request to obtain information from this patient's health insurance plan.

Name and address of health insurance plan:
Trinity Health Plan of the North
2345 South East Blvd.
Anytown, MA 11111

The health insurance plan is determining payment for a skin biopsy that was completed. The ROI staff member needs to answer the following questions:

After opening the chart, go to the 'Notes' tab and obtain the information from the following patient note:
MEDIC: PROCEDURAL REPORT, FAMILY CLINIC, EIGHT DOCTOR
1. What is the site of the biopsy?
2. What type of biopsy was performed?
3. Was the patient on any anticoagulant medications?
4. Were there any complications after the procedure?
5. Where was the patient discharged to?

Case 2—Patient Aftab, Ulfat

Dr. Johnston, from the oncology center of another facility, has requested that the following information be released for the above patient.

Name and address to respond to:
Dr. Johnston
Oncology Care of the West
9802 West Coast Ave.
Anytown, CA 20394

After opening the chart, go to the 'Notes' tab and obtain the information from the following patient note:
MED: NEW PT H&P, FAMILY CLINIC, ONE DOCTOR

1. Where was the initial diagnosis made?
2. What was the initial diagnosis?
3. What was the initial treatment?
4. Has there been any additional cancer diagnoses since the initial diagnoses?

Case 3—Patient Utne, Allison

The patient's insurance company has requested an answer to the following questions.

Name and address of the insurance company:
Value Health Care Plan
298 Great Lakes Blvd.
Anytown NY 30495

After opening the chart, go to the 'D/C Summary' tab and obtain the information from the Discharge Summary (this is different than the Discharge Note found in the Notes tab).

1. What was the patient's discharge diagnosis?
2. Were there any additional diagnoses for the case? If so, please list them.
3. What was the principal procedure?
4. Was this a planned procedure?